THE GRE
SACRIFICE

THE GREATEST SACRIFICE

Fallen Heroes of the Northern Union

Jane and Chris Roberts

Scratching Shed Publishing Ltd

Cover photography:
© Thaut Images – stock.adobe.com
Robert Randerson, Batley © Green Howards Museum,
Richmond, North Yorkshire
John Linton Ewart, Halifax © Andrew Hardcastle
Page viii: George William Midgley's name
displayed on the Menin Gate © Jane Roberts

A catalogue record for this book is available from the
British Library.

Typeset in Warnock Pro Semi Bold and Palatino
Printed and bound in the United Kingdom by

Unit 600, Fareham Reach, Fareham Road
Gosport, Hampshire, PO13 0FW

Dedicated to the memory of our Dads –
Kevin Hill and Ted Roberts

Contents

THE KING'S LIVERPOOL REGT

CAPTAIN
ORCHARD E E C
WARD T S

LIEUTENANT
BAKER E B
CHAVASSE A
DOLL P W R
FAUSSET S S
FURNEAUX P T
GEMMELL K A
TURNER W S
WILSON T W

SECOND LIEUT
BARBER J C
BARGH G
BIGG A G
BULLEN W I
CHINNERY R C
COLLEY D J
COPLAND G H
DEY H F
DIMOND F R
DUNLOP C D H
GLEDSDALE A
GOLDSPINK E N
GRAHAM W J
GRIFFIN E S
HARRIS A S
LANE F A
McCABE D J B
NICKEL G G
ORME A L
PRENDIVILLE L A
ROBINSON H P
SHIELD W J
SIMPSON J W , M.C
WALLACE H B
WHITE J P
WRAY F A

COY. SJT. MAJOR
CONNOLLY J
FLETT D
GILLANDERS H S
HORBURY J H

SERJEANT
BIRCH J
BOWERS W
BRADY C G
BRISCOE H R

LANCE CORPORAL
COPPLEN A
DAVIES E H
De VALVE I G
ELLISON W
FOSTER E C
GILLER W R
GRIFFITHS W M
HALL T
HALL W
HARGREAVES A
HARGREAVES H
HOLMES W A
HORRIGAN J J
HURLEY M
JONES A
KNOWLES A
LANIGAN E J
LEECH R
LOVETT J
LUDWIG J A
McCABE P
McKNIGHT G
McWHINNIE W J
MAKINSON H
MARSDEN T
MEYER S
MIDGLEY G W
MOORE R
MORRIS A
MUNNINGS F J
NICKLIN F L
OSBORN J
PARKER J
PHILLIS F
PILKINGTON J J
PURTON G L
QUINE H
RALPH J
ROBINSON A
ROBINSON T
ROGERS T
SAVAGE N B
SHANNAHAN S
SHARP T
SMITH T
SPEERS J G
TALLON J
THOMPSON J B
THORNE H
VANCE A P
WATERWORTH
WEATHERSPOOL

Introduction

Jane and Chris Roberts

The 10 March 1919 edition of the *Athletic News* provided a stirring introduction to a list of some of those players from the Northern Union (the forerunner to the Rugby Football League) who lost their lives in the Great War of 1914-18. It read as follows:

> 'Let every person connected with the Northern Union think first of the nation's honour and needs.'

This was the inspiring message sent out by the Ruling Council soon after the outbreak of war, and, be it said to the credit of the players, it was responded to whole-heartedly. At the beginning of September 1914, over 2,500 senior and junior players from clubs owing allegiance to the Union had volunteered for active service.

As the war went on, hundreds of other players answered the call, and all played their part nobly in the Greater Game. And now hostilities have ceased, we can look with pride at the great roll of honour. It is a glorious record, and should be illuminated and hung in every clubroom. Happily, scores of prominent first-class players have returned from the battlefields, but, alas, many who were the idols of the crowds – men who loved their game – will never be seen on our playing fields again. They have played their last game, but their memory will always be with the Rugby enthusiast.

The Northern Union has reason to be proud of its soldier players, for long before compulsion came into force they donned their khaki and shouldered their gun. They played valiant parts, and gallant officers and brave men of rank and file yielded up their lives.

These were fitting sentiments indeed, and ones that summed up the mood and emotion being felt in the immediate aftermath of the conflict. But where were those Rolls of Honour and glorious records honouring the fallen heroes of the Northern Union?

Within months of the signing of the Armistice on 11 November 1918 and the end of the Great War, the memories of those players who had sacrificed their lives were beginning to fade. There was no grand Rugby League Roll of Honour, there were no glorious records. There was almost nothing.

While some other sports did everything they could to keep the memory of their fallen alive, it was a different sorry story within the world of rugby league. It was as if that same Northern Union Ruling Council who back in 1914 had urged its players 'to think first of the nation's honour and needs' were now, just months after the end of the first global conflict, prepared to abandon such strong nationalistic feeling, turn its back on the sacrifices its players had made and instead advocate a policy of looking forward.

In their eyes, it seemed that dwelling on the past would achieve nothing – even if it meant the memory of those brave men who swapped the rugby field for the battlefield to fight for their King and country would be forgotten before the dust had settled on the killing grounds of France, Belgium and beyond.

This clearly was not right. These men were in the peak of physical condition and at the very top of their profession, adored and idolised by thousands throughout the northern heartlands. They were the sporting superstars of their day. Yet in the blink of an eye – forgotten.

As a result, rugby league has never produced a dedicated Roll of Honour to those professional Northern Union players who were a part of their clubs' senior competitive set-up in 1914 but then laid down their lives for their country during the course of a four-year conflict which unleashed unimaginable horrors on those involved.

Many individual clubs have worked tirelessly over recent years in a bid to discover which of their own players made the ultimate sacrifice. It has clearly not been an easy task given the lack of information generally available, particularly until recently.

But now that will end. It is time to finally unveil the 1914-18 Northern Union Roll of Honour. It pays tribute to those first-team players who competed at the highest level in the domestic game on the eve of the Great War and were on the senior playing register as the 1914-15 season was about to get under way. As war dawned, these were the cream of the rugby league playing elite.

As a general principle, in every Commonwealth War Graves Commission cemetery across the world which contains over 1,000 graves, there stands a Stone of Remembrance designed by the British architect Sir Edward Lutyens, inscribed with the phrase 'Their Name Liveth For Evermore'. These are the words from Ecclesiasticus in the King James Version of The Bible and suggested by the author Rudyard Kipling, whose only son Jack was among the 704,803 soldiers of the 5.7million from the British Isles who served during the Great War to lose their lives.

So now is the time to make sure the famous names of the Fallen Heroes of the Northern Union will 'liveth for evermore.'

In an ideal world, they would have been joined on this Roll of Honour by all of rugby league's players who lost their lives in the conflict – those professionals who had already retired prior to the eve of war season, as well as reserve team and amateur players. Their sacrifice was just as great.

But it has taken over a year of painstaking research to produce a list of the game's 1914 first-team stars who died during the conflict, let alone attempt to include a full list of retired and reserve team players as well. It's terribly sad that this is the situation, but for many the information simply is not out there.

And who is to say there is not at least one Northern Union player who for some reason or another has never been recorded in the past as having died during World War One and really should be joining the others on this Roll of Honour?

Hopefully, this is not the case.

G. R.

Your Country Wants You.

NOW, HUNSLET !

THE LORD MAYOR IS ASKING FOR 5,000 RECRUITS.

We want the "Lads Abaat" to rally round the old Flag and show they are willing and ready to serve their Country.

DO IT NOW!

"We've swept the seas before boys,
And so we will again."

RECRUITING HEADQUARTERS:

Swinegate, Leeds

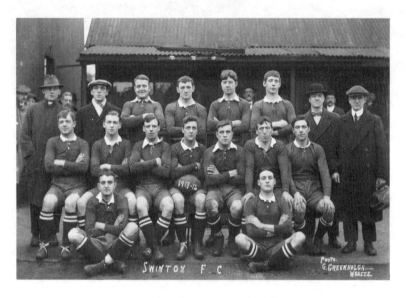

Swinton, 1913 – Jack Daley is the last player on back row, far right

courtesy of Ian Jackson

This Means War

1

The summer of 1914 was expected to be just like any other for England's professional rugby league clubs. Plans were in place for the start of the 1914-15 Northern Rugby Football Union season, with Salford eager to defend their first League Championship title and Hull looking to retain the Challenge Cup.

Salford were understandably riding the crest of a wave after their 5-3 League Champions final triumph over Huddersfield, while Hull were buoyant after a 6-0 Challenge Cup final win over Wakefield.

All had high hopes of making the 1914-15 season 'their' season, particularly Huddersfield's famous 'Team of All Talents', who had been the dominant power throughout the 1912-13 campaign and were determined to restore their status as the leading club. Admittedly, they had finished the regular season as the league leaders, with Albert Rosenfeld scoring a record 80 tries in a season, but they wanted to achieve much more. They were setting their sights on snatching back both the League Championship crown and Challenge Cup.

But Huddersfield's pre-season plans, and those of their 24 competition rivals, were to change in the wake of one fateful moment in the Bosnian capital of Sarajevo on Sunday 28 June 1914. Long-standing tensions in the Balkans – a volatile region around 1,500 miles away from the north of England – erupted back into life when 19-year-old Bosnian Serb nationalist Gavrilo Princip shot dead Archduke Franz Ferdinand, the heir to the Habsburg Austro-Hungarian throne, and his wife Sophie. The assassination did not cause any major ripples in England at the time. Yet a month later it was a different story.

On 28 July, Austria-Hungary finally retaliated by declaring war on Serbia and bombed Belgrade, sparking into life Europe's major pre-war alliances. This Austria-Hungarian action had been encouraged by Central Powers partner Germany, who knew the Russians would come to the Serbs' aid, and so Kaiser Wilhelm II's Germany declared war on Russia on 1 August. Germany then declared war on Russia's Entente ally, France, on 3 August and also invaded neutral Belgium the same day – an act which proved the final straw for Britain.

They, in 1907, had become a member of the Triple Entente alongside France and Russia as a result of the growing tensions with Germany which centred around a fierce naval arms race.

It was Britain who eventually emerged victorious in that particular challenge following their introduction in 1906 of the revolutionary big-gunned Dreadnought battleship which immediately made all other fighting vessels obsolete. Such was its impact, in fact, that Wakefield Trinity were later to adopt the nickname 'The Dreadnoughts' in homage to the lethal and lightning-fast floating killing machine. So, too, were York, for that matter.

In 1839, Britain signed the Treaty of London pledging to protect Belgium's neutrality in the event of any invasion, and so, on 4 August, Britain declared war on Germany. The Great War had begun.

In the early days of the conflict, many were confident it would be a short war, a war that would be over by Christmas. The British Liberal government under Morley-born Prime Minister Herbert Asquith adopted a 'business as usual' philosophy – a phrase believed to have been coined by Winston Churchill – on as many fronts as possible, including on the sporting front. It was their belief that by attempting to keep things as normal as possible at home, the more likely it was that morale would stay high and the greater the likelihood victory would be achieved over the enemy on the newly-created battlefields of Belgium and Northern France.

That may well have been why the Northern Union committee, as well as the decision-makers from several other sports – although not the Rugby Football Union and Cricket authorities who almost immediately called a halt to any future fixtures while the war was on – responded to the outbreak of the conflict with no real urgency.

They were fully supportive of the nation's 'business as usual' approach, which was clearly behind the Northern Union governing body's decision on 11 August to continue preparations for the 1914-15 season, with all the major competitions being planned accordingly – although it was soon apparent there would be nothing 'normal' about the forthcoming campaign.

Within days of Britain's declaration of war, rugby league players, officials and supporters joined thousands of their fellow countrymen in answering the call to arms, many prompted by Secretary of State for War Lord Horatio Kitchener's request on 7 August for the 'First 100,000' volunteers for his New Armies.

Unlike so many others, Kitchener believed from the start that the Great War would last at least three years, hence his volunteer appeal and the iconic 'Your Country Needs You' poster designed by Alfred Leete, with Kitchener pointing directly at potential new recruits. The fact Britain was the only belligerent nation that did not have conscription at the outbreak of the war and could not immediately mobilise a huge army made Kitchener's policy critical. His strategy worked a treat.

Between 4 August and 12 September a total of 478,893 signed up, many of whom were to form the locally-raised 'Pals' battalions, where men from the same community or workplace joined together in order they could train and fight as one – with obviously heart-wrenching consequences on the opening days of the Battle of the Somme less than two years later.

And although the decision of the Northern Union to go ahead with the 1914-15 season appeared to suggest its officials were fully behind the 'business as usual' approach, the sport's governing body certainly made no attempt to prevent those involved in the game who wished to join up from doing so.

In fact, Northern Union secretary Joseph Platt declared in early September that it was "the bounden duty of every player as well as every football enthusiast of suitable age and capacity to give his best to the nation."

As a result, a new 'sport' was very soon born, with local newspapers producing lists of which players from which clubs had signed up. The 'scores' made interesting reading for the general public. A first list was produced in the

Yorkshire Evening Post on 12 September, under the heading 'Professionals for the Front'. In summary it read:

> The professionals of the Northern Union clubs are rallying to the colours, as will be seen from the following list - by no means a complete one - of men who have enlisted from some of the clubs in Yorkshire and Lancashire –
>
> WAKEFIELD TRINITY – E. Parkin, H. Finnigan, G.H. Bolton, W. Parkes, T. Glynn, A. Harris.
>
> HUNSLET – Offield, Wishart, Duckworth.
>
> LEEDS – W. Jarman, J. Sutton, A. Sykes, S.C. Abbott.
>
> BRAMLEY – E. Broadhead, J. McManus, F. Watson, Reginald Carter, P. Unsworth, J. Lawson, G. Midgley, A. Braham.
>
> HULL KINGSTON ROVERS – J.C. Brain, P. Boltman, A. Moore, E. Boulton, T. Bateman, C.I. Gillie.
>
> OLDHAM – G. Cook, W. Biggs, T.O. Jones.
>
> ROCHDALE HORNETS – J. Twigg, W.J. Roman, J.E. Robinson.
>
> WIGAN – Sydney Jerram.
>
> DEWSBURY – L.B. Todd, G. Sharples, G. Millburn, J. Howgate, J.H. Walker, J. Waters.
>
> WARRINGTON – A. Naylor, S. Nicholas, A. Skelhorne, T. Broadhurst, W.H. Blundell, W. Clarke, G. Shepherd, J. Chesters, A. Brown.
>
> WIDNES – E. Swinton, A. Barrow, W. Carter, J. Cummings.
>
> HULL – J.H. Holden, A.V. McDonald, J.P. Smith, E. Whitehouse, J.A. Holliday.
>
> HUDDERSFIELD – R. Rowe.

HALIFAX – Percy Emmett, R. Emmett, J.A. Stirling, Norman Smith, Wilfred Haigh.

Then a week later, in the *Yorkshire Evening Post* of 19 September more names were added. This time it was under the banner 'Khaki-clad Footballers: What Rugby Men Have Done for Recruiting'. This article said:

> Rugby footballers, both of the amateur [*Rugby Union*] and professional [*Northern Union*] codes, have done their duty, as we never doubted they would do. Last week was published ..... a considerable list of players of Northern Rugby League clubs who have joined the colours, and from a further list to hand this week it seems probable that nearly 200 players on the League register are now in khaki.
>
> The additional names for which we are indebted to the various club secretaries are as follows -
>
> BATLEY – J.C. Tindall, Robt. Randerson, J.W. Debney, H. Hodgson, F. Newsome, W. Crosland, W. Catterall.
>
> BRAMLEY – Added to the eight names from last week are Oliver Anderson, Harold Smith, Harold Walsh.
>
> BROUGHTON RANGERS – W. Barnes, Williams, R. Craven, F. Daniels, H. Rebbitt jun., J. Beetham.
>
> RUNCORN – E. Toole, C. Inman, J.W. Lewis, S. Watton, E. Shaw, W. Potter, J.R. Burgess, F. Youd, J.W. Coleshill, J. Boyers, C. Thornton, J.T. Ashley, O. Cowley, J. Hughes, J.W. Hope, F. Mort, S. Nicholls, J. Plant, A. Sayle, H. Jackson, J.H. Tilley.

HALIFAX – Added to the first list are Joe Chadbourne, J.W. Cotton.
BRADFORD NORTHERN – H.B. Wray, H. Schofield, J. Ruck, W. Burrell, F. Craven, R. Mortimer, J. Simpson, J. Aspinall, F. Longthorpe.
ROCHDALE HORNETS – Added to last week's list are T. West, B. Burton, F. Pritchard, W. Bibby, J. Burton, A. Ryan.
ST HELENS – J. Manchester, J. Mosedale, P. Molyneux, T. Trenwich, J. Pope, J. Flanagan, J. Prescott, H. Mercer, H.S. Turtill, T. Browning, A. Waddell, A. Kelly, W. Woods, J. Ackerley, H. Heaton.

It was clear clubs across the competition would be fielding weakened sides in the 1914-15 season. And the lists kept getting longer and longer. As well as players from the professional ranks, amateur district league players were also quickly at the front of the queue to enlist, with Joseph Platt able to announce by April 1915 that 1,418 amateur and professional Northern Union players had answered the call.[1]

The departure of so many players almost immediately started taking its toll on the 1914-15 campaign. With clubs forced to field increasingly weakened teams and play in front of dramatically reduced crowds – which was hardly surprising given the number of Northern Union supporters who had volunteered to follow their sporting heroes into the recruitment offices – the financial strain began to tell.

At a Northern Union meeting on 20 October it was revealed Halifax were the only club not to see a decline in gate receipts, while in contrast crowds at Leeds and Hunslet had been halved, and Wigan had lost two-thirds of its season-ticket holders. As a result of the drastic reduction in income, a decision was taken to cut the wages of players and referees by 25%. In protest, individuals from both groups either went on strike or threatened to go on strike in early November, forcing the game's governing body to climb down.

It was a clear sign of how difficult it had become for the Northern Union to successfully uphold the government's 'business as usual' mantra, with professional players continuing to sign up for war all the time and clubs struggling to remain competitive as a consequence. It also did not help that the general enthusiasm for the game waned as casualties on the battlefield mounted, and the initial assumption that this would be a short war faded.

The fact Huddersfield swept all before them in winning every competition they entered, including an almost predictable 37-3 Challenge Cup final thrashing of St Helens in front of a crowd of just 8,000 at Oldham on 1 May 1915, added to the feeling within the game that domestic rugby league was fighting a losing battle.

Within a month of that unsatisfactory 1914-15 campaign coming to a close, the decision was taken to suspend all professional competitions until the Great War came to an end. That prompted more professional players to enlist, while others were to follow in another significant step after January 1916.

Even though a total of 2,466,719 joined the British Expeditionary Force (BEF) as volunteers between August 1914 and December 1915, the numbers were still not enough to sustain the nation's challenge in the first industrialised war. An attempt was made to continue to boost the figures voluntarily through the introduction of the Derby Scheme, whereby military-aged men were asked to 'attest their willingness to serve', in other words volunteer to be called up when needed. But this was unable to halt the steady decline throughout 1915, meaning the government was finally forced to introduce conscription through the first Military Service Act of 27 January 1916 for single men between 18 and 40. A second Military Service Act then came in on 25 May 1916 to call up all married men between those ages.

Again, rugby league inevitably took a hit. Although the sport's major cup competitions were placed on hold for the duration of the conflict, an attempt was still made to keep the professional sport going in some form through the Northern Rugby Football Union Wartime Emergency League, beginning with the 1915-16 season. After all, despite almost six million men ending up being called to the front during the course of the conflict, there were still plenty left at home to be involved in a relatively competitive league.

As well as players returning home from leave to play the odd game, many others remained in Britain because they were employed in the so-called 'reserved occupations'– jobs deemed vital to the nation's overall war effort. No doubt many of these such men would have been more than willing to have joined their teammates on the frontline, but the likes of coalminers and those working in the iron and steel industries which produced the ammunition and equipment for the fighting front could equally legitimately use their skills on the home front instead.

Yet even though there were still players around to take part in the inaugural Wartime Emergency League competition, its format was far from satisfactory. Factors such as ease of travel to reach an away fixture, or the obvious weekly availability of players, proved a major hurdle to overcome. It resulted in clubs playing a varying number of fixtures. For instance, eventual champions Dewsbury played 36 games, while Barrow a meagre 13. Due to that fact, the final League positions were based on success rate, with Dewsbury leading the way with 83.33%.

In that first year, Wakefield Trinity, Warrington, Widnes and Keighley did not participate, with St Helens Rec, Featherstone Rovers and Brighouse Rangers 'promoted' to be part of a 24-team competition. The following season, the same format was in place, with Featherstone pulling out, but Wakefield, Warrington and Widnes back in the fold. Dewsbury were again champions with 81.25%.

In 1917-18, it was again the same scoring system to determine the champions, although on this occasion Huddersfield, Oldham, Wakefield and York withdrew their services. That paved the way for Barrow, with 90.91%, to be crowned champions for the only time in the club's history – although their success was hardly the biggest surprise given the climate in which they were operating.

Barrow's Vickers shipyard was at the heart of the naval arms race in the build-up to the global conflict. As well as helping to produce modern battleships, the town also produced millions of shells as part of its massive munitions industry. Many Barrow residents were employed in the shipyard industry before and during the war, as well as in the iron ore mining industry, with thousands more – both men and women – arriving from outside town to help boost production. This meant Barrow's rugby league club was able to call on the services of many of their existing players involved in one of the 'reserved occupations' and were also able to add to their squad with the arrival of new talent from outside the area who had been recruited for their knowledge and experience in the steel and coal industry.

With yet more players joining the fighting forces, the 1918-19 League season became even more watered down, particularly with Huddersfield, Oldham, Wakefield, York,

Keighley, Widnes and Runcorn not involved. Many of those fixtures which did take place were not officially recorded.

Following the Armistice on 11 November 1918 which meant the gradual return of demobilised former servicemen, official games finally got underway again in January 1919 with shortened Yorkshire and Lancashire League and Cup campaigns as clubs began the process of re-building their squads ahead of the resumption of the 'normal' League structure later in the year. Rochdale Hornets earned the bragging rights in Lancashire by winning both competitions, while in Yorkshire, Hull were League champions and Huddersfield lifted the Cup. These county cup duels showed professional, competitive rugby league was up and running, and back in business.

But, sadly, when the 1919-20 season did get under way, many pre-war rugby league stars would not be there.

George Vinton of Broughton Rangers, the first senior
Northern Union player to lose his life in the Great War
Picture origin unknown

1914 – Baptism of Fire

2

At the outbreak of the First World War, only a handful of professional rugby league players went straight to the front. When the initial disembarkation of the BEF to France was completed on 16 August it consisted primarily of the nation's well-trained professional soldiers, who may have been small in number but were very highly regarded.

Around 90,000 were available to make the trip across the English Channel straight away, which was all the support Britain could offer its Entente partners in terms of troops until Kitchener's volunteer New Army was ready to start entering the fray the following year.

Britain's main contribution early on was to help finance France and Russia's war effort and impose an economic naval blockade on the Central Powers.

But while the vast majority of the BEF were the full-time professionals, they were also joined by Reservists – the former soldiers – and some members of the Territorial Army.

The bulk of the Northern Union volunteers, however, went instead from the rugby training ground to the Army training ground.

There was clearly no disputing the fitness and discipline of the players, but it was another matter when it came to learning the art of being a soldier. Many of them had no experience of what was required to be in the Army whatsoever. Over a period of many months, the men spent their time living and sleeping in training camps learning all aspects of the art of warfare.

At this stage, and while still based in Britain, it was all about teaching the fundamental military skills required to be an effective member of the Army. Days would start with Reveille, the bugle call at 5.30am to order the soldiers to duty. At 6.30am, recruits would parade for 90 minutes to improve their fitness, with Northern Union players clearly having a huge advantage in this respect. After breakfast, the morning was spent drilling on the parade square, learning how to march. After lunch, they would return to the drill ground until 4.15pm. This would last a couple of weeks before training became more advanced, with soldiers learning basic movements in the field and being introduced to night operations.

Then it was on to weapons handling – teaching recruits how to use the British Army's standard Lee Enfield rifle and its bayonet – as well as marksmanship and digging trenches. This was followed by several weeks or months of specialist training, such as learning how to become a machine gunner or signaller, before the soldiers would be shipped to the Western Front for final preparations in readiness to go into battle.

This would have been the standard procedure for the British Army's volunteers, as well as the conscripts to follow later in the war. Although initially there were some teething issues as the number of recruits swelling the ranks outstripped supplies and equipment.

But it was a different story for rugby league's relatively small band of Army Reservists, who already possessed the necessary skills to be called up almost immediately to the front.

As part of the BEF, they were at the heart of the action in the Allies' success in thwarting Germany's Schlieffen Plan, which aimed to defeat France within six weeks and then turn its full attention to Russia. The Germans knew they needed this to be a success to avoid fighting a war on two fronts, with its failure virtually ruling out a Central Powers' victory by the autumn of 1914. It was, of course, as a result of the implementation of the Schlieffen Plan and Germany invading Belgium that Britain entered the war.

The BEF played its part in slowing down Germany's initial rapid advance with its actions at the Battle of Mons in Belgium on 23 August – Britain's first involvement in what was to be a 1,564-day conflict – and the Battle of Le Cateau further south in France three days later.

But it was at the Battle of the Marne between 7-12 September that the British and French forces combined to push the Germans back – albeit still deep within French territory.

Having already gained so much ground, the Germans were determined not to retreat too far, digging in on the higher ground around the banks of the River Aisne to signal the start of trench warfare, with the invading forces ready to defend their gains in northern France's industrial region and most of Belgium.

While France and Germany focused on strengthening their lines down to the Swiss border, the British, French and

Belgians took on the Germans in the 'race to the sea' through Belgium. The combatants were neck and neck all the way up to the coast, with the Belgians' final act of defiance being to flood the northerly plains in order to stop the Germans in their tracks.

But winning that race was achieved at a price, with the original BEF suffering high casualties from day one and the first engagement at Mons. It was a baptism of fire for the British, with Northern Union players among those to suffer. In fact, it was not long before the public back home began to receive casualty reports. This included professional rugby league players.

On 12 October the *Athletic News* reported that Runcorn's former St Helens half-back Eddie Toole was the first Northern Union player to be killed – during the Mons engagement. Fortunately for Toole and his family, this proved to be incorrect. Toole was reported missing by his regiment, and it was soon discovered he had in fact been captured by the Germans and taken a prisoner of war. Inaccurate initial reports regarding the welfare of soldiers to loved ones back home were not unheard of throughout the conflict.

On 3 November 1914, the *Liverpool Daily Post* reported the following under the headline 'St Helens Footballer A Prisoner':

Rumours have been circulated in St Helens and Runcorn for many weeks to the effect that 'Teddy' Toole, the well-known rugby half-back, had been killed in the war. But yesterday his wife and mother were relieved to receive a postcard from him stating that he was in the hands of the Germans. The postcard was dated August 31.

At the same time, there were similar reports circulating around the Bradford area that new Northern signings James Simpson and Ralph Laycock had also fallen at Mons. According to the Bradford Bulls' Foundation Birch Lane Heroes Project, these two 30-year-old good friends had served together with the British Army in India for seven years before returning home to sign for Bradford Northern.

They would have been hopeful of making it into the first team for the 1914-15 season, but before they had the chance to prove themselves, war broke out and they returned to their old regiment, the Duke of Wellington (West Riding Regiment) as Reservists.

It was later discovered that Laycock had been captured by the Germans in Belgium, but on 11 November 1914 Simpson was pronounced missing presumed dead and is remembered on the Menin Gate in the Belgian town of Ypres. Laycock eventually returned home in December 1918 and made his one and only Bradford appearance in a 22-0 defeat at Halifax on 22 February 1919.

Simpson, sadly, never got the chance to fulfil his first-team potential with Northern.

But that was not the case for Broughton Rangers' George Vinton, who was to become the first senior Northern Union player to lose his life, on 27 August 1914.

The 30-year-old, born in Hull on 10 March 1884, was one of George and Caroline Vinton's eight children. The family moved to Cadishead in Lancashire in the 1890s. It was following the move that George Jnr was able to prove his sporting prowess with the Cadishead Rugby Club as a stylish three-quarter.

He soon began to emerge as a star of the team and, according to *A District at War – Irlam and Cadishead's Part in the Great War*, he was nicknamed 'Sugar' because of his high energy levels and was reputed to have carried a small child on his back while training with his teammates!

But whether that was fact or fiction, his exploits on the competitive field with the amateurs of Cadishead eventually caught the attention of Broughton Rangers, who he joined on 17 December 1912. Within four days, Vinton was making a tryscoring Northern Union debut in an 11-0 win at Swinton, and his professional career was under way.

Between then and the end of the 1912-13 season, he went on to play 14 more times for Rangers, with his final appearance of the campaign coming in a 19-10 triumph at Widnes on 12 April 1913. Playing on the wing, Vinton was to cross for eight tries during that time, an impressive strike rate of more than a try every other game. The highlight was an individual four-try haul in a 59-0 Challenge Cup destruction of amateurs Barton on 8 March.

Yet despite such a promising start to his professional career and the fact Broughton were eager to retain his services for the following campaign, he found himself on the senior fringes, having to play a bit-part Northern Union role as cover for those who had, all of a sudden, jumped ahead of him in the pecking order.

Although he was registered with Broughton for the 1913-14 season, he instead spent much of his time maintaining his match fitness with Cadishead, waiting for a call back into the first team that never came.

As a consequence, it probably was not the greatest rugby wrench in the world for Vinton when he was called up to serve his nation as a Reservist as soon as war was declared. Having been a professional soldier with the Royal Munster Fusiliers for several years before embarking on his professional rugby league career, Vinton was always going to be one of the first Northern Union players to see action at the front. Immediately before the war and while he was a member of Broughton's first team, he had worked with his father as a coal trimmer at the Partington coaling basin at Manchester Ship Canal. At the outbreak of war Vinton Jnr rejoined the 2nd Battalion of his old regiment, stationed at Malplaquet Barracks, Aldershot. He was shipped out to Boulougne from Southampton on the troopship Dunvegan Castle on 13 August.

Within days of arriving on mainland Europe, he penned what was possibly his last letter to his pregnant wife Edith Mary (née Beck) who he married in 1908. Baby Edith, a sister for Robert, Eva and George, was born in January 1915, after her father's death. The letter, which is published in *A District at War – Irlam and Cadishead's Part in the Great War*, said:

> Dear wife and children, just a few lines to let you
> know I am getting on all right at present ..... I am
> not allowed to tell you where I am. Remember
> me to all the family. I am sorry I cannot let you
> know about the place – not allowed, but will
> when I return, if the Lord spares me.

Unfortunately, the Lord did not spare him. Just days later, on 27 August 1914, Vinton, serving with the Battalion's 'D' Company, was killed during the BEF's famous rear-guard action against the full might of the advancing German Army at Etreux.

The Munsters had not been involved in the first day's fighting at Mons and had remained in reserve. Instead, they were charged with the task of attempting to contain the enemy's progress and allow III Corps of the BEF to continue its retreat south to Guise.

On the morning of 27 August 1914 the Munsters acted

as rear-guard to hold the village of Fesmy until ordered to retire, or they were driven out. However, the extra firepower brought to bear by the Germans forced them to continually pull back and try to reach the rest of the Brigade at Etreux while facing an enemy onslaught. Eventually, by late afternoon, they reached the area near to Etreux railway station, and then some orchards, where they were attacked from the east, south and west – much of the village was already in German hands. Throughout this time they hoped to be helped out by the Brigade but eventually, at 9.12pm, when facing attacks on all four sides with dwindling ammunition and reinforcements of Germans arriving from the north, the remnants surrendered. As an extract from a letter of 14 December 1914 from the battalion's Captain Gower stated:

> I could hear no firing to show any relief coming and was only losing men and doing no good. Also fresh machine guns getting into position, I surrendered with 3 officers and 256 men – other men tried to get away but 100 more brought in next morning and after 9 days there were 444 prisoners. We had exactly 100 wounded and 150 killed and 9 Officers killed and 6 wounded.[1]

They had been fighting for over 12 hours against a German force that outnumbered them by about six to one. The main objective of allowing III Corps to carry on retreating though had been achieved. There was no denying it was a brave last stand that earned the full praise of the far larger German Army.

Under German supervision, the battalion's survivors – some of the first British prisoners of war – were allowed to bury their comrades the following day in the same apple orchard in which they fired their last shots. Unfortunately, Broughton Rangers player Vinton was one of those who did not make it. He, along with many of his comrades, are now buried in the Etreux British Cemetery located in the spot of that very orchard.

At this stage the Vinton family held on to the slim hope George was amongst those captured. They were one of many families making enquiries via the Red Cross, whose records show him reported missing in action at Mons. It was not until May 1915 that the Vinton family finally received official confirmation their relative had been killed rather than taken prisoner. The official notification to his wife dated 7 May 1915 states:

> Madam, It is my painful duty to inform you that a report has been received from the War Office notifying the death of No 7806 Private George Vinton, 2nd Battalion, Royal Munster Fusiliers, which occurred on the 27th of August, 1914, and I am to express to you the sympathy and regret of the Army Council at your loss. The cause of death was killed in action..... [2]

It was confirmation that George Vinton was the first current senior Northern Union player to lose his life in the war.

On 7 October, the competition would suffer its second loss in Hunslet's George Wishart.

And the death of the 22-year-old Scottish forward brought the final curtain down on a short life that had known far more bad times than good.

Born in Arbroath on 22 April 1892, George had a difficult childhood. He was the son of journeyman plasterer

Alexander Wishart and his wife Betsy. The lives of the Wishart children were turned upside down when their mother died suddenly of pneumonia in November 1902. Unfortunately, their father was unable to cope with looking after his young children and turned to alcohol as an escape.

It was not long before his drunkenness and subsequent neglect of his children (some reports say four, others five) resulted in him appearing in court, as the *Dundee Courier* on 6 February 1904 reported:

> ARBROATH PLASTERER ILL-TREATS HIS CHILDREN. A very wretched home in Arbroath is kept by Alexander Wishart, plasterer, who was charged in Dundee Sherrif Court yesterday with neglecting his four young children for a long period. The evidence was conclusive as to the dirty nature of the house and the drunken habits of the father, who, notwithstanding, complained of a lack of work. The inspector said he had no hopes of this man improving in his habits but the Sheriff thought he would have a better chance of reforming outside than prison.

The case was deferred for a month but it seems George's father was sadly incapable of changing his ways, for when he appeared in Court the following month his behaviour had shown no signs of improvement.

Unfortunately, and perhaps unsurprisingly, George himself began to stray from the straight and narrow. By the age of 12, he too was featuring in the wrong columns of the newspapers, appearing in court for a number of minor offences, including the theft of 50 cigarettes from an Arbroath tobacconists and breaking into two shops to steal small sums of money and a shirt. There was also the small matter of involvement in a jewellery robbery, with Wishart turning in his partners in crime. This case came to court after the town's legal chiefs had already sent Wishart to the Baldovan Industrial School, where he was ordered to stay until he was 16.

Upon leaving the school he worked for a time as a shipyard labourer, but on 17 May 1909 he enlisted with the Royal Field Artillery (RFA). The 1911 census shows him with the 30th Brigade, in military barracks at Dundalk, Ireland.

After such a troubled upbringing, the strict discipline of Army life was probably just what the young Wishart needed. In fact, had it not been for that experience, it is highly unlikely he would have been handed the opportunity to prove himself on the rugby field and earn a professional contract with a Northern Union club.

After returning to Scotland following his military service and competing locally in the 15-a-side rugby code, his talents as a strong-running forward were spotted by Hunslet. And it was not long before the South Leeds club made Wishart an offer and he was moving down to the north of England, officially signing from hometown club Ardenlea on 22 July 1913. After such a sorry upbringing, George Wishart's life was finally starting to change for the better. It did not take him too long to adapt to the 13-a-side code and, after proving his potential with several powerful 'A' team performances, he was given the nod to make his first-team Northern Union debut for Hunslet in a home League game against Runcorn on 11 October 1913.

It could not have gone much better for Wishart and his new senior teammates, with the young Scot donning the No13 shirt and helping his side power their way to an impressive 37-0 triumph. As a result, Wishart held onto his jersey the following week, although this time Hunslet suffered a 19-8 Yorkshire Cup home defeat to Dewsbury. The evidence suggests that did not help the new boy's cause.

Wishart had been handed his chance against Runcorn and Dewsbury due to injuries to more established first-team players and, as they returned, the Scot returned to the 'A' team to continue his league education. He would no doubt have hoped that, with age on his side, he would develop into a first-team regular in the 1914-15 season. But the war put an instant stop to that.

Having previously served in the Army, Wishart was immediately called up to join as a Reservist, and went out to France in mid-August 1914. He subsequently served as a Gunner with the 56th Battery, 44th Brigade RFA.

The Battery was involved in fighting around the Mons area, and in fact briefly engaged the enemy at Etreux on the 26 August, where fellow Northern Union comrade George Vinton was to lose his life. They were also involved in the Battle of the Marne between 5-12 September and the first major battle on the River Aisne in mid-September. At some point he was injured, although no details of the circumstances are known.

Wishart was taken to the No6 General Hospital in Nantes in north-west France, where medical staff were unable to save his life and he passed away on 7 October 1914. He is buried in La Bouteillerie Cemetery in France.

George Wishart's name does not appear on Arbroath's Roll of Honour. It would appear, therefore, that one of the few public notices that he had fallen in battle was recorded in the *Yorkshire Evening Post* on 9 January 1915, in a small article relating to a Hunslet club Roll of Honour, which had earlier appeared in a club matchday programme. It included a list of 13 players from the club who had enlisted. Wishart was the first name on that list, simply stating: 'G Wishart, Royal Horse Artillery (reported died from wounds).'

While Wishart and Vinton were buried in northern France, Bramley's George William Midgley was to die in Belgium on 26 October 1914 and is remembered on the Menin Gate in Ypres.

A Lance Corporal in the 1st King's (Liverpool Regiment), 26-year-old full-back or winger Midgley was a highly-regarded member of the Bramley team, with his death reported in the *Yorkshire Evening Post* on 28 November 1914 under the headline 'Bramley Footballer Killed in Action.' It read:

> Mr. and Mrs. Ernest Midgley, Brickfield Place, Stanningley, have received official intimation that their eldest son, George W Midgley, was killed in action at Ypres on October 26.....
>
> According to a letter received a few days ago from Private Charles Parsons, a comrade of Midgley, the latter was shot in the head and succumbed to his injuries in five minutes. He was buried in the trenches with six other men, including an officer. Midgley was well known in football circles, having played for the Bramley Northern Union Club, and also for the Stanningley Football Club. He was unmarried. A younger brother, Thomas Ernest Midgley, is a private in the Royal Welsh Fusiliers.

Thomas was to survive the war.

George was born to parents Ernest and Elizabeth Midgley (née Archer) in 1888 and baptised at Meanwood Holy Trinity on 21 October that year. As a youngster, he cut

25

his rugby teeth at Horsforth and initially signed for Batley, before switching to Bramley on 17 September 1912. That move from Mount Pleasant was made after he had impressed in a couple of trial appearances for the Leeds club, including his debut on the opening day of the 1912-13 Northern Union season as his new club fell to a heavy 32-3 defeat at Wakefield Trinity. Midgley was clearly not held responsible for that early setback, with the youngster starting the first seven games at scrum half. In all, he made 24 first-team appearances in his debut campaign, featuring at full-back, wing and stand-off, as well as in the No7 shirt.

By the start of the following season he appeared to have established himself as a first-choice first-team winger, starting in Bramley's 9-5 opening-day home win over Wakefield Trinity on 6 September 1913 and going on to make four more senior starts in the opening months of the season.

However, less than two weeks after making his fifth appearance in an 11-3 home loss to York on 6 December, Midgley enlisted with the Kings (Liverpool Regiment) in Leeds on 16 December 1913. His trade at the time was a fitter. Earlier, in the 1911 census, his occupation was a striker in an iron foundry. Although he remained on Bramley's books, he had decided to pursue a career in the Army, no doubt hoping to do enough during his time on leave to make the odd senior appearance for the Villagers here and there. That wish was never to come true.

Instead, having enlisted to train to be a professional soldier, he was one of the initial members of the BEF to travel across the Channel on 12 August 1914. Serving in Belgium with the regiment's 1st Battalion, he was amongst the first to experience the full force of the German fighting machine.

Having survived the opening onslaught, Midgley was not so fortunate during what was to become known as the first Battle of Ypres between October and November 1914. In his battalion's Unit War Diary for 26 October 1914 – the day he died – it became clear he lost his life during an incredibly grim struggle during what was effectively an interlude between two phases of the Battle, although he was not named individually. The action took place in the area around Molenaarelsthoek and the Becelaere-Reutel Ridge in Flanders, when he was one of the 49 non-commissioned officers (NCOs) killed and wounded according to the Unit War Diary. It went on to record:

> The rifle fire at the corner of the village was the heaviest I have ever been under, how any one got through I can't make out.[3]

Two days later, Midgley's battalion received a message from General Officer Commanding 6th Brigade which said:

> I appreciate fully what a very important part your battalion has taken in the last few day's operations and am very sorry your officers and men should have been hit so hard.[4]

As a mark of respect, when news reached West Yorkshire of Midgley's death, the Bramley club flag at their Barley Mow ground was flown at half-mast for their Leeds derby against Hunslet on 28 November 1914, the day the newspapers reported he had lost his life. The sombre mood was reflected in a lack-lustre Bramley performance as they suffered a 13-5 defeat at the hands of their arch local rivals, with a considered piece in the *Leeds Mercury* on 30 November suggesting the loss of Midgley could have been a major influence.

Whether the Bramley players were affected by the news that a former comrade, G.H. [*sic*] Midgley, had lost his life in the war, we cannot say, but it is certain they played with nothing like the confidence and dash shown lately in matches at home. The forwards seemed flurried and disorganised, while amongst the backs Abbey had a very bad time, and the others suffered in consequence. Hinton was sent off in the last ten minutes.

The impact of the Great War was beginning to hit home.

1915 – Time to Attack

3

By the start of 1915, it was obvious this would not be a short war. Having contained the initial German attacks on the Western Front, both sides began to dig in and quickly developed a system of trenches that would remain virtually static for almost four years.

The British, French and Belgians had lost hundreds of thousands of men keeping the German advance at bay. But with the aggressors still occupying vast swathes of gained territory, the French and Belgians were not prepared to accept the status quo. Quite rightly, they wanted the Germans out of their land, particularly as millions of their men, women and children were now being forced to endure a life under a foreign power. And that meant the only real option for the French and the British – the small Belgium Army was already virtually destroyed – was to launch a counter-attack in a bid to win back the occupied land.

It was not going to be easy.

The huge French Army would clearly have to shoulder much of the responsibility, with the British looking to re-build the BEF which had been so severely weakened in the 1914 defence of Belgium, and continue to knock their volunteer force into fighting shape back home.

But under pressure from French Army Chief Joseph Joffre, British opposite number Sir John French agreed to his troops launching a support attack in early March, even though they were still relatively small in number and yet to be bolstered by Kitchener's New Army. This was the Battle of Neuve Chapelle.

It got under way on 10 March 1915 and was highly-innovative in its preparation, with aerial reconnaissance of German trenches used to help the artillery hit its targets. That bombardment was also incredibly fierce and intense, with the Royal Artillery firing more shells on the day than in the entire Second Boer War between 1899 and 1902.

Although the British did achieve initial success, the Germans countered strongly and, by the end of the battle on 13 March, just 4,000 square yards had been gained at a cost of over 12,000 casualties. One of those to die was Rochdale Hornets' forward John Twigg. Having been an Army Regular before embarking on his rugby career – and, therefore, a Reservist – he was quickly mobilised to the front.

Born in Coalville, Leicester to parents William and Emma (née Partner), his birth was registered in the March Quarter of 1888. He was baptised in the parish of Ibstock on 18 February 1890, but within a year of this event his mother died. In 1895 his father remarried – his third wife. He was already a widower when he married Emma in 1886.

Twigg enlisted with the Leicester Regiment in September 1904 and served with the 2nd Battalion in India for six years, where he represented his regiment on a Rugby

Union tour to Ceylon (Sri Lanka). Upon his return, he played for Coalville before signing for the mighty Leicester.

During his two years with the club, he also represented his county six times, including in the Midland Counties clash against Cornwall, where he was spotted by Rochdale Hornets directors on a scouting mission. They wasted little time persuading him to switch codes and move north, with Twigg playing his last Leicester game against Gloucester on 14 March 1914 and signing for Hornets two days later, when it was reported that on 'signing on' he received the largest bonus paid by Rochdale to a forward.

On announcing his capture, the *Rochdale Observer* described the new man as a 'strong, sturdy forward. He is six feet in height and weighs 13st. 8lbs.....' and then adding, '..... he should make a name for himself in Northern Union football.'[1]

However, Twigg's debut at Runcorn on 23 March 1914 was something of a rude awakening. In what was proving a mixed season for the Hornets, the forward was forced to switch to the three-quarters after two of his teammates were sent off – a significant factor in Runcorn securing a 13-5 home win. But, according to the *Rochdale Observer* on 28 March, Twigg was still able to prove his potential, stating he:

> ....made a satisfactory first appearance. The difference in the rules governing the two games naturally troubled him. Twigg worked hard and is the type of forward valuable in any team.

That was to be the first of eight senior appearances for Twigg – he failed to score a try – before his career was to end in the Great War. Yet in the short time he had been in Lancashire, he made a hugely positive impression. In one of the *Rochdale*

Observer reports following his death, the newspaper made it clear how well he was developing with the Hornets, revealing:

> Quick in following up and a good tackler, he was often much in evidence in the open and he gave signs of developing into a very good forward. While the displays that Twigg gave on the field were of that strong, robust kind which spectators like to see, he never unfairly took advantage of a player who did not possess such a fine physique. Sergeant Twigg had a cheery disposition which made him very popular amongst those with whom he came in contact.[2]

As well as fitting in well on the rugby sporting field, he also made a number of appearances for the first XI at Milnrow Cricket Club, where he was a left-hand fast bowler and left-handed batsman. So when Twigg announced he had re-joined his old Leicester Regiment at the outbreak of war – he was appointed a Lance Corporal on 8 August 1914 and arrived in France in the autumn of 1914[3] – there were certainly mixed feelings around much of the town. As a result, the letters he wrote 'home' during his time serving across the Channel were always well received.

One of his last communications – by which time he had been promoted to Sergeant[4] – was published in the *Rochdale Observer* on 6 March 1915, which concluded:

> At one time we were up to the waist in mud and water, but we don't grumble, as we are doing it for the old country's sake. I am quite happy. The only thing I miss is a game of Rugby football. I

am pleased that this war is not being fought in our country, for it makes one's heart ache to see beautiful houses, churches and factories knocked down by the German artillery. Once I was in an advanced trench with six men when they started shelling us. The Germans must have fired about 35 shells, as they were dropping all round us. We sat down and smoked cigarettes, expecting a shell dropping on us, but we were very lucky. I am pleased to see that my old team are on top of the league, and I hope they will win the Northern Union Cup.

Unfortunately, the *Rochdale Observer* announced on 24 March 1915 that Twigg had lost his life. Under the headline, 'Caught by a Shrapnel Shell', it stated:

Sergeant John Twigg, the popular Hornets forward ..... is reported to have been killed in action ..... Since going to France, Sergeant Twigg had regularly corresponded with friends in Rochdale, and as no word was received from him for nearly a fortnight it was feared that he had been disabled.

The news was confirmed when a postcard was received by Rochdale Hornets secretary Mr F.T. Hudson from Private John Clacey[5] of the 2nd Leicester Regiment, who had been wounded at the same time as Twigg was killed and was receiving treatment at the Second Western General Hospital in Manchester. He wrote:

I am very sorry to inform you that one of your

Rugby players in the person of Sergeant Twigg was killed in action at Neuve Chapelle in the heavy fighting on the 10th inst. in company with me, which was caused by shrapnel by the Huns.[6]

Eager to find out more, a reporter from the *Rochdale Observer* went to visit Private Clacey in hospital to gain an eye-witness account of what exactly happened to one of the town's most famous adopted sons. The interview was, the report states, conducted in the hospital grounds around which hoardings had been erected to shield the many injured troops from public view. And Clacey's recollections left little to the imagination.

Before our infantry were given the order to charge the artillery opened fire, maintaining a fierce bombardment. The Germans replied, and, one of their shells dropping into the trench where Twigg was, he was struck on the head with a big splinter and so severely injured that death was instantaneous. Shells were flying about, and our officer called out 'Who will volunteer to take a message to 'C' Company?' Just before this I had been struck on the left hand with a splinter, but I volunteered to take the message. It was while going on this errand that I saw poor Twigg. He was in a kneeling position with a horrible wound on the side of the head. Some of his comrades at once covered him over with garments, and he would be afterwards, no doubt, buried in a cemetery for fallen British soldiers a short distance away ..... When out there, Sergeant Twigg used to often talk about Rochdale Hornets and his friends at Rochdale, and he regularly received some fine hampers from that town.[7]

Although Clacey states Twigg was killed on 10 March, the Commonwealth War Graves Commission records his date of death as 13 March 1915.

He is remembered on the Le Touret Memorial in France, with the Army Register of Soldiers' Effects revealing monies owed to him were paid to a Martha Butterworth, who was the daughter of Abraham Butterworth, the licensee of the 'Tim Bobbin' in Milnrow. Martha married Nicholas Rigby in 1919.

Even though Twigg and so many of his British comrades were killed or wounded at Neuve Chapelle for very little gain, it failed to deter Allied Army Chiefs from attempting new offensives just two months later. Joffre, in particular, was convinced the March assaults had weakened the German lines, while at the same time a fresh offensive would help alleviate some of the pressure on Eastern Front allies Russia and Serbia. Britain's contribution was to come at the Battle of Aubers Ridge on 9 May 1915, in the form of a supporting attack to another larger French assault.

It was to prove another bleak day for the British, with over 11,000 casualties suffered, making it one of the highest rates of loss during the entire war. Many were once again killed, including one of Batley's star men, Jack Tindall.

The 24-year-old three-quarter was at the height of his Northern Union powers when he left for the front. In the 1912-13 season, he set a Batley club record 29 tries in a season – a massive nine more than the previous best set by Wattie Davis in 1899-1900 – and this remained unbroken until 2010 when Johnny Campbell crossed 30 times.

Two of Tindall's tries during his record-breaking

campaign came in Batley's 17-3 Yorkshire Cup final triumph over Hull at Headingley on 23 November 1912, in front of a 16,000 crowd which produced gate receipts of £523. It was to prove to be the 'Gallant Youths' one and only County Cup success, with Tindall's heroics that day and over the season earning him legendary status at Mount Pleasant. But it was in the 15-a-side code that Hull-born Tindall initially made his mark.

John Clarence Tindall was born in January 1891, the son of Frank and Edith Tindall (née Allen). The family subsequently moved to Bramley. Having played rugby union whilst serving with the Territorials of the 8th Battalion Prince of Wales Own (Leeds Rifles), he signed for Otley Rugby Union Club in 1910 and was soon proving a real talent.

As a report in the *Yorkshire Evening Post* of 13 May 1915 stated:

> As a wing three-quarter, Jack had few peers. He was ubiquitous on the field, and once he got hold of the ball he was so fleet of foot that he could easily outdistance his pursuers.

Tindall immediately helped Otley secure two successive Yorkshire Challenge Cup triumphs and looked destined for great things in the 15-a-side code. But in the 1911-12 season, he turned his back on the sport after suffering what he saw as a major injustice, which was also described in the same edition of the *Yorkshire Evening Post*. It revealed:

> An unfortunate incident in a match with Horton, on the old ground at Fagley, led to Tindall forsaking the Rugby Union. He was one of the most inoffensive of players. But at the Horton

match he was sent off the field for striking – a clear mistake on the part of the referee. Being of a most sensitive disposition, Tindall never forgot the injury, and the following season he joined the Batley Northern Union Club.

The switch was even quicker than suggested. The incident happened in March 1912 and by the following month he was playing for Batley. In his debut 1911-12 season in the professional 13-a-side code he made five appearances and scored three tries – his first start was in a 10-3 defeat to Wakefield on 2 April 1912 – before setting that club tryscoring record the following year.

He was now a genuine star of the game and, such was his high status, that in the next campaign he became the first ever 'billed' Batley poster boy, with the club announcing: 'Jack Tindall is playing to-day.'

Unfortunately, however, given his four years with the Territorials from 1908-1912, it was not long after war was declared that Tindall was heading overseas to fight. He did make four appearances and scored one try in the 1914-15 season, including his last – and 79th – Batley game whilst on leave in a 7-2 home win over Halifax on 6 April 1915. But just over a month later, he would be dead in France – and under controversial circumstances.

Confirmation of his death was reported in the *Batley News* of 15 May 1915 with the information coming from a number of sources, although his father Frank stated the family had received no official news. This was still the case the following week when the *Dewsbury Reporter* provided an update from Frank, saying:

We have no official news as yet, but have a letter

from the son of one of our near neighbours, who sends his deepest sympathy, and says, 'I stayed with him till he died, and the last words he said to me were, "I am going, kid".' He goes on to say, 'I don't think he had much pain. We buried him in a grave and put a little wooden cross over him. It was very hard to see an old pal go under.'

It was only later that more details emerged as to how Tindall had died. In the early hours of 9 May Tindall and his battalion were in an advanced position in the British line, awaiting the instruction to go 'over the top'. But 15 minutes into a fierce opening bombardment, a shell fell directly into the dug-out, killing and wounding several men, before a second landed shortly after. Tindall was in the very midst of the explosions.

A graphic eye-witness account of the sight inside the trench was later provided by a Bandsman Sanderson, a former Colliery Ambulanceman who was operating as a stretcher-bearer. It came to light in a 1983 University of Leeds School of History thesis by Patricia Mary Morris, entitled *The Leeds Rifles and their Antecedents, 1858-1918*. The account said:

Accustomed as I was to all kinds of mine accidents, I had never before been called on to handle men who were mutilated as these men were mutilated ..... One of the men I attended to was J Tindall, the Batley footballer. He had received terrible injuries to his shoulder and back, and was in great pain. I did my best for him, but I was too late to save him, and when I saw that to prolong his life was only prolonging his agony to no purpose, I allowed him to bleed to death.

Once the deadly barrage came to an end and the men who survived it had time to gather their thoughts, it soon became clear that the shells which caused so much death and destruction had come from their own artillery.

Within days of the news of Tindall's death, his father Frank joined up in a bid to exact revenge on the Germans, signing up at the age of 48 with the Army Service Corps, helping to keep the frontline troops fully supplied.

In the winter of 1915, Tindall Snr found himself on the Balkan Front and was able to report back home via a letter published in the *Yorkshire Evening Post* on 15 January 1916. It came under the heading: 'Father Serving in the Balkans. Trying to do the bit my son left unfinished.' Frank's letter began:

> Somewhere in the Balkans, December 27, 1915 .....
> 'I am writing these few lines from our post, which is the most advanced on these lines of communication ..... I enclose our menu for Xmas dinner. We spent a really enjoyable day under the circumstances. In the afternoon we played a match ..... Probably as you may be aware, it was a new departure for me to have a hand in at Socker [*sic*], the game of my youth. The past three Xmas days were to me Batley v. Leeds, and Boxing Day Dewsbury v. Batley. Anyhow, I am trying to do, as far as lies in my power, the bit my dear son left unfinished.'

Frank survived the war, as did Jack's younger brother, Eric, who was also eager to make the Germans pay for what they had done – although he was thwarted in his initial attempt to reach the front. Like his father, as soon as news came through that Jack had died, Eric enlisted claiming to be 19. He was in fact only 16, well below the requisite age to serve overseas. This was but one case of a recruiting officer appearing to turn a blind eye in a desperate bid to bolster the Army ranks. Subsequently in 1916, the War Office agreed if families could prove a soldier was under age, they would not serve overseas and those already there could be brought back home. Eric's older sister, Edith, immediately contacted the military authorities to inform them of her brother's true age and requested he be retained in England. She provided his birth certificate as proof. As a result, it was not until early 1918 that Eric finally had his first taste of frontline action.

Unfortunately, the lessons of Aubers Ridge and the death of soldiers like Jack Tindall failed to be learned by the Army's High Command. Two failed attacks at Aubers resulted in that offensive being halted, but further pressure from the French led to the British mounting another diversionary attack in the form of the Battle of Festubert, which was launched on 15 May 1915.

It was another disaster, with the inexperienced British still struggling to adapt to the demands of fighting a modern war. And it was the campaign that would cost the life of Widnes winger Ernest Swinton, whose bravery earned him the distinction of being 'Mentioned in Despatches'. This was a junior form of recognition, whereby a list of men nominated as worthy of mention for their actions was periodically sent by the Commanders-in-Chief to the War Office. The award was subsequently announced officially in the *London Gazette*.

The 25-year-old had the distinction of sharing his name with Major-General Sir Ernest Swinton, who played a key role in the development of the tank which made its debut in September 1916 as part of the Battle of the Somme. He was also the government's official war correspondent on the

Western Front. But rugby league's Ernest Swinton was in his own right a leading – and brilliant – light in two particular fields when he went out to fight at the earliest possible opportunity.

He was born in Widnes on 5 December 1889, the son of Thomas and Alice Swinton (née Ashton). On 12 August 1914 Swinton enlisted as a Sapper in the Royal Engineers and was posted to serve with the Lancashire (Fortress) Royal Engineers. Initially he went to Buncrana, County Donegal, to work on the maintenance of searchlights for the defence of the port of Lough Swilly. With effect from 5 December 1914, his 25th birthday, he received his commission as a 2nd Lieutenant in the Royal Field Artillery (Special Reserve), as announced in the *London Gazette*[8], and left for France a few days later.

It seemed a natural move for such a well-educated professional Northern Union player.

As well as excelling in sport, Swinton also excelled academically, having been a pupil at Farnworth Grammar School between 1902-1907. Afterwards he attended the Secondary School at Widnes, where he was a prefect. He passed his Oxford Senior Local Examination in July 1909 before accepting a place at Liverpool University three months later.

After successfully completing his four-year studies in mechanical and electrical engineering, he was awarded a Diploma in Electrical Engineering. During his time at Liverpool, he acted as president of the University Engineering Society, taking up his position in March 1911. He was also awarded a Medal and prize by the Liverpool University Engineering Society for a paper on 'Electrical Drive' and held the role of editor of the Society's magazine.

On top of that, he unsurprisingly shone on the athletics

front as well, proving the star player in the university's rugby union first team and winning the Northern Universities' 100 yards flat race.

After graduating, he became Assistant Engineer at Liverpool Corporation's Lister Drive Power Station and was also an Instructor in Electricity at Widnes Technical School, although by that time he was already firmly established in the town's senior rugby league side.

Swinton made his tryscoring debut on the right wing in a 19-0 home triumph over Ebbw Vale on New Year's Eve 1910, with the youngster immediately catching the eye. In fact, the *Athletic News* of 2 January 1911 reported:

> Swinton, of the 'A' team, was given a chance on the wing. He made an excellent first appearance and scored a very fine try. He is a well-built young fellow, full of dash, and goes for the line.

The winger continued to impress as the year went on, with the *Athletic News* of 24 April 1911 stating:

> One player who, in another season, should make a valuable three-quarter back is E. Swinton. A student at Liverpool University, he was formerly an Association player, but he was persuaded to try the Northern Union game, at which he at all events showed prominence. His methods are as yet crude; but he has a fine physique, more than a fair turn of pace, and the power to boot the ball.

He remained a regular in the line-up throughout that first season, with the highlight being a hat trick of tries in a 29-0 triumph over Dewsbury. His final appearance before going off to fight was another tryscoring affair in the final fixture of the 1913-14 campaign at home to Batley on 18 April 1914, with the hosts securing a 10-5 triumph. That was to be Swinton's 84th in a Widnes shirt, during which time he crossed for an impressive total of 42 tries.

The winger was, therefore, at the top of his game when he took the decision to sacrifice his glittering career and turn his attention to using his engineering skills to help his country defeat the Central Powers. And, unfortunately, on 28 May 1915, he sacrificed his life.

Before suffering what were to be fatal injuries at Festubert, Swinton had seen action at Neuve Chapelle and Aubers Ridge. He had served with distinction on both fronts, but nothing was to prepare him for the challenges at Festubert. It was here, on 18 May, that he received his wounds, although he actually passed away days later after being repatriated to London for medical treatment.

During the early phase of the battle, the officer commanding the 1st Trench Mortar Battery of the 7th Division was badly wounded, with Swinton immediately volunteering to take charge of the dangerous task of directing the fire of the mortars towards the Germans. His services were accepted on 16 May. Over the next two days, the trench mortars under his command provided valuable assistance in helping the infantry push into German territory.

However, on the morning of the 18th, he went forward to reconnoitre a position for his mortars and, whilst doing so, was severely wounded by shrapnel from a German shell that burst near him. He was taken to hospital in Boulogne for treatment. As infection spread it became necessary to amputate his right leg and arm. He was transferred back to St Thomas's Hospital, Westminster, where he died from his wounds on 28 May.

Following his death, Swinton was brought back to his hometown of Widnes, where a funeral was held in the town on 2 June 1915 and he was buried with full military honours in St Luke's Churchyard, Farnworth.

A comprehensive report in the following day's *Liverpool Daily Post*, read:

> The military present were detachments of the 5th Welsh Regiment doing duty in Widnes, R.F.A. (West Lancashire) ..... and a firing party of twenty from the South Lancashire and twenty from the 5th Welsh Regiment. A number of soldiers on furlough and those at home wounded took part in the procession all under the command of Captain Kilpatrick.....
>
> The procession was headed by mounted men of the Widnes Division under Superintendent Foster, and Handel's 'Dead March' in *Saul* was played by the South Lancashire Regiment. Among others present were Sir A. Dale, (Vice-Chancellor of the Liverpool University) ..... and the Mayor of Widnes (Mr. D. Lewis).....

What the reports of the day did not say, however, was the bitterness Swinton's father Thomas – the proprietor of the Queen's Arms Hotel, Widnes – was feeling towards the British authorities in regard to the death of his son.

Fuelled by grief at the loss of his son, Swinton Snr wrote an explosive and understandably angry letter to the War Office on 30 May. He was not only enraged that he had to make his own arrangements to get his son's body back home for burial, but also blamed the authorities for his boy's death.

The letter was uncovered in Swinton's service records and was addressed to the 'Secretary War Office.' It read:

My son Second Lieut Swinton R.F.A. passed away on Friday last the 28th inst at St. Thomas's Hospital, London.

I received a wire from the Hospital on Thursday last to come at once as my son was seriously ill, he was shipped from Boulogne on the day previous. I journey [*sic*] to London on the day following and saw him in the Hospital and I was grieved to find that he was in such a weak state, as when I was at Boulogne on the Monday the 24th inst the Doctor he told me that he would not be able to leave Boulogne for at least three or four weeks, and to my surprise when I returned home on Tuesday the 25th inst, I received a wire from [*my*] son that he was coming to England on the Wednesday ..... which in my opinion cost him his life.

When I heard of his death, I was in London at the time. I immediately went to the St. Thomas's Hospital and received from a Doctor in charge the usual certificate, and at once applied to the War Office for his removal home, but could get no satisfaction, with the result that I had to make the necessary arrangements myself, which I consider is a crying shame for a father who had lost a son who fought and died in honour of his King and Country.....

As soon as I receive a[*c*]counts for the remo[*v*]al [*of*] my son Second Lieut Swinton from St. Thomas's Hospital to his home ..... I will forward them along to you and I shall expect reparation for the loss and trouble I was put to in his removal.[9]

A reply from the War Office was quickly posted on 3 June 1915.

> The Secretary presents his compliments to Mr. Swinton, and, in reply to his letter of 30th May, begs to inform him that the Authorities at St Thomas's Hospital had not communicated the fact that his son, Second Lieutenant Swinton R.F.A., had died on the 28th, and when the telegram was sent home on the 29th it was believed that he was still abroad. The Secretary need hardly say how much he regrets having given Mr Swinton this great trouble and he begs him to accept on behalf of Lord Kitchener his sincere sympathy.[10]

His request for expenses was rejected, despite a further appeal.

In a further letter dated 26 July 1915 to Swinton's parents, a staff officer of his Division wrote:

> I am directed by Lieutenant-General H.P. Gough, lately in command of the 7th Division, to inform you, that he brought to the notice of the Commander-in-Chief [*Sir John French*] the distinguished conduct of your son, Second-Lieutenant E. Swinton, Royal Field Artillery, in the action in which he was fatally wounded[11], in the following terms.

'At Festubert, on the May 16th, when in command of the Trench Mortar Battery, showing coolness and courage of a high order and thereby assisting considerably the advance of the Infantry.

'Next day he again went forward with his mortars and was severely wounded while reconnoitring for a position.

'He deserves the greatest commendation.'

Lieutenant General Gough desires me to express to you his sense of your son's gallant devotion to duty and his most sincere sympathy in the loss which you have sustained.[12]

A further letter was received by the family from the Assistant Military Secretary informing them that Swinton was mentioned in a Despatch from Field-Marshal Sir John French on 30 November 1915, for his gallant and distinguished service in the field. It ended:

His Majesty trusts that their public acknowledgement may be some consolation in your bereavement.[13]

The official announcement was published in the *London Gazette* supplement dated 1 January 1916.[14]

The gravestone of Harold Whitfield – Runcorn

Jane Roberts

1915 – New Deadly Weapons

4

While it was the Allies on the attack in northern France, it was a completely different story in Belgium, where it was the Germans who were on the offensive in the early months of 1915. They were still determined to make a breakthrough in the north in an attempt to destroy the British supply lines from the coast and encircle their enemy in the south.

The Germans made their intentions clear in the Spring by launching the first gas attack on the Western Front at Ypres on 22 April 1915, although they had used it earlier against the Russians at the Battle of Bolimov in January. This new form of modern warfare encapsulated the brutally of the conflict, with the Germans determined to use every means at their disposal to gain the upper hand.

It meant the British were placed under immense pressure to hold their lines, with Northern Union players among those to suffer the consequences. They included Runcorn winger Harold Whitfield, who was not killed by gas but by a sniper's bullet. His loss had a profound effect in his native Runcorn, where he was such a well-known and well-liked figure.

Born in the spring of 1892 to parents John and Eliza Whitfield (née Royle) and baptised at Runcorn All Saints on 15 May that year, Harold was brought up in Loch Street by his mother, his father having died whilst he was young. He attended the town's Granville Street Board School from August 1897 and quickly began to excel as a junior rugby player with the local White Star club. He was also a prominent member of the Runcorn Grappling Corps.

It was certainly no surprise, therefore, when the promising winger was snapped up by his professional hometown club on 6 September 1911 at the age of 19. He did, however, have to play something of a waiting game to be handed a first taste of Northern Union action, having to prove himself in the reserves before making his first-team debut in the first game of the 1912-13 season.

That came in a 12-6 win at Coventry on 7 September 1912, with Whitfield then reappearing in a 7-0 home defeat to Rochdale Hornets a month later. He wore the No2 shirt on both occasions. It was also around this time that he married Emmeline Buckley.

But although everything was going well on the domestic front, Whitfield was unable to make any progress on the Northern Union front, struggling to get back into the first-team frame and having to again bide his time in the reserves.

By now working as a window cleaner, Whitfield was one of those who served with the local Territorials, the 1/5th (Earl of Chester's) Battalion Cheshire Regiment. After declaration of war, the battalion spent time training at Northampton and Cambridge before they set sail from

Southampton to Le Havre on 15 February 1915, with Whitfield amongst them.

After a couple of days in rest camp, they made their way by train and foot to the Belgian town of Neuve Eglise, arriving on 19 February. Within days they were in the trenches with one or two men in the battalion either killed or wounded there on a daily basis, a pattern which continued as they switched to Kemmel and then reached Ypres on 8 April 1915. On 22 April half the battalion moved to Kruisstraat – a journey Whitfield would not make.

That day he was shot through the head by a German sniper and died instantly, with the simple note in the unit war diary of the day stating: '1 man killed in trenches near Ypres'.[1]

The news of his death was first reported in the *Runcorn Guardian* on 29 April 1915, although the publication had the misfortune of calling one of their most well-known sons at the time – a description the paper itself used for Whitfield – Leonard Whitfield rather than Harold. The article was recorded under the headline: 'Territorial Killed: Shot Through the Head'. It read:

> Mrs Done, of Brunswick-street, Runcorn, received a letter on Tuesday from her soldier husband, in the course of which he said that Private Leonard Whitfield of the 5th Cheshires (Runcorn Territorials), a single man, residing in Loch-street, Runcorn, had been fatally shot through the head on Friday. The sad news was confirmed by the following letter received by the mother on Wednesday morning:-
>
> 'I regret to have to inform you of the death of your son, Private Whitfield. He was killed in action at 6.30am on the 22nd, doing his duty with

gallantry and devotion. He was one of my best men. His end was quite peaceful. His comrades from Runcorn join with me in offering our sincere sympathy to you in your sorrow. He has been decently buried in a cemetery, with prayers – H.F. Davies, 2nd Lieutenant, 5th Cheshire Battalion.'

Private Whitfield was well known in the town. At one time he was on the Public Hall staff, but had latterly followed the occupation of a window cleaner. He was 23 years of age, and was 'born and bred' in Loch Street. He took a great deal of interest in Northern Union football matters, and some time ago was given a trial with the Warrington second team.

The report also states Whitfield was a single man, and the soldiers' effects register records his mother Eliza as the next of kin for any monies owing. Emmeline, of 20 Cross Street, Widnes, is however recorded on the Commonwealth War Graves Commission register as his wife. It does appear she re-married later in 1915.

Private Harold Whitfield is buried at Spoilbank Cemetery, just outside Ypres.

Also losing his life in Flanders was rising Leigh star Ernest Doorey. When he signed his professional papers for his hometown club as a 22-year-old from the Firs Lane amateurs on 2 September 1914, it was anticipated throughout the game that he would make an immediate Northern Union impact.

The tall, well-built forward proved his worth straight away by starring in Leigh's 'A' team and was quickly promoted to the first team, where he featured on several occasions in friendly fixtures in the build-up to the 1914-15 campaign.

The Leigh club made it publicly clear that they expected Doorey to emerge as a top Northern Union player and also a potential future Great Britain star. There was a strong belief around the Leigh area, therefore, that he could very quickly become one of the professional game's hottest properties, in other words he would be the next 'big thing' in the game.

But as well as being an incredibly-talented rugby player, he was also exceptional in the world of bowls, having won the Spring View Inn Bowling Club Championship Cup around four years before his death. In fact, the whole Doorey family were outstanding bowlers, with his father Thomas having once claimed in the *Leigh Journal* that he and his sons Ernest, John and Harry would beat any father-and-three-son combination in the world!

Yet just as Ernest was poised to take the Northern Union by storm, war was declared and he lost the chance to become a major rugby league star. Instead, he joined the King's Own (Royal Lancaster) Regiment. The 1911 census showed the 19-year-old as a Private with the 3rd Battalion in their Bowerham Barracks, Lancaster. He did not have to wait too long to get to the front, arriving in France to join up with the 1st Battalion on 19 January 1915 and serving as a Corporal, shortly after marrying his sweetheart, May Saunders.

Just prior to his death the battalion were in Belgium where things were tough, as a letter to his family which was printed in the *Leigh Journal* in early May described:

I am sorry I haven't had much time to write before. I am just getting round after the German gasses. We have been fighting very hard around Ypres this last week or two, as I dare say you have read in the papers. Ypres is all in flames, and it is terrible to see a place like this in this state. I am very sorry to tell you that Jimmy (Sergeant Finnigan, his cousin) has been wounded. I think he will get home all right with it, as he has got a very nice one. I was very lucky the same day, as I got a bullet through my hat. But never mind, I am still going and in the pink, but I might tell you we have had a very rough time of it this last three weeks. Well, I hope you are all going on all right and still carrying on with the bowling and enjoying yourselves (I don't think). Well, I think Jimmy will be in England by now, and will not be long before he is home. Wishing you all the best of luck.

It was to be one of his last letters home. On 24 May 1915, he was killed in action during the Battle of Bellewaarde Ridge, the closing phase of the Second Battle of Ypres.

The German operation was noteworthy because of the length of the front attacked, the weight of the bombardment and the scale on which gas was used. According to the unit war diary of the 24 May, the Germans launched an attack at 2.30am that morning using gas shells and heavy, sustained rifle fire. One of the places the Germans made an impression was the area around Shell Trap Farm (later renamed Mouse Trap Farm) held by the Dublin Fusiliers and next to them the Royal Irish Regiment. All but one company of the Royal Irish withdrew, allowing the Germans to occupy some of the vacated trenches. These were to the right of Doorey's battalion, who had to step into the breach. The ensuing action lasted all that day, with Doorey and his colleagues struggling to contain such a strong German assault. They held their position until receiving the order to fall back later that night, for which they received praise. Little is known about the exact circumstances of Doorey's death.

Official news of his death was confirmed the following month and reported in the *Leigh Journal*:

> An official communication has been received by his parents at Plank-lane, Leigh, that Sergeant Ernest Doorey[2], C Company 1st Battalion King's Own Royal Lancaster Regiment, British Expeditionary Force, France, has been killed in action. Sergt. Doorey, who was only 22 years of age, and has not long been married, was 6ft 2in in height and styled 'the young giant' of Plank Lane. He had been at the front since January ..... He was a playing member of the Leigh Football Club, and one of a family of bowlers. His death will be greatly regretted at Plank Lane.

Ernest Doorey has no known grave and is remembered on the Menin Gate in Ypres.

Then a day after Doorey's death, vastly-experienced former Welsh and Great Britain centre Phil Thomas also died in the Ypres area. The 36-year-old was one of the Northern Union's most respected senior servants, having played for Oldham, Leeds, Hull KR and Coventry. He had also been the subject of a rugby league transfer record when he switched from Oldham to Leeds for the princely sum of £250 in 1904.

When Thomas enlisted early in the war, serving with 'A' Squadron of the 1/1st Yorkshire Hussars (Alexandra Princess of Wales's Own) Yeomanry, he had, in fact, only recently been transfer-listed by Hull KR. It was his second spell with the east coast club, having made nine appearances and scoring three tries in the first half of the 1913-14 season, before losing his place to younger teammates. At the outbreak of war, the transfer-listed Thomas was maintaining his match fitness with Harrogate Northern Union Club.

As a youngster, the Welshman impressed in the forwards in local junior rugby union teams. Neath recognised his talent and signed him up as a 16-year-old. He was quickly turned into a strike centre, using his speed and strength to terrorise rival defences. After three seasons he moved to Tredegar, where he was made acting captain in his second season and finished top scorer for his club with 37 tries, as well as four drop goals. Not surprisingly, he was regarded as hot property throughout the Principality, being tipped to become a Welsh international.

But it was then that the Northern Union and the Oldham club stepped in to make their move in 1902, with a special feature in the *Yorkshire Evening Post* of 23 September 1905 shedding some very interesting light on how many of the Welsh deals were being done at that time through the 'Flying Barber', including the Thomas deal of three years earlier.

> The story of his transfer to Oldham furnishes an interesting insight into the methods adopted by Northern Union clubs to secure Welsh players. It appears there is a character known locally as the 'flying barber', whose activity in negotiating the transfer of players from Wales to Yorkshire is well-known.
>
> 'Well,' says Thomas, in describing his own case, 'this "flying barber" came to get me to join Oldham, and though I refused two or three times to have anything to do with the Northern Union,

I finally consented. One Friday night when he came for me I prepared to go with him to the station to go right away to Oldham. That's how I got away to Oldham and next day I played against Hunslet and scored two tries. If I had not gone to Oldham I dare say I should have got to Newport, for Arthur Gould, the famous three-quarter, had been down just previously to try and arrange for me to go there.'

Thomas quickly established himself in Oldham's first team and gained a first Lancashire County cap against Cumberland in 1903, with the lure of cash and a record-breaking transfer deal at the heart of the move to Leeds just under two years later in August 1904, as recorded by the *Bradford Daily Telegraph.*

The transfer fee of £250 is undoubtedly a Northern Union record. The previous biggest transfer fee was, by a remarkable coincidence, also paid by Leeds to Oldham. This was in the case of the transfer of T.D. Davies, the sum being £130.[3]

It was then revealed in the *Leeds Mercury* later in the month that:

The Dewsbury executive are greatly disappointed in not having secured the transfer of Phil Thomas, of Oldham, for whom they offered £200. He has gone to Leeds for a still higher figure.[4]

The move to Leeds, however, proved fruitful, with Thomas immediately becoming a first-team fixture and a Headingley hero. During his time in the blue and amber, he was capped several times for Yorkshire, starred for Wales against England in 1908 and also played for Great Britain against New Zealand the same year.

Yet that proud Leeds record, which also included being promoted to club captain, still did not prevent him from making another move, this time to Hull KR, in January 1909, in a deal revealed in the *Yorkshire Evening Post*.

> To followers of the Northern Union game, the most sensational piece of football intelligence to-day is that 'Phil' Thomas ..... has now been transferred to Hull Kingston Rovers. A brilliant player when at his best, Thomas will prove a very useful man to Hull Kingston in their present extremity. The transfer fee is reported to be something over £100.[5]

Some of the Rovers' faithful were fearing Thomas's best years may have been behind him when he joined the Robins, although a *Hull Daily Mail* report of 21 February 1910 proved otherwise.

> The form Phil Thomas is showing is quite an eye-opener to the many critics who said that the days of the Welshmen [sic] had gone, never to return. His tackling on Saturday was of the highest order, and I know of no more artistic tacklers than Thomas and Devereux. They time their efforts to a nicety and, seemingly, without effort, bringing down the strongest of their opponents with an apparent ease, which is remarkable.

Yet despite winning over his critics and starting up his own business as a coal merchant, Thomas was again soon on the move, briefly joining the ill-fated Coventry club in 1912. That proved a poor decision to make, with Coventry folding at the end of the 1912-13 campaign and Thomas making a rapid return to Hull KR, where fresh questions were being raised over the 'veteran's' contribution to the cause. The *Yorkshire Evening Post* of 29 September 1913 stated:

> Hull Kingston Rovers scored freely against Bradford Northern at Craven Street [*winning 23-12*], but they left much to be desired in the work of their backs. There was little effective combination, Phil Thomas doing nothing to warrant his recall and fitting in very indifferently with Shiel in the centre.

Within weeks Thomas was shunted onto the first-team fringes, placed on the transfer list at the end of the season, and went to assist the Harrogate Northern Union club. He enlisted with the Army in October 1914. While on home leave during his training, late in January 1915, he married Dorothy Jackson, a barmaid at Harrogate's West Park Hotel. He arrived on the Western Front on 17 April 1915, being thrown into the thick of the action at the Second Battle of Ypres in Belgium.

The unit war diary mentions Private Thomas by name as having been killed by shell fire on the morning of 25 May. The diary also noted they had been ordered to move in broad daylight from their trenches to Vlamerting(*h*)e. He was one of three to die during that bombardment.

Amongst the first public reports of his death to reach

home was an article in the *Yorkshire Evening Post* of 31 May 1915 which said:

> A private letter from the front received in Leeds states that Phil Thomas ..... was killed in action on Whit-Monday. He was in the Yorkshire Hussars, who went to France five or six weeks ago.

Then, five days later, the *Yorkshire Post* and *Leeds Intelligencer* printed an eye-witness account from Trooper N.H. Barr of the Hussars of the events surrounding the death of Thomas during a German shell raid. It included the following passages:

> My next rush brought me over a little bridge that filled up the ditch to let carts pass into the fields, and at the other side I found two wounded men. I looked down and saw one was Judd, the trumpeter for our troop. As I jumped down, he said: 'Oh, Barr, do straighten my leg, it's broken.' 'Hulloa,' I said, 'hit?' 'Yes,' he answered, 'and there's Thomas here – he's done.' I looked, it was Phil Thomas, and both his legs were broken just above the ankle. His eyes were closed, and his face as pale as our tanned complexions are able to pale.....
>
> We then got our friend [*Judd*] on the stretcher and were able to set off. As we lifted him, I had noticed Thomas's breast give a big, deep heave, so knew he was still living. We reached the dressing station safely, and there the doctor ..... dressed the wounds, while I gave drinks of hot cocoa, out of a big mug. All the time Judd did

finely and even remarked ..... he would get a holiday in England. We took him another half mile down the road to a large building that was being used as a hospital, and there I met Mr Walker (our officer). I told him what I knew, and that Thomas was living, so he and I and three Red Cross men went back again with two stretchers to see if anything could be done. However, by then, Phil Thomas was passed beyond our aid..... Of course, we did not attempt to bury those who had fallen – to do so by daylight would be asking for death.[6]

Thomas has no known grave and, like Doorey, he is remembered on the Menin Gate.

While Doorey had been in the Flanders area when the Germans used gas for the first time on the Western Front, one of his comrades from a rival Northern Union club was to experience first-hand the full horrors of another deadly new weapon used on a widespread scale for the first time – flamethrowers, or liquid fire as it was more commonly known at the time. Again, the area around Ypres was to be the German testing ground, with Warrington's Howard Davis unfortunately in the wrong place at the wrong time.

The attack on British trenches at Hooge on 30 July 1915 caught the troops totally by surprise, although many of the casualties did not die from burns but mainly as a result of soldiers being flushed into the open to escape the flames in the trenches and then killed or injured by enemy bullets or shells. This was the case with Davis.

The 27-year-old Davis had not experienced the 'usual' Northern Union upbringing – that of the stereotypical working-class variety. Born in Handsworth, near Birmingham, to parents Edwin and Susan Davis in 1888, he and his brothers and sisters had instead enjoyed a privileged start to their lives, with the 1891 census revealing Edwin managed what must have been a successful print business, as also living in the Davis household at the time were two servants.

Davis was educated at Aston Grammar School, where his talents as a rugby player almost immediately shone through, although he also excelled at cricket as a fast bowler, running and the high jump. At the age of 10, he joined the Grammar School rugby team and soon earned a reputation as a free-scoring three-quarter.

After leaving school, he played for Aston Old Edwardians' first XV. When his work commitments as a clerk took him to Coventry, he impressed the city club's second team before his promotion to Coventry Rugby Union Club's first team as a three-quarter or stand-off.

When the club took the decision to switch codes and become a Northern Union club for the start of the 1910-11 season, Davis chose to switch with them, although as the Coventry Herald reflected in their publication after his death was announced, he, and his club, experienced some tough times.

In fact, in the three years Coventry were competing in the professional 13-a-side code, they managed just 12 League wins, finishing bottom in their final season with just one draw and 26 defeats to their name. One of Davis's Coventry teammates during that time was, of course, Phil Thomas. The *Coventry Herald* on 27 August 1915 said of Davis:

> When in form, there was not a more attractive exponent of the game. He played with the Coventry Northern Union Club during the three disappointing seasons of its existence, and his

displays as a three-quarter, either wing or centre, and as a stand-off half, was one of the relieving features of what were often otherwise poor games. He was a prolific scorer, fast and gentlemanly. Howard Davis was always a prominent figure on the field. He stood about six feet and was built for speed.

After Coventry folded at the end of the 1912-13 campaign, Warrington quickly moved in to acquire the services of Davis, who registered with the club on 22 July 1913. He made his debut at centre in a 23-4 home League win over Leigh on 6 September the same year. That was to be the first of 22 senior appearances in the Warrington colours – he crossed for one try during that time – with his final game coming in a 25-0 defeat at St Helens on 2 January 1915 during his time on leave.

By now, Davis was already impressing as a soldier. He attested on 3 September 1914, serving with the 8th Battalion of the Rifle Brigade (The Prince Consort's Own). He quickly rose through the ranks from Private to Corporal and was finally confirmed as a Sergeant on 25 January 1915, after holding the role in an acting capacity since the previous November. Davis arrived in what was termed the France and Flanders theatre of war on 20 May 1915. And it was at Flanders where Davis suffered his serious injuries on 30 July 1915, succumbing to them the following day.

Captain E.F. Prior, his Company Commander, wrote after his death:

I valued him very highly as a sergeant, and as a man of very strong character, and I placed great reliance on him.[7]

Those sentiments were echoed by Lieutenant E. Boughey, who added:

> I can't tell you what a good soldier he was, and
> what an enormous help he was to me.[8]

But the account of how Davis suffered his fatal injuries was given by Colour-Sergeant Hill, one of the last to see him on the fateful day. According to De Ruvigny's Roll of Honour, Hill wrote that he:

> .....last saw him on 30 July, when the enemy used
> liquid fire, when he was wounded in the arm. In
> spite of this, he crawled about in the open field
> dressing other wounded men before attempting
> to go into safety himself. He was hit in the chest
> later on by shrapnel bullets, which caused his
> death the next day.[9]

Before the wounded Davis lost his life, he was evacuated to the Casualty Clearing Station at Lijssenthoek, around 20km behind the front line at Ypres. He is buried at Lijssenthoek Military Cemetery.

One of the earliest announcements to the public back home of Davis' death was in the *Birmingham Mail* on 13 August 1915. It read:

> Mr Edwin Davis, of Davis, Ltd., Great Charles
> Street, has received intimation that his second
> son, Sergeant Howard Davis, of the 8th Rifles
> Corps (Winchester), has been killed..... Sergeant
> Davis, who enlisted as a private in September,

was well known in Rugby football circles, having
played for Coventry, Warrington, and Aston Old
Edwardians.

Davis was the second union convert to be killed in July 1915,
with Salford winger Jimmy Cook having already fallen at
Cambrin in France on 3 July. But unlike his Warrington rival,
not as much is known about Cook's death, although he was
killed by the effects of shrapnel in the frontline trenches
during a heavy shelling raid by the Germans on the area
around Cambrin.

According to the unit war diary for Rifleman Cook's
battalion, the 1st King's Royal Rifle Corps:

Germans shelled Cambrin somewhat heavily,
and also put some pip-squeaks over our front
line.[10]

Although the diary gives no indication of the number of
casualties suffered that day and the nature of their injuries, it
appears Cook may have been one of the many victims of the
'pip-squeak' or 'whiz bang', which the British nicknamed the
shells from a German 77mm field gun.

But whatever the nature of his death, his family did
have the consolation of knowing his body was recovered and
is buried in the Cambrin Military Cemetery in Pas-de-Calais.
His parents, Charles Henry and Ellen Cook, also had the
consolation of having his personal effects returned to them
at their home at Buller Road, Exeter. These contained
photographs and letters, as well as a copy of the New
Testament, which his father had given his only surviving
child.

The news of his death was widely reported in his native

south west, as well as in the Northern Union heartlands, with the *Western Times* amongst the first to confirm his demise, under the headline: 'Killed in Action: Old Exeter Rugby Footballer's Career Ended.' It stated:

> 'Jimmy' Cook, the old Exeter Rugby footballer, has been killed at the Front. The sad news reached his parents, who live in Buller Road, St Thomas, yesterday, and was conveyed in a sympathetic letter from the officer of his regiment, which stated that their son had been killed by a bomb in the trenches. Jimmy Cook was one of the most popular as he was also one of the most brilliant three-quarters who did his duty for Exeter half a score years ago. On the small side, he was one of the fleetest-footed wing 'threes' in the county at a time when Devon could boast many first-class men. His nippiness and speed were his great asset, and many a thrill has he sent through the crowd on the County Ground when, placed in possession of the ball, he has jumped off the mark to leave the opposition virtually standing still. 'Jimmy' was a prolific try-getter, and it caused much regret locally when his brilliant football talent led to his seeking further laurels in the [*Devonport*] Albion ranks. Later, Cook migrated, as so many other fine products of the West have done, to the Northern Union, and became attached to the Salford club, with which team he had a wonderfully successful career. After the outbreak of war he joined the King's Royal Rifles, to the roll of honour of which splendid regiment his name is now added. His

death will be deplored by his numerous friends, whose sympathy, too, will go out to his parents.[11]

It was clear Cook was well-known and well-liked back in his native Devon. His birth was registered in 1886 in the Honiton District of Devon under the name James Henry Cook. The youngster quickly made a name for himself as a talented junior rugby player.

He may have been small in stature – his stated height when he joined the army was just 5ft 3½ins – but his lightning pace made him an elusive player, which soon brought him to the attention of Exeter. As the *Western Times* report stated, Cook made the move to Devonport Albion in 1906 in a bid to further his career.

But the following season, he made the move north to join Salford, signing for the Manchester club, as reported in the *Exeter and Plymouth Gazette* of 25 September 1907, announcing:

> J.H. Cook, the Devonport Albion three-quarter, has signed on for Salford, one of the professional clubs under the Northern Union, and will play for that club against Headingley on Saturday..... The sum to be paid for his services has not transpired.

The newspaper was right about Cook making his debut at Leeds, although the winger may have regretted his decision to join Salford, given the way they played that day. While stating Leeds had played well in beating Salford 23-2, the *Athletic News* were equally damning in their assessment of the visitors' performance and had some sympathy for the 21-year-old Cook.

> [*Leeds'*] general work was capital, and in striking contrast to the scrappy work of Salford, who were seen at their worst. They, too, tried a young Rugby Union player in J.H. Cook of Devonport Albion, but this wing three-quarter back was neglected, and got few chances. He is a little chap, but fast, and should be of service to Salford, who, however, are never seen to advantage on the Headingley ground.[12]

Fortunately, their prediction that Cook, a carpenter by trade, could be a good Salford servant proved to be right. Between his September 1907 debut and the outbreak of war, Cook went on to make 161 first-team appearances and scored an incredibly impressive 98 tries. By the 1913-14 season, his senior chances had started to become limited.

But even if he had been competing on a weekly basis, his playing career would still have ended immediately war was declared, with Cook another of the Northern Union Army Reservists, after his time with the Exeter Rifle Volunteers before his move to Salford.

That was why Cook joined the 1st Battalion of the King's Royal Rifle Corps and why, unfortunately, he was to become the first from the Salford club to lose his life, as the *Manchester Courier and Lancashire General Advertiser* of 21 October 1915 confirmed by copying an extract from the club's official programme.

> Our boys are doing their duty. One (Jimmy Cook) has already laid down his life, and it is reported that another (G. Russell)[13] is also killed, but so far we have no confirmation. Many others are with

the forces: Billy Brady, now a sergeant in the
A.S.C. (he has written a most stirring letter to us);
Alec Culshaw, David Preston, and others, not to
speak of followers.

There will be more about legendary Salford scrum-half
Preston later.

Batley's Captain Robert Randerson, *right*, in the trenches
courtesy Green Howards Museum, Richmond, North Yorkshire

Gallipoli 1915 – A Wider War

5

Despite the monumental efforts made by both sides to force a breakthrough in the opening months of the war, there was complete stalemate on the Western Front by early 1915.

Some among the Allied powers believed a new strategy needed to be implemented in a bid to break the deadlock. These were the so-called 'Easterners' and included the likes of future Prime Ministers David Lloyd George and Sir Winston Churchill among their ranks. That strategy involved attacking Germany's ally Turkey by forcing open the Dardanelles Straits – the strategically vital waterway that connects the Mediterranean and Black Sea – and joining forces with Entente ally Russia, who would then be able to release their trapped Black Sea naval fleet into open water and mount a united attack on the Central Powers on the Eastern Front as well as on the West.

Such an attack would also underline British and French support for their Russian partner, as well as help capture

Constantinople (modern day Istanbul), the spiritual capital of the Turkish Ottoman Empire. And First Lord of the Admiralty Churchill was in no doubt as to the significance of success at Gallipoli, as he proclaimed in one of his famous quotes:

> This is one of the great campaigns of history. Think what Constantinople is to the East. It is more than London, Paris and Berlin all rolled into one are in the West. Think how it has dominated the East. Think what its fall will mean.

The initial sea-based attack on 18 March 1915 proved a complete failure, meaning a Plan 'B' approach of landing on the adjacent Gallipoli peninsula would be undertaken. Troops began to land on 25 April and were soon bogged down in the face of determined Turkish resistance. For the next eight months, the Western Front stalemate was replicated on the unforgiving Gallipoli scrubland before the humiliated invaders were forced to withdraw, with Churchill having lost his job.

During that time, a total of 21,255 British soldiers were to lose their lives, including the first Northern Union player to obtain a commission in the Great War – Batley's Robert Randerson.

In March 1915, there had been some debate among the Yorkshire and Lancashire press as to who had won rugby league's race to be the first officer. Some were championing Wakefield Trinity's William Lindsay Beattie, who was appointed temporary 2nd Lieutenant in the Border Regiment on 15 March 1915, while others pointed to Wigan's Great Britain tourist Gwyn Thomas, who was made an officer in the Northumberland Fusiliers towards the end of 1914. The papers had overlooked the actual 'winner' in the form of the Batley winger.

The York-born Randerson, a member of the Leeds University Officer's Training Corps (OTC), enlisted shortly after Britain's entry into the war, with the *London Gazette* announcing on 25 August 1914[1] he was one of the OTC cadre appointed as a temporary 2nd Lieutenant. Promotion quickly followed. In January 1915 the *London Gazette* announced his appointment to temporary Lieutenant with effect from 10 December 1914[2]. The same official journal announced his promotion to the rank of temporary Captain from 15 May 1915[3].

By that time, the press had corrected their records and acknowledged Randerson's status as the Northern Union's first commissioned officer, something the Batley club was delighted to announce at its annual meeting in May 1915.

> Randerson ..... was the first N.U. player to receive a commission. This honour had been claimed by others, but it belongs to Lieut. Randerson and the Batley Club.

Within months of the confirmation, Randerson was dead.

Born on 4 November 1890, he spent his childhood in York with his parents Robert and Annie Randerson (née Wilkinson) and four brothers Benjamin, William (who died aged nine), John and George and sister Annie. The family were comfortably off with Robert Senior earning his living as a master corn miller, then as a grocer and corn merchant. The family also had strong Catholic links, with young Robert's uncle being a priest, and siblings also following religious vocations.

After his education at Archbishop Holgate's Grammar

School, Randerson trained to be a teacher in Catholic schools at St Mary's College, Hammersmith, where he quickly demonstrated his all-round sporting ability. For instance, in an inter-college sports contest he broke all previous records for the 100 yards flat race, covering the distance in fractionally over 10 seconds.

He was appointed an assistant master at St Mary's School, Batley, in 1913, and soon became involved in the wider Parish community, holding the role of choirmaster at St Mary's Church. But he became known beyond the town's Catholic population when he signed for Batley. He was spotted by the club after doing sprint training at the Batley Athletic and Cricket Club, part of the rugby team's set-up. After seeking permission from the Borough Education Committee, he signed on as a pure amateur initially, according to his diary, because he hoped to soon return to York.

After impressing in the reserves, he signed as a professional, with the flying winger making his first-team debut in an 11-0 Challenge Cup defeat at Halifax on 14 March 1914, where his centre partner was a certain Jack Tindall. In what the local press described as a 'creditable debut', Randerson's diary notes stated: 'I was disappointed to lose my first match without a score'.

Even though Randerson started his senior Batley career with a loss, he maintained his place in the side and opened his tryscoring account with two in the 21-5 home Northern Union victory over Keighley the following week. Those were to be the first two of his five senior appearances, during which time he crossed for a total of four tries, before the outbreak of the war cut short a very promising start to his Northern Union career. As soon as war was declared, his sense of duty kicked in and he became the first Batley player to enlist, stating:

I am not a fighting man; I don't like to fight, but
I ought to go and fight at a time like this.[4]

He served with the 6th (Service) Battalion, Alexandra, Prince
of Wales Own (Yorkshire Regiment), which was one of
Kitchener's New Army volunteer battalions and is better
known today as the Green Howards. His enlistment
necessitated a re-arrangement of the St Mary's Boys
Department timetable, an event noted in the school log book.

It was during his training in Grantham that Randerson
made his final Batley appearance against Keighley at Mount
Pleasant on 10 October 1914. He informed club secretary
Kershaw Newton it would be his last game due to the
growing demands placed upon him as an officer. He
explained in a statement produced in the *Batley News*:

> 'I have 60 men under me and I am responsible for
> them, and will have to lead them to war. To make
> them and myself efficient requires all my time
> and energy, and I do not think it would be right
> to risk laying myself up with an injury.'

He poignantly added:

> 'I will come and hope to see many of my old
> friends round the railings as a sort of good-bye
> until we get the serious business through and
> when honour and justice are satisfied I trust to
> have many a jolly game on the hill' [*of Batley's
> Mount Pleasant ground*].[5]

Randerson was among the tryscorers against Keighley in a

19-0 triumph, although ironically, given his concerns about injury before the game, he suffered a kick to the head. This blow confined him to a darkened room for a few days on returning to his Belton Park Army training camp. Yet even though he signed up for war almost immediately, it was not until early July 1915 that Randerson and his battalion left Liverpool bound for the Dardanelles.

They initially landed at Lemnos then Imbros during July to acclimatise and practice night landings and attacks, and then on the evening of 6 August they disembarked in the Gallipoli peninsular at Suvla Bay with the aim of taking Lala Baba. As soon as they moved off from the sea shore, they were plunged into total darkness, unable to see their comrades around them. It was then that the Turks struck.

Lala Baba was eventually taken, but the unit war diary records a heavy price paid, with 16 of the battalion's officers killed or wounded.[6] Robert Randerson was one of those killed, dying on 7 August 1915, within hours of the landing. The War Office telegram to the family read:

> Deeply regret to inform you that Capt R Randerson Yorks Regt was killed in action Aug 7 Lord Kitchener expresses his sympathy.[7]

According to a fellow officer, Randerson met an instantaneous death as the result of a gunshot wound to the head. In a letter to Robert's father, which was published in the *Batley Reporter and Guardian*, he wrote:

> We made our landing on the evening of the 6th August below the Salt Lake. The 6th Yorks covered the landing of the rest of the brigade. We disembarked from the barge with little

76

opposition and started up the peninsular to take a hill called Talla Baba, and there we lost a lot of men. I got there just before midnight. Some of our men had gone over and some were held up by the Turks entrenched on top and there were several of our officers wounded and killed there. I was told your son had been killed there and the sergeant who told me said that he had been shot through the head, so his death seems to have been instantaneous.[8]

Shortly after his death, there was also a tribute in the *Batley News* of 21 August, which summed up the way the public throughout the town viewed Randerson.

A pattern of good conduct on the rugby field, handsome appearance, of excellent physique, and a splendid teacher, his demise removes from the Heavy Woollen District one whose manifold example commends itself to the rising generation.

The entry in the St Mary's school log book simply read:

News received that Captain Randerson, Assistant Master from this school, was killed in action at the Dardanelles on August 7th.

His mother wrote two desperate letters to the War Office begging for the return of his personal belongings. It appears from records none were forthcoming. Robert Randerson does, however, have a named grave, at Lala Baba Cemetery, Gallipoli.

Randerson was not the only Northern Union player to

be part of the Suvla Bay landings on the evening of 6 August. Bradford Northern forward John Wilkinson was also involved, although not directly alongside his Batley rival. The 33-year-old Wilkinson was in the 8th Battalion of the Duke of Wellington's (West Yorkshire Regiment) who, incidentally, also did their initial training in Grantham.

Born in Keighley on 1 January 1882 to parents Joseph and Mary Wilkinson and baptised at St Mary's, Eastwood, on 11 February 1885, he married Harriet Ann Dresser on 14 April 1900 at Holy Trinity, Lawkholme. A painter of iron machines, the young John proved a highly-promising forward, and the *Yorkshire Post and Leeds Intelligencer* of 11 December 1907 reported that Keighley had secured Wilkinson's registration.

By the end of his debut season, Wilkinson made the short move to Bradford Northern for the start of the 1907-08 Northern Union campaign, where he remained until the outbreak of war and made his ill-fated trip to the Dardanelles. But unlike Randerson, Wilkinson survived the Turks' initial fierce act of resistance as the British landed on their shores. Those who were fortunate enough not to be hit were forced to dig in and hold their ground until reinforcements started to arrive. For three days, Wilkinson and his colleagues were virtually 'trapped' close to the shoreline, until they were ordered to advance on the Turks at 4am on the morning of 9 August.

It proved to be heavy and dangerous going, with the unit war diary describing how the enemy were also advancing in force and 'the fire now became very hot and heavy casualties were rapidly being sustained.'[9] With around only 350 men left, practically no officers remaining and ammunition running short, Wilkinson and his battalion were compelled to repeatedly withdraw to more suitable positions before finally being forced to regroup at their brigade headquarters the following day, as part of the reserve. But they had little time to rest as the Turks then counter-attacked, with the order going out for the battle-weary British to fix bayonets and advance in a bid to fill a gap in the line. This they successfully did.

By this time, however, it was obvious no further progress could be made against their brave foe, who may have been suffering far more casualties than their invaders but were in no mood whatsoever to hand over any of their territory. It was no surprise, therefore, when the order was received on 11 August for the 8th West Yorkshire Regiment to fall back to the beach and re-organise yet again. This the soldiers had to do under heavy enemy shell fire, with Wilkinson reported as missing presumed dead during this engagement at Suvla Bay. The date recorded for his death is 12 August 1915.

News he had probably died was reported in the *Shipley Times and Express* on 10 September 1915. Under the heading 'Keighley Soldier Missing. Played for Bradford Northern', it said as follows:

> Mrs. Wilkinson, the wife of Private John Wilkinson, of the 8th West Ridings, and of Hanover Street, Keighley, has been notified by the War Office that her husband has been posted as missing since August 12th.
>
> Private Wilkinson was a Rugby forward. He played for Keighley Olicana, Keighley Zingari, and Keighley clubs, and some seasons ago was transferred to Bradford Northern, in which team he figured pretty regularly when they played at Greenfield. Whilst there he figured against the All

Blacks (Baskerville's famous team of New Zealanders).

Wilkinson, along with several other Keighley lads well known in football circles ..... joined the forces soon after the outbreak of war, and with the 8th West Ridings went out to participate in the Dardanelles campaign. He took part in the landing at Suvla Bay, and the tidings that he is missing date back to the time of the great battle which succeeded it. Whether he has suffered the fate of his colleague Wiggan, or whether he has been wounded and taken prisoner by the Turks, only time will show.

Although the report stated Wilkinson was a regular in the Northern side, his appearances in the first team were relatively limited. Despite signing for Bradford for the start of the 1907-08 season and remaining on the first-team register until the outbreak of the war, he made just eight senior appearances during that time. And, in fact, he found himself involved in a little controversy early in his Northern career, as the *Yorkshire Post* of 3 March 1908 revealed. It read:

An objection was made by Brighouse St. James's against the result of their match with Girlington in the first round of the Halifax Charity Cup, on the grounds that they played J. Wilkinson who, they contended, was ineligible because he failed to produce a permit to play from the Bradford Northern Club. It was shown that Wilkinson had the permit, and the objection was not upheld, though the deposit of the Brighouse Club was returned.

His loss was later confirmed in an article in the *Yorkshire Post and Leeds Intelligencer* on 2 November 1915, which stated:

> A comrade now in hospital at Alexandria has written to say that he saw him fall.

Wilkinson is commemorated on the Helles Memorial, Gallipoli. He left a widow, Harriet Ann, and seven children.

Although Randerson and Wilkinson were the only two current first-team players to have featured at Northern Union level to lose their lives during the doomed Dardanelles campaign, two other men who were well-known within the game are well worthy of mention.

One was just about to embark on what many predicted would be a highly-successful Northern Union career, while the other had achieved greatness in both codes of rugby. They were Leigh's 24-year-old Harry Ward and the 34-year-old former England Rugby Union international and Oldham star William Moore Bell Nanson, who were both killed during the ill-fated third battle of Krithia on 4 June 1915.

Ward had caught the eye of Leigh directors for a string of impressive performances for local amateur club Parkside Rangers, with the youngster signing around the same time as his Parkside teammate Tom O'Neill. He was very quickly a key member of Leigh's 'A' team, starring regularly in the hooking role, although his first-team opportunities were blocked as Leigh boasted one of the best No9s in the game at the time in Joe Cartwright.

The exceptionally-gifted Cartwright's pedigree was underlined by the fact he went on to earn Great Britain international honours and toured Australia in 1920, which meant Ward was denied the chance to demonstrate his undoubted talent on the Northern Union stage.

In comparison, Nanson had seen it all. The Carlisle-born forward was twice capped by England at rugby union in 1907 against France and Wales before joining Oldham the following year. Within months he had helped his new club reach the 1908 Lancashire Cup final, where they suffered a 10-9 defeat to Wigan, and also represented Cumberland in a pioneering game against the first Australian touring side. But injury then restricted his appearances, and within a couple of seasons he had been forced to retire and resume his working career in slating.

By September 1914, both Ward and Nanson had enlisted.

Although both men lost their lives at the same time and in the same battle, they were not from the same regiment. Able Seaman Ward was in the Anson Battalion, part of the 63rd Royal Navy Division. This Division included surplus Royal Navy reservists and Royal Marines who were not required for service at sea so fought on land alongside the Army. Sergeant Nanson served in the 1/10th Battalion Manchester Regiment.

After the failure of the first two Battles of Krithia, there was hope among many of the allies that the Turks were about to crack, with a bombardment of Turkish strongpoints at 8am on 4 June, followed by an infantry advance just over three hours later. As the shells were launched overhead, the British troops made their way up to the front-line trenches, waiting for the moment to 'go over the top,' just like many of their colleagues were doing on the Western Front. As described by Ordinary Seaman Joe Murray in an article on The Gallipoli Association website,[10] men were unable to lie down, standing in the boiling sun amid an overpowering stench and maggots and flies from dead bodies strewn around. It was a hell hole from which Ward, Nanson and many others did not escape.

News of Ward's death was reported in the *Leigh Journal* of 21 July 1915 under the headline: 'Another Leigh Footballer Killed'. It stated:

> On June 21st, 1915 [*his death was later officially recorded as 4 June*], Able Seaman Harry Ward, R.N.V.R., was reported as missing in Gallipoli. His parents,[11] who reside at 10, Norbury-st, Leigh, have just received word that he was killed on that date. Able Seaman Ward was with the second draft of men that landed in Gallipoli, and was with the 'Anson' Battalion. He enlisted on September 4th 1914 when he was working at the Plank Lane Collieries. He was a single man ..... A man of fine physique, he played as a forward with the Leigh 'A' team.'

It was another professional rugby league career cruelly taken away before it had begun. Like Bradford Northern's John Wilkinson, Nanson and Ward are remembered on the Helles Memorial.

For the British, the Gallipoli campaign was a complete disaster and is often overlooked when discussing the history of the First World War. But in Australia and New Zealand it is seen as a defining moment in their nations' history. When war was declared in August 1914, Australia had been a federated nation for just 13 years, and its people were desperate to prove their relatively new-found status on the world stage. Gallipoli would be their chance.

As members of the British Commonwealth, both Australia and New Zealand's forces were immediately called to arms, with a role at Gallipoli the chance to show their fellow allies just what they could do. The soldiers of these two countries would be fighting together for the very first time as the Australian and New Zealand Army Corps – the ANZACs.

This new force landed on Gallipoli on 25 April 1915 and were met by fierce resistance by their Turkish defenders. On their very first day of military action, the ANZACs suffered heavy casualties, setting the tone for the disastrous eight-month campaign. By the time the campaign had ended, Australian casualties were 8,709 dead and 19,441 wounded, and New Zealand's were 2,779 dead and 5,212 wounded.

As a result, Gallipoli had a profound impact on the two nations, with 25 April adopted as their Remembrance Day for all their fallen in all conflicts from 1915 to now.

And rugby league does, of course, play its part, with the annual Australia v New Zealand ANZAC Test on 25 April now a major sporting occasion which is staged in honour of all those from that part of the world who made the ultimate sacrifice.

1915 – French Pressure Mounts

6

Even though the 1915 Spring offensives had achieved little for the allies, the British were still put under considerable pressure from the French to mount a major Autumn offensive. The plan was for the British to mount a large-scale attack at Loos in northern France on 25 September. It was not a battle they wanted to fight.

Forced to attack on a wide and open front, they lacked the guns and shells required to inflict the required damage. Nevertheless, after using gas for the first time, the British did make initial gains, which Sir John French failed to exploit by holding back his reserves too long. It was a mistake which would ultimately cost him his job – Douglas Haig took over on 19 December the same year – but tragically the British failure at the Battle of Loos cost many men their lives, with casualties of over 50,000 being suffered.

Among the dead was Oldham's Daniel Shannon, who was killed on the opening day of the battle at the age of 29 and is remembered on the Loos Memorial. Born in Hawick in 1886, the son of John and Jane Shannon, he made his name in rugby union with his home town of Hawick before registering with Oldham on 15 October 1912. The fresh-faced, fair-haired, diminutive half-back, who stood at just under 5' 4", was described as a pocket Hercules. He had caught the eye of several Northern Union clubs, including Hull KR as well as Oldham, for his natural ability to shine in the seven-a-side form of the union code – a form that seemed naturally suited to league. In fact, Shannon had been key to helping the Hawick VII set a new Borders Sevens record in 1912, winning five seven-a-sides competitions on five successive Saturdays. Shannon played throughout.

It was something that had not gone unnoticed 'down south', with Oldham winning the race to land his signature later that year. His capture was announced in the 11 October 1912 edition of the *Hawick News and Border Chronicle*, who predicted big things for Shannon in the Northern Union, although they were to prove heartbreakingly accurate in their assessment when they stated he would be a success in the new code 'barring accident'. The newspaper reported:

> Danny Shannon, the popular Hawick half-back, has accepted an offer to play for Oldham, and left Hawick. The fact that Shannon has at last gone over to Northern Unionists has occasioned keen regret in the town and the 'Greens' are the poorer for his departure. It will be remembered that Hull Kingston Rovers were said to have been desirous of securing Shannon last season, but nothing came of it. Oldham have gone one better than the Hull people and 'for better for worse' Shannon is 'over the Border an' awa'.' He is said to have

received £50 down, and the promise of £2 per
match with an extra 10s for a win, while work
will be found for him. Shannon is not a youngster
and by no means a veteran of the game; he is of
sturdy build, and should have several seasons of
football (bar accident) in front of him.

But his initial impact in the Northern Union was far from
dramatic. Despite signing for Oldham in October 1912, he
had to learn his league trade in the reserves before eventually
making his Northern Union debut at stand-off in a 16-0 defeat
at Widnes on 15 February 1913. He then had to wait until 24
March to make senior appearance No2 and a 13-8 defeat at
home to Broughton Rangers, before featuring at scrum half
for the final five fixtures of the campaign. Returning to
Hawick in May 1913 he described the Northern Union game
as 'a bit faster, but otherwise not so much different to that
played in Scotland'. He failed to score in any of his seven
first-team games in his first season. He also failed to cross in
his one solitary 1913-14 start in an 11-7 home defeat to
Broughton Rangers on 17 January 1914.

Shannon remained on the club's books throughout that
campaign and was still on their register at the outbreak of
war. However, his lack of success seems to have initiated a
move back to Hawick to run a fish and chip business in the
Howegate area. At the outbreak of war he wasted relatively
little time answering the nation's call and joined the 7th
Battalion Cameron Highlanders as a Private in November
1914, sailing to Boulogne on 8 July 1915.

Unfortunately, he joined a battalion who were to
experience some very fierce 1915 fighting weeks later in the
Battle of Loos.

At 5.50am on 25 September, the first day of the battle,

the gas was turned on, although it proved ineffectual because of the lack of wind. Forty minutes later the 7th Camerons went forward as part of the 44th Brigade's 15th Scottish Division's assaulting column in support of the 9th Black Watch and 8th Seaforths. They passed through the German third line trenches, cutting through wire unaffected by the earlier artillery bombardment, and streamed through Loos, the ground behind them strewn with the dead and wounded. In Loos they had to bomb and bayonet the Germans from their positions in the ruined town's cellars, before proceeding to Hill 70 where they were pinned down. According to the 7th Cameron's official history their casualties for that day were 548 officers and men killed, wounded or missing.[1] Shannon was amongst them.

As a result of the chaos of battle, it was some time before reports of what had happened reached back to Scotland, with one of the earliest accounts of Shannon's demise printed in the *Hawick News and Border Chronicle* on 8 October. It read:

> Private D. Shannon of the 7th Cameron Highlanders, is reported to be seriously wounded and missing since 25th Sept. The information was contained in a letter to his sister from J.G. Dawson, a Hawick man in the same regiment, who writes as follows:
>
> 'Your brother was a great favourite with us all. We all hope he will turn up yet, for they are still bringing them in from the battlefield. We have had a very big fight, about the biggest that the world has ever seen, and have made a mark that will never fade. General French addressed us to-day (28th Sept), saying that no praise could be

good enough for the way we had come through; and I can tell you it has been terrible. It is not finished yet, for we have the Germans on the run and are giving them something they have never got before. We also have got a terrible cutting-up; not many of us are left now, for you never know the minutes here. As I write, shells are dropping around us every now and again.'

From later information received by his relatives, it is feared that Private Shannon has been killed. Private D. Shannon (who is a son of Mr John Shannon, 9 Beaconsfield Terrace) was a well-known Rugby footballer and foot runner. After doing splendid work for the Hawick 'Greens', Shannon went over to the Northern Union, playing under the Oldham colours for a short time.....

The family made enquiries through the Red Cross, but his death was officially accepted by the military authorities in September 1916. Later in the war, his brother Andrew lost his life on 3 December 1917 whilst serving with the Durham Light Infantry.

As well as Daniel Shannon, Runcorn's John 'Jack' Thomas Ashley also lost his life on 25 September. Born in around 1889 to parents Francis and Mary Hannah Ashley (née Joyce), he was baptised at Runcorn All Saints parish church on 24 March that year. The young Jack proved a shining light on the local junior rugby league scene, primarily with the Runcorn White Star. It was no surprise, therefore, when the forward was snapped up by his hometown Northern Union club during the 1911-12 season.

Ashley made an ill-fated senior debut in a heavy 60-0

thrashing at Oldham on 30 March 1912. It was a defeat that summed up Runcorn's wretched season, with the team's main objective at that time to avoid finishing the campaign in the bottom three. In the end, they managed that relatively comfortably – Keighley, Bramley and Coventry were the three below them, with Coventry bottom of the pile – but Ashley unfortunately paid the price for being involved in such a heavy loss on his Northern Union bow and was immediately dispatched back into the reserves. He was also briefly de-registered by the club, but was then re-registered with the first team as a back-up player. Despite remaining on Runcorn's first-team books, he was continually overlooked for a second Northern Union start, and wasted little time enlisting when his country went to war.

Ashley, a worker at the Manchester Ship Canal Company, signed up with the 9th Battalion Cheshire Regiment within weeks of Britain's declaration and arrived in France on 19 July 1915. Initially, the battalion's time overseas was relatively quiet as they began to prepare for the major offensive ahead.

Details regarding the exact nature of how Ashley received his fatal injuries are scant, but records show he died of wounds and is buried at Lillers Community Cemetery in the Pas de Calais region of France. News of his death was reported in the *Liverpool Echo* on 1 October 1915 under the headline 'Runcorn Footballer Killed'. The report read:

> News has been received in Runcorn that one of the local Rugby footballers has fallen in action. The information was communicated by a chaplain to the forces to the parents of Private John T. Ashley, of 109 Shaw-street, that their son has died of wounds in France received in an

engagement on the 25th [*September*] ..... He was 26 years of age, and was an old choir boy at St Michael's Church. His brother Frank lies in a base hospital in France suffering from wounds received in action on the same date whilst serving with the Royal Lancaster Regiment. There is another brother serving with the forces.

Only four days after Shannon and Ashley had fallen, Rochdale's 33-year-old three-quarter Tom West lost his life. Ernest Thomas West, to give him his full name, was born in 1882, the son of Walter and Emma West of Twerton near Bath. He began playing rugby for Oldfield Park and from them joined Bath, quickly proving a leading light in the club's second team where his natural prowess as a sprinter helped establish him as a strike three-quarter. His promotion to the first team was almost inevitable, debuting against Taunton in 1903. He had a brief spell at Gloucester after taking up a job in the city.

His defection to Gloucester was among the topics discussed in the *Bath Chronicle and Weekly Gazette* in their review of Bath's season on 25 April 1907. It said:

> .....it was satisfactory to have such speedy three-quarters as Meister, Lewis and West with which to commence the season ..... Lewis, Harding, and West turned out with praise-worthy regularity until the exigencies of employment transported the last-named to Gloucester, where his speedy absorption into the Gloucester premier fifteen was a compliment not overlooked by his Bath friends.

Unfortunately, in the half a season he was there, he struggled to get into a first team packed with England internationals, so he returned to Bath and was very quickly promoted to club captain for the 1907/08 season. During this time, he played alongside winger Jack Robinson, who was also to join Rochdale and was selected to tour Australia and New Zealand with Great Britain in the autumn of 1914, along with Hornets teammate Walter Roman. There will be more about Roman later.

Whilst captaining Bath, West made six county appearances for Somerset, who were captained by another future Rochdale signing in Tommy Woods. West then switched codes and signed for Hornets in 1908 – and was given a good job in the Corporation Electricity Works at Rochdale – making his debut at centre in a home game against Leigh on 7 November that year.

A crowd of over 3,000 were there to watch the contest, with the Cricket and Football Field stating in their match preview of the day that West's debut had created some interest, revealing the Hornets were:

> .....hopeful of repeating their last season's victory of 11 points to eight over the Mather Laners as they had got together a strong team, including Tom West, a new centre three-quarter from Somerset County, who last season captained Bath.

Unfortunately, things did not go according to plan, with Rochdale losing 11-0 and triggering a considered piece in the *Cricket and Football Field* the following week which proclaimed:

> Tom West, Rochdale Hornets' latest capture, did
> not make a very satisfactory debut against Leigh.

But West was soon to make the publication eat their words as he became a mainstay of a successful Hornets side. He went on to make a further 138 appearances, mainly on the wing, scoring 48 tries and kicking four goals, and becoming a very popular member of the squad in the process. The highlight during that time was his appearance, alongside fellow Somerset men Roman and Woods, in Rochdale's 12-5 Lancashire Cup final triumph over Oldham on 2 December 1911, in front of a capacity 20,000 crowd at Broughton Rangers' Wheater's Field ground. But even though he was such an influential member of the Hornets' squad, he was a relatively early volunteer at the start of the war, joining the King's Royal Rifle Corps in early September 1914.

He was killed in action on the morning of 29 September 1915, whilst serving with the 10th Battalion's 'A' Company. He was on sentry duty alongside former Bath teammate Bert Lewis (who was to die in December 1915) when hit by a German sniper bullet that killed him instantly. His death was recorded in his battalion's unit war diary, although he was not named in person. The diary entry for 29 September records in a matter-of-fact manner:

> A very wet day, work being done as quickly as
> possible to make the parapet bullet proof. Had
> one man shot through it.[2]

Amongst the first newspapers to announce his death was the *Manchester Courier and Lancashire General Advertiser* of 5 October, which said:

> Private Tom West, King's Royal Rifles, a brilliant Rugby football player, and a former member of the Rochdale Hornets team, has been killed in action.....

And the following day there was a far more comprehensive report in the *Rochdale Observer*. It read:

> Rifleman T.I. Pomfret of the King's Royal Rifles, in a letter to his mother, who lives at 191 Rooley Moor Road, Spotland, announces that his 'greatest chum' Tommy West, the well-known Hornets player, was killed in action in France on Wednesday of last week. The writer says: 'I regret to inform you that Tommy West met his death this (Wednesday) morning whilst doing his duty. The bullet passed through the side of his face, and there was no hope for him. He died immediately without saying a word. The trenches are awful, we being up to the knees in mud.'
>
> The late Rifleman T. West and Rifleman Pomfret enlisted together in September of last year, leaving Rochdale on the seventh of that month. They were members of the same regiment and had been companions while undergoing their training. Deceased, who was a native of Bath, joined the Hornets club in the year 1909 [*sic*] and played regularly for the first team for several seasons. Before coming North he assisted the Bath and Gloucester clubs, and at different times played for Somerset County against Glamorgan, Yorkshire, Devon, Cornwall, Gloucester and Middlesex. West was a most unassuming player

and he has often rendered conspicuous service as a wing three-quarter. Of rather small stature, he was a very speedy and plucky player.

Deceased ..... was employed as a mechanic at the Rochdale Electricity Works.....

Rifleman W.R. Coupe of the King's Royal Rifles, writes to the 'Observer' Office as follows: 'It is with deep regret that I send you the sad news of Rifleman Tom West's death. He was killed in the early morning of Wednesday last whilst on sentry, and died in a few minutes without regaining consciousness.

'Everyone in the platoon feels the loss very much, as he was a bright and cheerful fellow, and was liked by all. Being Tom's friend, he asked me to advise his chums in Rochdale if anything occurred to him, as we enlisted together on September 5th. He asked especially to be remembered to Vic. Slade, his chum in Rochdale.'

As well as the official Army letter sent to his parents telling them he had died, they also received what would have been his last, unsent letter home to them, as revealed in the *Bath Chronicle and Weekly Gazette* of 9 October.

.....The officer who wrote to them said that West was killed instantaneously, and remarked: 'He was a good soldier, a kind friend, faithful in his duty, and will be missed by all.' Enclosed was a letter which West had written to his mother but had not lived to despatch. It began with the following pathetic[3] passage: 'I may not have the opportunity of writing to you for a little while, so you must not worry if you don't hear from me. I shall be quite all right. We are all keeping in good condition.'

Tom West is buried at the Royal Irish Rifles Graveyard at Laventie, France.

As the cold winter months approached, the plans for further offensives were put on ice. But that did not produce a halt to the killing. Soldiers on both sides continued to die on a regular basis, with shelling, sniping and trench raids all contributing to producing a cumulatively high death toll. And around Christmas-time, Northern Union players Herbert Finnigan from Wakefield Trinity and George Thom of Salford were to lose their lives.

Finnigan died of gas poisoning in Belgium on 19 December after the Germans used phosgene gas for the first time – chlorine had been used in earlier attacks – while Thom was to die from his wounds back in England on 30 December.

The 26-year-old Finnigan was a Wakefield lad through and through. Born on 29 September 1889, he was the son of Thomas and Harriet Finnigan of Outwood. It was the locality with which he retained strong associations throughout his relatively short life. He was baptised in the local church of St Mary Magdalene. He then went on to play as an amateur with Outwood Church ARLFC, where his ability as a three-quarter was spotted by Wakefield, who handed him a professional contract on 8 October 1912.

He made his 1913-14 first-team debut the following September in a 9-5 League defeat at Bramley, going on to make eight appearances in total on the wing or at centre before joining up. He also crossed for two tries during his relatively brief time in the Northern Union spotlight, in an 8-

3 defeat at Widnes in February 1914 and then a heavy 33-5 home loss to Huddersfield a month later.

Finnigan joined the local Wakefield Territorials in 1908, the 4th King's Own Yorkshire Light Infantry (KOYLI). They were at their annual summer camp at Whitby when war was declared and the order to mobilise was issued. Finnigan had no hesitation in enlisting to serve overseas with his fellow 1/4th KOYLI chums. Training in earnest followed, including a tragic raft building and bridging exercise whilst based in Gainsborough, Lincolnshire in February 1915 when seven men died.

Finnigan went out to France in April 1915, his battalion forming part of the 49th Division. They were initially in northern France before moving to Flanders on the Ypres-Boesinghe front. There they spent the summer constructing and repairing trenches and strong points which were constantly damaged by enemy shelling, and although sustaining regular casualties, there were no major incidents. As a qualified carpenter, Finnigan was certainly well suited to the task at hand.

Unfortunately, however, nothing was to prepare them for what was to come in December, after sixth months in the sector. Early that month, intelligence reports and information collected from captured German soldiers suggested the enemy was about to mount a gas attack. Gas cylinders had been seen along the German front, opposite the 49th Division's position. And at just before 5am on the morning of 19 December, the attack began, as described in the KOYLI's unit war diary for the day.

> 4.50am: A hissing noise like a fast running motor car was heard in the German lines. Very shortly after, the presence of cylinder gas, said to be

Fossgene [*sic*], was detected in the air. Warning was given, tube helmets put on and rapid fire opened on the enemy's parapet with rifles and machine guns.[4]

The 1/4th Battalion did manage to keep enemy attacks at bay, but as they were being relieved that evening, a fresh bombardment was launched using shells filled with the lethal phosgene. Given the casualty toll, it was shockingly clear the British gas helmets were not equipped to deal with this new deadly gas. Finnigan was one of those to suffer. The unit war diary for the day records one officer and 23 men killed through gas poisoning with a further two officers and 149 other ranks wounded. Another officer was wounded and subsequently died and a further 19 other ranks wounded in the enemy attacks.

By this stage in his Army career, Finnigan had reached the rank of signalling Sergeant, and he was successfully able to raise the alarm to battalion headquarters and keep the lines of communication open before he was overcome by the fumes. It proved a heroic act, and one that would later receive official recognition at the highest level, with Finnigan going on to be Mentioned in Despatches for his selfless deed in the *London Gazette* of 13 June 1916.

The Wakefield man was one of 19 members of his battalion to be named individually in the Despatch – some of whom died, others surviving the attack – which read:

The following despatch has been received by the Secretary of State for War from General Sir Douglas Haig, G.C.B., Commander-in-Chief of British Forces in France: 'SIR:- I have the honour to forward herewith the names of those under my command whom I wish to bring to notice for gallant and distinguished conduct in the field. I have the honour to be, Sir, Your obedient Servant, D. HAIG, General, Commander-in-Chief The British Forces in France.....

King's Own Yorkshire Light Infantry (Territorial Force) ..... Finnigan, No. 287 Serjt. H. (killed)[5]

Confirmation of his death was reported in the *Leeds Mercury* on 1 January 1916, under the heading 'Gas Attack Victims.' It read:

Official news has been received in Wakefield of the deaths of about 20 local men belonging to the 1st/4th Battalion K.O.Y.L.I. (Wakefield and District Territorials), the following having succumbed to gas poisoning ..... Sergeant H. Finnigan, who lived at Leeds Road, Outwood, was 26, and was a Wakefield Trinity three-quarter. He had been in the Territorials about eight years and had taken many prizes for shooting and signalling.

In contrast to Finnigan's burial taking place close to where he picked up his injuries, at Hospital Farm Cemetery near Ypres, Salford stalwart Thom would have his funeral at 'home' and be laid to rest in Salford (Weaste) Cemetery. Not surprisingly, it proved to be a major event in the city, given his stature and status in the area.

George William Anderson Thom was born in Salford in 1885, the son of policeman George Thom and his wife Mary (née Hodge). In November 1907 Thom married Annie

Rebecca Titley at St Luke's parish church, Weaste. The couple had three children, though one son died before the outbreak of war. In civilian life Thom worked as a motor engineer.

Having signed for Salford in 1908, the hooker soon became a regular in the senior side and by the time he joined the Royal Army Ordnance Corps at the outbreak of war, he had made 157 appearances and scored six tries. His career highlight came in the 1913-14 season when he helped Salford secure their League Championship success, although he had to wait until after the completion of the season to receive his medal, having suffered a season-ending leg injury at home to Broughton Rangers on Christmas Day, 1913. It was to be his 14th and final game of that glorious campaign for his hometown club.

News that Thom's efforts that season had been belatedly recognised by the Northern Union appeared in the *Yorkshire Post and Leeds Intelligencer* of 13 May 1914.

> The Committee granted permission to present extra League championship medals to G. Thom, G. Callender and G. Currie, of Salford, players who had qualified by playing in six or more matches in the League Championship.

But the young Thom originally had designs on becoming a footballer rather than a rugby player, spending much of his youth with the Weaste Amateurs. That all changed when he took part in a Broughton Rangers' workshops competition, and was immediately signed up by Salford's arch Manchester rivals from Wheater's Field.

Thom underlined his potential with several strong performances in Broughton's 'A' team before he made the move to his 'local' Salford club. After just four reserve games, he was promoted to the first team. It would be the start of a long and illustrious career which made him one of the most prominent players on Salford's books. Not surprisingly, therefore, there was no shortage of praise regarding his rugby league exploits in the newspaper columns when the news of his death filtered through. The *Manchester Evening News* of 3 January 1916 announced:

> The death has taken place of Artificer Staff Sergeant George Thom, in Fort Pitt Military Hospital as the result of an accident whilst on active service in France. A Salford forward for a good number of years, he was one of the oldest members of the team, and prior to an accident to his leg on Christmas Day 1913, was one of the best scrimmagers the Salford club ever had. His death will be deplored not only by the Salford patrons and directors of the club, but by all followers of the Northern Union game in general.

Tributes in other papers included ones about his fine understanding of the game, as well as his rare tackling and keen scrimmaging skills despite his short stature for a forward – he was 5ft 9in and weighed between 12 and 13 stones. He was also praised for being one of the most gentlemanly players who ever stepped onto the field.

Thom, who had gone out to France at the end of August 1915, suffered his injury whilst on the roof of a building observing German troop movements ahead of him. As light began to fade, the Salford man attempted to climb down, but missed his footing and fell heavily to the ground, forcing his left leg to give way under him.

Such was the severity of his injury that he was

evacuated back to England for treatment at Fort Pitt Military Hospital at Chatham.

He spent several weeks in hospital at Plymouth undergoing many operations in a bid to save the leg. These failed and the decision was taken to amputate it just below the knee. By mid-December, the news being received back in Lancashire from his wife, who was at his bedside in Chatham, appeared positive. The official Salford matchday programme on 11 December 1915 reported her writing 'George was much better and still improving'.

Before the end of the month, however, he was dead as the strain from undergoing so many operations took its toll. The only consolation for Thom's relatives was they were able to hold the type of family funeral denied to so many others whose sons, husbands, fathers and brothers were buried overseas; or to those other families whose loved ones had no known final resting place.

Thousands took to the streets for one of their favourite son's farewell, including many notable dignitaries. Among those were leading councillor F. Hampson, several members of the Salford club and senior officers from the Salford Police, where Thom's father had served as an inspector. The funeral cortege was accompanied by a band and a firing party, with the 'Last Post' played as his coffin was lowered into his grave.

287 SERJEANT
H. FINNIGAN
KING'S OWN YORKSHIRE L.I.
19TH DECEMBER 1915

HIS MEMORY
LONG WILL LIVE
LONE IN ALL OUR HEA...

Herbert Finnigan
(Wakefield),
Hospital Farm
Cemetery

Jane Roberts

Arthur Llewellyn (Leeds)
*Leeds Rhinos Foundation
Heritage Committee*

Arthur Douglas West
(Oldham)   *Michael Turner*

Belfred Ward (Leeds)
*Leeds Rhinos Foundation
Heritage Committee*

Billy Jarman (Leeds)
*Leeds Rhinos Foundation
Heritage Committee*

Billy Simpson, *bottom right*, in Wakefield's 1909 cup team
Trinity Heritage

Daniel Shannon (Oldham)
Michael Turner

David Harkness Blakey
(Leeds) *Leeds Rhinos Foundation
Heritage Committee*

David Preston (Salford)
Graham Morris

Ernest Doorey (Leigh)
Mike Latham

Ernest Swinton, *second left, second row,* with Widnes   *Steve Fox*

Fred Perrett (Hull FC) – also
played for Leeds in 1913
*Leeds Rhinos Foundation
Heritage Committee*

Fred Longstaff
(Huddersfield)
David Longstaff

Fred Longthorpe
(Bradford
Northern) is
pictured on his
wedding day,
with new bride
Emily Lincoln
Marie Cousens

George Thomas
(Warrington) with
the Challenge Cup
Warrington Wolves

G. THOMAS

WARRINGTON FOOTBALL CLUB

George Thom (Salford)
Graham Morris

Harold Ruck (Bradford)
Birch Lane Heroes

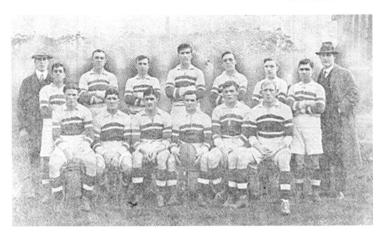

George Wishart (Hunslet), *pictured front, second from right*
www.albertgoldthorpe.info

Harry Basil Wray (Bradford)
Birch Lane Heroes

Harry Ward (Leigh)
Mike Latham

Howard Davis (Warrington), *fourth right, back*, with Coventry RU *Mike Latham*

Howell Rees (Keighley)
Bradford Telegraph & Argus

Jack Harrison's medals on display
Leeds Rhinos Foundation Heritage Committee

James Debney, *third right back row*, and Jack Tindall (both Batley), *third right front row*, wearing cap
Batley Bulldogs

Jimmy Sanders (Leeds)
*Leeds Rhinos Foundation
Heritage Committee*

John Twigg (Rochdale)
Rochdale Rugby League Heritage

Joseph Child
(Batley)
Batley Bulldogs

Jimmy Cook (Salford)
and also inset, *left*
Graham Morris

The First Half of 1916 – Calm Before the Storm

7

In 1915, the majority of the British soldiers who fought and died were the professional soldiers, reservists or Territorial soldiers. By 1916, it was becoming a totally different story.

A small number of Kitchener's volunteer 'New Army' had been thrown into active service in 1915. But the majority of the volunteers would be seeing frontline action for the first time in 1916.

Having said that, the early months of 1916 were relatively quiet, giving little indication of what was to follow on the Somme later in the year. As a result, it was not until 29 April that the first senior Northern Union player was to fall that year – Rochdale Hornets' Charles John Inglis Burton.

Although Burton – he was known by everyone as Jack – was a professional rugby league player, it was almost inevitable he would volunteer to join up early in the war. After all, he had military blood coursing through his veins. One of nine children, he was born on 26 April 1889 at the

Athlone Barracks, Ireland, where his father Charles was a Sergeant Major with the 1st Wiltshire Regiment. A career soldier, he married Charles' mother, Catherine Leavy, whilst serving in India.

Burton Junior, however, initially chose not to follow in his father's footsteps, instead embarking down the sporting route. At an early age, he excelled in sport, representing Ruabon Grammar School in Wales at both football and cricket. And when the family moved to Wigan around the turn of the century, he took up rugby, initially playing with Wigan RFC as both a junior and a senior where he was vice-captain of the 3rd team. In Wigan, Burton was employed in the commercial department of Messrs Strowger and Sons Printers. It was also around this time, in 1906, that his well-known Wigan Freemason father died, leaving Jack's mother Catherine to bring up the children.

His big rugby break was to come early in 1911. After trialling at Warrington where he played in the Combination side, Burton signed for Hornets on 28 February and made his first-team debut at, ironically, hometown club Wigan at centre on 1 April. Unfortunately, that would prove to be one of just two senior Rochdale appearances, with Burton going on to command the somewhat unenviable tag of a 'stalwart of the Hornets 'A' team', although he did remain on the first-team's books up to the outbreak of war. The club knew he could be relied upon to answer the Northern Union call if required.

Yet even though Burton remained on the fringes, he regularly appeared in the newspaper columns for his role as 'reserve team leader', although one incident in which he was involved gained attention for all the wrong reasons. Under the headline 'Local Player Badly Injured' the *Wigan Observer and District Advertiser* of 1 October 1912 reported the following:

The meeting between [*Rochdale A and Wigan A*] was marred by one very regrettable incident, and which ought to lead to some immediate action. It appears that Jack Burton, an elder brother of Bert Burton, who assisted the Rochdale senior team at Wigan last Saturday, and who has since been confined to his home through a severe knee injury, was the victim of an action by one of the Wigan players, whose identity is unknown save to a very restricted number. We gather that J. Burton had successfully evaded the attentions of the Wigan defence, but was hotly pursued by several opponents and as he approached the line received a severe blow on the temple. He retained his feet for some few seconds and then suddenly collapsed. Medical aid was summoned with all possible speed, and it was deemed necessary to remove the unfortunate player to the Rochdale Infirmary, where he lay unconscious for fully three hours. Burton expressed appreciation of the kind treatment he was accorded whilst in the Institution, but was anxious to return home, and made the journey from Rochdale on Monday. His condition was found to be worse than at first thought, although there is no cause for anxiety. The referee was unable to discern the transgressor, owing to the congestion of players in the vicinity.

Soon after war was declared Burton enlisted with the 5th Dragoon Guards before transferring and serving as a Private with the 3rd Battalion Worcestershire Regiment where he was attached to the grenade section. After completing their training, Burton and his comrades arrived in France on 13 July 1915, although it would be eight months before the Rochdale player would lose his life during one of the relatively 'minor' skirmishes – as opposed to major battles – that were taking place all the time. And the action that proved fatal for Burton, as well as several of his colleagues, was described in the unit war diary of 29 April 1916.

> Two platoons of A Company, supported by two platoons of B Coy, were ordered to gain and consolidate the near lip of [a] crater of [a] mine exploded on the 28th. The assault was made at 8.15pm after artillery preparation, but owing to very heavy Machine Gun fire and rifle fire from the crater, no headway was made. A second attempt was made at 1.45am with the same result.[1]

Initial reports back home suggested Burton had been badly wounded rather than killed, among them the *Wigan Observer and District Advertiser* of 6 May, which said:

> It is reported that Pte. Jack Burton has been very badly wounded in action. He has been on active service for about 11 months. Private Burton is well known as a footballer, having played with Wigan and Rochdale Hornets.....

Then one of the first reports of his demise appeared in the *Yorkshire Post and Leeds Intelligencer* of 11 May, confirming:

> Pte. C.J. Burton, a popular three-quarter back of Rochdale Hornets, has been killed in action.

Burton, who was a native of Wigan, was in the Dragoon Guards. He is the third Hornets' player who has been killed in action, the others being J. Twigg and T. West.

He is buried at the Ecoivres Military Cemetery, Mont-St-Eloi, Pas-de-Calais, France.

And a day after Burton fell, Leeds centre Belfred 'Belph' Ward was also to lose his life. Born in 1895 in Pontefract, the son of George and Elizabeth Ward (née Miller), he came from a well-known and well-respected rugby-playing family. His father and his uncle Belph were both top players with Pontefract Rugby Football Club – and they were both as hard as nails. In fact, uncle Belph went beyond the call of duty to prove how brave – or foolhardy – he was, when the *Yorkshire Evening Post* of 3 November 1892 reported:

> At one of the wild beast shows at Pontefract last night, Belph Ward, one of the best forwards of the Pontefract club, and a pioneer in the Volunteers, entered a lion's den with one of the lion tamers, before a large crowd of spectators. Two huge lionesses were put through their facings, and Ward came out of the cage no worse amidst loud cheers.

His nephew, Belph, was also an exceptional rugby player and arrived at Headingley from Featherstone Rovers in February 1914 during what was proving a transitional period for the Leeds club. They were looking at the 1913-14 campaign as the chance to re-build and challenge the mighty Huddersfield, who had emerged as the major Yorkshire force. As a result, they started the season with three promising new signings in top Welsh representative forwards Fred Perrett and Patrick

Gould, and John West from Cross Keys. This trio alone were unable to change Leeds' fortunes for the better and, as a result, even more new faces started to arrive, including Ward, Abertillery duo Joseph Hopkins and Arthur Llewellyn, Neath's Ivor Jones, Durham's David Harkness Blakey and outstanding 'A' team prospect Thomas Harkness. Unfortunately, some of these names will be re-visited later.

Of those who did arrive in early 1914, Ward was arguably the most well-known in the area. All of his brothers, including Leeds forward George, had already established themselves as top professional rugby league players, as the *Yorkshire Evening Post* pointed out on 21 February 1914.

> Good judges Pontefract way congratulate the Leeds Northern Union Club on a smart stroke of business in signing on Belph Ward, a centre three-quarter, of Pontefract.
>
> This player, who recently joined the Featherstone club, and has been transferred by them, comes of a famous football family. He is one of four brothers, all of whom are still playing football. They are Tom Ward (the once famous Hull Kingston and Pontefract centre), Bob Ward (a former Leeds half-back), George Ward, and Belph.
>
> He is 18 years old and began the Northern Union game this year with the Pontefract 'A' team. After a few matches with them he was transferred to the first team and has played some fine games with them. He weighs 11st 1lb and stands 5ft 11in.....
>
> His brother Tom, who is a competent judge, expresses the opinion that the youngster will be the 'star' of the family.

Later reports in the *Yorkshire Post and Leeds Intelligencer* suggested Leeds paid Featherstone £76 to acquire his services.

It was not long before the teenager was underlining that potential. He made his debut at centre in a 22-5 home League win over Hull KR on 21 March 1914 and went on to make five further Northern Union appearances before the end of the season, including a tryscoring display in a 22-5 home success over Bradford on 11 April. As well as playing centre, Ward also operated on the wing and was switched to the flank as Leeds beat in-form Wigan 11-2 at Headingley on 28 March 1914 with the *Yorkshire Evening Post* match preview making it clear that the Leeds fans were never slow in venting their frustrations if they felt a player was under-performing. The preview started:

> The fight for the first four places in the Northern Union League is now almost at an end. Huddersfield are certain of heading the table and of entertaining Hull in the League semi-final at Fartown, but the question of whether Wigan or Salford will finish second has been rendered more open by the former dropping a point against Dewsbury..... In this match, 'Will' Davies will resume his place in the Leeds three-quarter line, and 'Belf' Ward will operate on the wing in the place of Ganley, who feels very acutely the 'barracking' which he received from the crowd last Saturday.

The following season Ward's senior appearances were limited. He featured just seven more times for Leeds, with his final appearance coming on the wing in a 7-3 home win over Oldham on 3 April 1915. He enlisted initially with the Yorkshire Regiment but shortly afterwards transferred to the newly-formed Machine Gun Corps. He was on his way to France in the early spring of 1916. Within weeks of arriving he died, on 30 April 1916. That day the Germans launched a gas attack just inside the Belgium border at Wulverghem. The mixture of chlorine and phosgene gas released across a large front claimed hundreds of casualties, including fatalities, across a range of units in the area. One of those affected was the 72nd Machine Gun Company. Their diary entry reported:

> Enemy released GAS on a front of 3500 yards N of Wulverghem. Owing to our artillery fire the enemy was only able to make small raids on the Brigade's frontage, which were easily dealt with and repulsed.[2]

It went on to say that one officer was slightly wounded and gassed, along with five other ranks wounded and a further six gassed. Ward was one of those affected. He was treated by Number 1 Canadian Casualty Clearing Station for wounds on his right side and gas poisoning. Based at Bailleul, just six miles across the border from Wulverghem in France, their unit war diary records they felt the effects of the early morning German gas attack. The diary also records the admission of 85 patients and 15 deaths. One of those fatalities was Ward, with the Chaplain writing to his mother informing her of the news.

His death was reported in the *Leeds Mercury* of 13 May as follows:

News has been received of the death in action of

Pte. Belf Ward, of Pontefract, who was well-known in Leeds Northern Union football circles. Pte. Ward, who was twenty-one years of age, joined the Leeds Club as a three-quarter back from Featherstone Rovers, and played in several positions for the Headingley team with success. He was formerly employed at the Prince of Wales Colliery at Pontefract.

Ward is buried at the Bailleul Communal Cemetery Extension in France.

Exactly two months later, on 30 June 1916, another Northern Union player with the potential to be a major star of the future died. This time it was Leigh's 21-year-old half-back Robert 'Flop' Topping.

Local lad Topping was born in Abram in 1894 and lived on Talbot Road, Plank Lane, Leigh with parents William and Jane (née Clegg) and brother Albert. It was while he was there that he emerged as a precocious young rugby talent, helping Plank Lane United Methodist Church secure several junior honours. He then moved to Firs Lane, from where he was handed a professional contract with Leigh on 28 February 1913.

Topping may have been small in stature but was big in heart, with his displays in the 'A' team under captain and former first-team regular Dick Gallop soon making him a firm crowd favourite. And the *Leigh Chronicle and Weekly District Advertiser* was clearly impressed with what they were seeing, stating in one report:

Little Topping, or 'Flop', as he is called, from Firs Lane, gave a rattling good account of himself at scrum half, and varied his passing to a nicety. He was always in the vicinity of the ball, and as he is only 18 years old he should do very well.

His performances also caught the eye of Leigh's first-team coaching staff, and on 11 October 1913, Topping was handed his Northern Union debut in a home game against Broughton Rangers while still a teenager. Unfortunately, his debut was overshadowed by the first appearances of big Welsh signings Jack Evans and Fred Hockey, who were charged with the task of halting a mini start-of-season four-game slump. Neither man failed to make any difference as Rangers triumphed 8-0.

But even though Topping had made a far more promising start to his Northern Union career, he joined the Welsh duo in being made scapegoats, and was quickly relegated back into the 'A' team where he stayed for the rest of the campaign. There was at least some comfort on the personal front for the youngster during the second half of the season, however, as he married Ellen Holcroft in Leigh on 1 January 1914.

Topping was also in the 'A' team when war was declared, and within a month the coal miner enlisted, initially with the Army Cyclist Corps, before being attached to 11th Battalion Royal Sussex Regiment as a Private. At the Front in 1916 he undertook the dangerous task of a dispatch rider and was killed in action in the Battle of Boar's Head, Richebourg, where he is buried at St Vaast Post Military Cemetery. It was to prove a significant battle for the Sussex regiment, with the men of the 11th, 12th and 13th Southdowns Battalions being part of a diversionary raid ahead of the start of the Battle of the Somme the following day.

By the end of the action, all three battalions had suffered significant casualties. The 12th and 13th suffered the most as they led the assault, losing 429 and 800 killed and wounded respectively. But the 11th lost 116 casualties whilst supporting the attack, with Topping one of those to lose his life.

On the news of his death, the *Leigh Journal* reported:

> Another Leigh footballer to lay down his life in defence of his country is Pte. Rob[er]t Topping, who lived in Talbot-rd., Plank Lane. Pte. J. Stone discloses the information that he was killed in action on June 30th. He saw him taken away to be buried, and says he died a hero's death. 'He was liked by everybody, and his chums are very much upset. If he had lived he would have lost his leg. He was not killed instantly, but he died before they got him away.'

His widow gave birth to their second child at the end of 1916. She remarried later in the war, her new husband being Fred Wilcock.

Unfortunately, the death of Topping was a taste of things to come.

Joseph Henry Hopkins made his Leeds debut in 1914
courtesy of Leeds Rhinos Foundation

The Somme 1916 –
Headingley's Heavy 1 July Toll

8

In early December 1915, the Allies met at French General Joseph Joffre's headquarters in Chantilly to plan their strategy for 1916. The general consensus was the key to success against the Central Powers was to stretch their interior lines to the limit. The impressive transport links through Germany and Austria-Hungary meant they were able to switch reserves quickly from the Western Front to the Eastern Front and vice versa, depending on which needed to be strengthened.

It made good sense, therefore, for the British, French, Russians and Italians to attack simultaneously in order to leave the Central Powers defending all of their front lines at the same time, therefore stretching their troops to the absolute limit and with no hope of being relieved by fresh reserves from elsewhere. It was felt this pressure would lead to the front breaking at some point and, ultimately, pave the way to victory.

It was decided the British and French would launch their attack in the Somme region of northern France in the summer of 1916. Joffre had been waiting for some time for the British to get their Army up to strength in order to fight an effective land battle, and believed that time had now come. The plan was for the British and French to fight side by side, even though General Sir Douglas Haig, who had replaced the ineffectual Sir John French as the commander-in-chief of the BEF on 19 December 1915, did raise concerns over thrusting his inexperienced and untried conscript Army into such an important and potentially dangerous offensive.

But before the final battle plans could be formulated, the Germans threw a massive spanner in the works by mounting a major attack against the French further south at Verdun on 21 February 1916 in a bid to 'bleed France white'. All of a sudden, the British knew they would have to take the lead for the Somme offensive, with the French now having to mount a determined defence against a new enemy onslaught that was to last for months. The scene was set for the Battle of the Somme, with the slaughter of so many British lives from its bloody, opening day on 1 July 1916.

A week-long barrage before the men were sent 'over the top' as part of the 'Big Push' towards the ultimate victory was supposed to destroy all the German front lines and make the advance a formality. As it turned out, that could not have been further from the truth. For a start, a large number of shells fired were duds and failed to explode, while many that did were shrapnel shells rather than high explosive shells. Shrapnel shells that sent thousands of lead pellets into the air were never going to cut through the barbed wire in front of the German trenches or cause damage to the enemy troops hiding underground in deep, concrete bunkers. If all the shells had been high explosive, then the damage would have been considerable, with the advance having far more chance of success.

As it was, the wire and German bunkers were still intact at 7.30am when the attack began and, sadly but predictably, by the end of the first day, the British casualties were 57,470, of which 19,240 were killed.

Northern Union stars were among them, with Leeds suffering the most as a club. By the end of the worst day in the history of the British Army, Headingley heroes David Harkness Blakey, Joseph Pickles and Joseph Henry Hopkins were dead. All three were relative newcomers to the Leeds club, with none of the trio making their debuts until 1914. They were all potential future blue and amber stars.

The first to sign was Welsh centre Hopkins, who made the move from Abertillery to Leeds on 30 December 1913 and made his debut in an 18-7 home Northern Union triumph over Bramley on 24 January 1914. Though he was not officially registered until the end of December, his capture was being discussed in some detail in the *Yorkshire Post and Leeds Intelligencer* on 20 December. It focused specifically on the impact the departures to the Northern Union of the likes of Hopkins was having on the union code in South Wales. Under the headline 'South Wales Serious Losses', the report said:

> South Wales Rugby football has sustained two serious losses by defection to the Northern Union. George Haywood, of Swansea, who has played for Wales six times, going to Wigan Northern Union Club, and Joseph Hopkins, of Abertillery, going ..... to the Leeds Northern Union Club. Hayward's departure especially has caused consternation in Welsh Rugby circles. Only a few

weeks ago a Northern Union club signed on Swansea's half-backs Owen and Jerram ..... By capturing Hopkins, the Northern Union have dealt another severe blow not only to the Abertillery Club, but also to Welsh Rugby football generally, for Hopkins is admittedly one of the most promising centres in Wales. Although he assisted the Abertillery Club on a few occasions last season, it was not until the end of September this year that his capabilities were fully revealed.

Born in 1893, one of Daniel John and Charlotte Hopkins' 12 children, he was baptised along with sister, Edith, at Llanfrechfa parish church, Monmouthshire on 4 June 1893. Joseph grew up in Abertillery and was quickly bitten by the rugby bug. Having excelled in the sport at school and in the town's junior club ranks, it was almost inevitable he would eventually join the senior Abertillery side. He broke into the first team whilst still a teenager and helped them reach the top of the Welsh League at the start of the 1913-14 season before making the move to West Yorkshire at the age of 19. The capture of the Welsh coal miner was also announced in the *Yorkshire Evening Post* on 20 December, with the paper keen to hail the new arrival.

The Leeds Northern Union Club have obtained the signature of Joseph Hopkins, a centre three-quarter who has been playing with distinction with the Abertillery Club, one of the most successful of the South Wales teams. Hopkins is 19 years old, 5ft 9½in in height and weighs 10st 10lb. He has scored 10 tries with the Abertillery teams this season.

It was clear when he made his debut in the 18-7 home win over Bramley on 24 January 1914 that he was a player with some potential, although far from the finished article and lacking in terms of general fitness, as the *Yorkshire Evening Post* match report of the day clearly demonstrated.

> .....some correspondents in the 'Evening Post' have been eagerly inquiring why Hopkins has not been played before in the first team, and the following remarks in the Leeds programme will probably supply the answer: 'All players who come from the Rugby Union frankly confess that they cannot at first keep up with the Northern Union game. Even Will Davies, probably the best man that has ever come to Leeds from a R.U. club, seemed palpably out of condition when he first played at Headingley. In his first appearance with the second team Hopkins lacked condition, but he has trained rigorously and improved accordingly, and he is now receiving a trial when he has gained experience of the game and is physically fit to do himself justice.'[1]

The report continued later in its match analysis:

> .....the Leeds backs had shown great skill in their angling and judged on first appearance ..... Hopkins and Llewellyn[2] are likely to strengthen the side, although the first-named would do better to use more discrimination in his kicking and passing.

Hopkins went on to make three further starts before the end of the campaign, but failed to feature in the 1914-15 season as he turned his attention to serving his country. Despite being a proud Welshman, Hopkins chose to enlist with the West Yorkshire Regiment (Prince of Wales's Own), with his training geared up to be ready to fight at the Battle of the Somme. He served as a Private with the 2nd Battalion, going out some time in 1916. His battalion was obviously one of many expected to play a key role on the morning of 1 July, with the unit war diary giving a comprehensive insight into how preparations were going.

In the week leading up to the attack, there was a daily update into the type of activities that were taking place, with one reference on 28 June of particular significance given the way the battle would unfold and the obstacles the soldiers would face. It reported:

> On the night of the 28th two patrols went out to see the condition of the German wire, one under 2/Lieut: A.W. Wilkinson, the other under 2/Lieut: E.H. Matheson. They reported wire to be still more or less intact.[3]

As history would show, and as already stated, that inability to destroy the wire made the task for Hopkins and his comrades almost impossible.

On the morning of the battle, the diary revealed the role of Hopkins' battalion in the attack was:

> .....to support the Devons and Middlesex if required to during the early stages and the capture and consolidation of the village of Pozieres was allotted to it as a special task.[4]

It proved a complete disaster. By midday, the battalion had been beaten back and forced to withdraw – with Hopkins and many of his colleagues nowhere to be seen following their attack that morning – as the diary continued:

> Out of the 21 Officers and 702 Other Ranks who went into action, 5 Officers and 212 men came out. The failure of the attack was probably due to the numerous enemy machine guns placed in deep emplacements or tunnels in the slopes of the hill on the La Boiselle side of the valley. Machine guns so emplaced could enfilade the whole Brigade attack.[5]

After the 22-year-old Hopkins went 'over the top' he was never seen again and is remembered on the Thiepval Memorial.

Back-row forward Blakey was another to arrive at Headingley from outside the traditional rugby league heartlands. Signed from the Winlaton Vulcans Rugby Union Club in Newcastle on 15 April 1914, the Gateshead-born Blakey quickly established himself as a first-team regular. Having been capped several times for Durham in the 15-a-side code, Leeds believed they had seen something special in the 'northerner'.

He made his debut as a senior trialist in a 22-5 home triumph over Bradford the same month and then followed it up with a second back-row start at Wigan two days later. That promising start continued into the new 1914-15 campaign, where he appeared in a 12-0 opening-day triumph at Batley and then went on to feature in eight of Leeds' first 10 matches – getting starts at prop and loose-forward, besides the second row – before he answered the call to arms.

The fact he had been a member of the Blaydon Territorial Army from 1909 until he moved to West Yorkshire clearly had some influence on his decision to enlist by January 1915. As someone who had been born in Felling, Gateshead on 9 November 1889 – where he was raised by father Henry and mother Isabella, Henry's second wife – it would not have been a great surprise if he had chosen to attest with a regiment from the north east.

Instead, however, he decided to join the Royal Inniskilling Fusiliers from Ireland, with that particular regiment having been running a series of successful recruiting campaigns in the Gateshead area at the time. And their English recruit certainly made a positive impression, having been promoted to the rank of Sergeant with 'D' Company, 11th Battalion by the eve of the Somme offensive.

On the first day of the battle, Blakey and his battalion formed part of the 109th Brigade of the 36th Ulster Division and assembled at the edge of Thiepval Wood, charged with the task of attempting to take the formidable Schwaben Redoubt German strongpoint. Although they made strong initial gains, they were unable to break through the Redoubt and were eventually forced back as the casualty toll mounted horrifically. Among those to fall was Sergeant Blakey who, according to subsequent letters to his wife, was last seen seriously injured in no man's land.

His heroic efforts did not go unrecognised, however, as he was awarded the Military Medal for 'bravery in the field', something which was chronicled in the 14 December 1916 supplement to the *London Gazette*.[6] In Blakey's absence, the decoration was pinned to the chest of his seven-year-old son Henry during a concert organised by the Winlaton Welcome Home Committee in August 1917. Winlaton was the home town of his wife, Sarah Kendall, who he married in 1908. No doubt the presentation was an emotional affair for the family, although to add to their grief, Henry would also be killed in action in the Second World War in France on 1 June 1940 during the evacuation from Dunkirk. He was 31, and had two sisters, Vivian and Isabella.

Yet this was not the end of the David Harkness Blakey story.

Due to the ferocious fighting in the early days of the battle, it was impossible for the bodies of those killed in no man's land to be recovered. As a result, it was assumed Blakey's body would be lost forever, with his name inscribed alongside over 72,000 others on the Thiepval Memorial to the Missing.

But in November 2013 – 97 years after his death – his remains were discovered just six inches under the ground during a road-widening project near Connaught Cemetery in the heart of the Thiepval battleground. Identification after such a passage of time can prove difficult, if not impossible. But a homemade metal identity tag believed to have been created by his wife was on the body, clearly showing Blakey's name, rank, number and regiment.[7] A Fusilier cap badge was also discovered.

In October 2015, his name was removed from the Thiepval Memorial and he was buried with full military honours at Connaught Cemetery, with three generations of his family there to see it.

Also to die on 1 July was 19-year-old Joseph Robert Pickles, who signed for Leeds from the York Phoenix club in Selby on 15 December 1914. He was expected to go on to be a major Northern Union star.

That deal came just three days after he made a tryscoring debut as a trialist loose forward in an impressive 36-0 home win over York. He was just 17 at the time, and clearly had the rugby league world at his feet. But despite such an eye-catching start to his Northern Union career, it was to prove to be Pickles' one and only Leeds appearance, with the Great War cruelly and abruptly cutting short what could have been the brightest of futures.

And hopes were certainly high that he would go on to become a real Headingley hero. After all, he had come from good rugby stock, with his father Joe having also worn the Leeds colours – something the *Hull Daily Mail* of 15 December 1914 were keen to point out when the younger Pickles put pen to paper.

> One of these new forwards is Pickles, who hails from the junior York Phoenix Club and who is a son of the veteran Joe Pickles, who was known in Hull's Holderness-road days as a redoubtable forward of Leeds St John's and later of Leeds. Young Pickles, who is a promising youth of 14 stones, is a veritable 'chip off the old block', for he signified his appearance with Leeds by playing just as his 'dad' might have done, and by scoring a rare try into the bargain.

In contrast, however, the *Yorkshire Evening Post* of 19 December rather played down his debut by focusing on the lack of strength of opponents York.

> We do not often find young players introduced into the ranks of Northern League football without first having to undergo a preliminary canter with the reserves. But realising perhaps the weakness of the opposition against them, the Leeds officials made last Saturday's game the

occasion for experimenting with the front line, and two youths were paid the compliment of coming direct into the team. One is the son of Joe Pickles, the old Leeds St John's and Leeds forward. Young Pickles has been attached to the York Phoenix club.

Yet however strong or weak the opposition may have been, the fact he had scored a try on his Northern Union debut at such a tender age would have made many within the game sit up and take note. But even though Pickles could have quickly earned hero status, he wasted little time showing his commitment to the nation's cause, serving with his local Territorial battalion, the 1/5th West Yorkshire Regiment (Prince of Wales's Own).

He was clearly a good soldier as well as a good rugby player, having risen to the rank of Sergeant by the time the Somme offensive approached – despite being one of the younger men in the battalion. His battalion's unit war diary sheds some light on their preparations and their objectives on the opening day, showing them based at Varennes on the eve of the battle. They were part of the 49th Division support to the 32nd and 36th Division assault from just south of Authuille to a point just north of Hamel, in reserve to be drawn upon to replace casualties. The diary gives a feel for the changing orders as 1 July progressed:

At 10am Batt[*alio*]n moved to assembly trenches in Thiepval Wood. 4pm Batt[*alio*]n assembled for attack on Thiepval village. Attack was counter-ordered and Batt[*alio*]n ordered to occupy British front line trenches. Batt[*alio*]n was withdrawn and ordered to occupy Schwaben Redoubt.

Redoubt reached by a small party ..... Remainder
of Batt[*alio*]n moved to Johnstones Post..... [8]

This was over the ground where Harkness Blakey and the
36th Division had fought earlier in the day. The diary then
went on to reveal five of the battalion's other ranks were
killed and 53 wounded. Pickles was one of those killed that
day. His death was announced in the *Yorkshire Post* on 10 July
1916.

Sergt. Joe Pickles, of the West Yorkshires,
youngest son of Mr Joseph Pickles, a foreman at
the Selby Olympia Oil and Cake Mills, has been
killed in action. He was only 19 years of age, and
had recently been promoted [*to*] sergeant. He was
well known in Leeds football circles.

Although the family resided at Selby at the time of his death,
Pickles was born in Leeds in 1897 and baptised at Holy
Trinity, Meanwood. He was one of Joe and Susannah Pickles'
(née Atkinson) seven children and, in fact, served alongside
his older brother George at the Somme.

Joseph's body was never found and he is remembered
on the Thiepval Memorial. While George survived the
Somme, he was to lose his life on 3 November 1918. Records
show he was captured by the Germans in around April 1918
during the German Spring Offensive and was held as a
prisoner of war in Crossen where he was shot by a camp
guard and died from his wounds later that day.

Back on the Somme, it was also announced at the same
time as the deaths of Hopkins, Harkness Blakey and Pickles
that another Leeds Northern Union player, forward John
Sutton, had been killed at the start of the campaign.

On 11 July the *Yorkshire Post* reported:

> J. Sutton, the well-known Northern Union forward, was killed in the big advance. Sutton was one of the strongest and ablest forwards in the Leeds team. At the outbreak of the war he joined the 2nd East Lancashire Fusiliers, and during his training he played occasionally with the Headingley thirteen. He was a Tyldsley man and came to Leeds from the Leigh club.

But 20 days later the *Yorkshire Evening Post* was having to announce that Sutton was, in fact, very much alive! Under a prominent headline it stated 'Sutton, the Leeds footballer, not killed' and continued:

> A month ago, the death in action of J. Sutton, the Leeds Northern Union forward, was reported; this morning, Mr James Goldthorpe, the Leeds secretary, received a letter from Sutton, dated July 27, enclosing a newspaper notice of his death and football career, and stating that he was in sound health and uninjured. How the mistake occurred is not known, but there have been several instances of the kind during the war.[9] Sapper John Sutton came to the Leeds club from Leigh and was regarded as one of the strongest forwards in the team. At the outbreak of war he joined the 2nd East Lancashire Fusiliers, but he has since been transferred as a sapper to the Royal Engineers. The letter announcing his safety has come from France.

Arthur Clarence Cockcroft of Wakefield Trinity
courtesy of Yorkshire Post Newspapers

1 July 1916 – Others Suffer on First Day of the Somme

9

The opening day of the Battle of the Somme hit the Leeds club hard. Sadly, however, Headingley trio Joseph Hopkins, David Harkness Blakey and Joseph Pickles were not the only professional rugby league players to die on day one. Several other Northern Union clubs shared their pain. West Yorkshire rivals Wakefield Trinity and Lancashire clubs Salford and Swinton had also lost men by the end of 1 July.

In the case of talented Wakefield three-quarter Arthur Clarence Cockcroft, he was one of rugby league's Army Officers to lose his life. Born in Hull on 21 May 1892, he was the son of grocer George Henry Cockcroft and his wife Sarah Ellen (née Curtis), one of their six children. By 1901 the family had settled in Knottingley.

Having the distinction of signing for Wakefield on the same day as Trinity legend Jonty Parkin on 15 April 1913, Cockcroft arrived at Belle Vue from hometown club Knottingley Albion with high hopes of becoming a major

Northern Union star. In fact, the details of Cockcroft's deal were revealed by the Wakefield Trinity Heritage Group in the club's minutes of a meeting on 12 March 1913, which said:

> Arthur C Cockcroft was signed on. The following from the terms £5 down and a further £15 is satisfactory after four matches if not to be struck off our register. J Parkin of N Featherstone was paid £5 and a further £5 promised after four matches if satisfactory for signing our forms and if not satisfactory to be struck off register.

In other words, given the respective personal terms offered, it would appear Wakefield rated Cockcroft higher than Parkin at the time!

Yet even though Cockcroft was being held in high esteem, it took him a little time to start to underline his potential. He made a tryscoring Northern Union debut in a 7-6 away win at Bradford on 19 April 1913 – the final game of the 1912-13 season – but was then unable to make any sort of breakthrough the following year.

That all changed at the start of the 1914-15 campaign, however, with seven of his eight senior appearances coming at that time. And the fact he crossed for a total of six tries from the centre berth in those relatively limited run-outs – including a 16-5 opening-day win over Oldham on 5 September 1914 – proved he clearly had something to offer.

Unfortunately, he was never able to fulfil his undoubted potential. Instead, he packed in his job as a clerk, answered the nation's call and signed attestation papers with the Grenadier Guards as a Private in Leeds on 31 October 1914 – exactly the same day he was being featured pictorially in the *Yorkshire Evening Post*, when it said:

Arthur Clarence Cockcroft, who has this season rendered excellent service for Wakefield Trinity as a wing three-quarter, was born at Hull 22 years ago, but has resided at Knottingley for the greater part of his life. He stands 5ft 10½in tall and weighs over 12½ stones.

The paper was then reporting the following week:

I am informed that A.C. Cockcroft, whose portrait appeared in last Saturday's 'Evening Post' in connection with Wakefield Trinity, has now joined the colours, having enlisted with the Grenadier Guards, and he has gone to Caterham (Surrey) for training, etc. His only brother, Horace, well-known as a promising Rugby player in the district, joined the yeomanry (Queen's Own Yorkshire Dragoons), in the spring of this year and is now with them near Market Weighton. Mr G.H. Cockcroft, of Chapel Street, Knottingley, the father, has now two sons and four nephews serving the colours.[1]

The Wakefield star was soon proving to be an excellent soldier and was granted a commission to Second Lieutenant with effect from 31 May 1915.[2] And he was no doubt helped in achieving that Commission by a glowing reference from the Rev. Thomas Howey Nichols, the headmaster of King's School, Pontefract, where Cockcroft had been educated. The testimony showed he was of a scientific bent and listed the extensive range of subjects he studied, including chemistry, physics, mechanics, algebra, trigonometry and geometry as well as traditional arts-related subjects like English, religious knowledge, history, geography and French (including spoken). It also read:

> Cockcroft came to King's School in Sept 1904 and left in July 1910 ..... and before leaving held the Matriculation Certificate of the Northern Universities and also 3rd Honours at Cambridge Senior Locals. He did exceedingly well in Games ..... and he has made a considerable name at Rugby football.[3]

Cockcroft's Commission was with the 11th Battalion of the King's Own Yorkshire Light Infantry, but he was subsequently attached to the 10th. It was whilst serving with them that, according to the unit war diary of 25 January 1916, '2nd Lt Cockcroft was wounded accidentally in the right arm' returning from a trench raid whilst operating near the French town of Armentieres.[4] It was a month to the day after his arrival in France.

He was back on duty in the build-up to the 1 July attack, and killed that day, possibly within the opening minutes as his battalion was one of the first to go over the top, as the unit war diary explained:

> The British offensive commenced this battalion leading the 64 Brigade assault. They left the trenches at 7.30am and took Crucifix Trench that morning and held it till early the next when they were relieved by the 1st Lincolns.[5]

A later eye-witness account confirmed Cockcroft was one of the first to fall. A note in his service records under the heading

'No Enquiry', says he was in 'B' Company and according to Private Sam Hepworth of the same company:

> .....on July 1st, 1916, at Fricourt, he saw Lieut. Cockcroft killed by a Machine Gun bullet, he was the first of the Company to fall. Reference: Pte. Sam Hepworth 21465, 10th K.O.Y.L.I., B. Company, home address: Barnsley.[6]

News, as well as details, of his death was announced in many newspapers including the *Sheffield Daily Telegraph* on 13 July:

> Second-Lieutenant Arthur Clarence Cockcroft, elder son of Mr. and Mrs. G.H. Cockcroft of Knottingley, was killed on July 3rd[7] by a bullet which passed through his head whilst leading a platoon of the K.O.Y.L.I. Educated at King's School, Pontefract, he was 24 years of age, and an athlete of some repute, being a playing member of the Wakefield Trinity Football Club. He enlisted in the Grenadier Guards in October, 1914, and was granted a commission in May last year. He went out to the front on Christmas Day last and exactly a month later was wounded in a raid on a German trench, and on that occasion the commandant. Lieutenant-Colonel W. Burton-Stewart wrote to his parents: 'He was the first man in – I have every intention of putting his name forward. He is a most capable and gallant officer – the best subaltern we have, and I shall be terribly disappointed if I don't get him back soon.'

He is remembered at Gordon Dump Cemetery, Ovillers-la-Boiselle, where he has a grave with the inscription: 'Believed to be buried in this cemetery'.[8]

Sadly, this was not the end of the Arthur Clarence Cockcroft story. Arthur's brother, George Horace, went on to survive the war. He named his son after his deceased brother. On 22 April 1945, Flight Officer Arthur Clarence Cockcroft was killed during a raid on the German city of Bremen during the Second World War. He was 21 years old. Both Arthur Clarence Cockcrofts are remembered on the Knottingley War Memorial.

Also losing his life on 1 July 1916 was veteran Salford half-back David Preston. Born in December 1879 to William and Ellen, Preston cut his rugby teeth playing for the Adelphi Lads Club. He signed for his hometown club at the turn of the century and made his debut in December 1902. He was still on the club's first-team books at the outbreak of war, by which stage he had been a member of the senior squad for an impressive 12 seasons.

At the latter stage of his career and with injuries taking a heavy toll, he was restricted to playing a back-up role to his far younger teammates, which meant he was limited to just one Northern Union start in the 1913-14 season – a 7-0 defeat at Barrow. That was to be his 256th and final Salford appearance, during which time he had crossed for 41 tries.

The beginning of the end of Preston's illustrious playing career could be traced back to a 14-8 home defeat over Leigh in February 1910. It was recalled in the *Athletic News* match report on 21 February, which described how:

.....a stroke of bad luck befell Salford, for Dave Preston, in stopping a rush, got injured, and it was ascertained that he had dislocated his shoulder blade. Of course, he took no further part in the game. Thom[9] was brought out of the scrum, and Salford had to be continually on the alert to keep Leigh out.

Although the injury did not prove as serious as first feared, it still meant Preston was unable to play on a regular basis. But as the *Manchester Courier and Lancashire General Advertiser* reported on 25 August 1913, the vastly-experienced Preston would still have been capable of doing a quality job whenever his services were required. Reporting on a Salford practice game, the publication said:

> The most notable feature at Salford was the re-appearance of David Preston, the well-known half-back who has been absent from the field through an injury sustained at Leigh some three years ago. He seemed to have lost none of his old skill in getting the ball from the scrummage.

Preston enlisted soon after the outbreak of war, joining the 15th Battalion Lancashire Fusiliers, the First Salford Pals. Interestingly, it may not have been the first time Preston enlisted with the Lancashire Fusiliers, as records appear to show he had attested on 2 August 1898 and was then discharged by purchase just 13 days later.[10]

Although Preston and his Salford Pals went to France in November 1915, they had up to now suffered very low casualty rates. This changed when they were thrust into battle on 1 July. Their objective was to attack the German trenches sitting in front of the village of Thiepval, and within minutes of the attack, it was clear it was going horribly wrong.

Preston's Pals were among the first to advance at

7.30am, with the unit war diary account making it clear how terrible it was for those in the first line who went over the top and those who followed.

> When the later lines followed on it was found that the German Front line was occupied. It was known that the earlier lines had penetrated. All attempts to get forward by the later lines resulted in the instant killing or wounding of the party moving forward. It was obvious by 9am that further efforts in this direction were only [a] useless waste of life.[11]

By the end of the day, out of the 24 Officers and 600-plus soldiers who left the trenches that morning, 449 men and 21 officers were either killed, wounded or missing. The vast majority were missing, including 'D' Company's Lance Corporal David Preston. In fact, it was not until June 1917 that his widow, Elizabeth, finally received information from the authorities that her husband was presumed to have been killed on 1 July 1916.

At the end of the war, the *Athletic News* paid tribute to a player who had been one of the Northern Union's longest and most loyal servants.

> David Preston was one of the best half-backs who ever worked a scrummage for the Weaste club. In company with John and Lomas he did great service for his club until he developed a shoulder injury which interfered with his career. His duels with the late Sam James, of Broughton Rangers, will be long remembered.[12]

Preston, who left a widow and children, is remembered on the Thiepval Memorial.

Swinton's Ernest Stephenson was another to fall on the fateful first day – in yet one more heart-wrenching family tale to emerge from 1 July.

Hailing from Salford, where he was born in April 1891, he was one of John and Sarah Stephenson's 13 children. By 1911 only five were still alive, with the family living in the Pendleton area of town and Ernest working as a labourer in a bleacher's works. The young Ernie, as he was affectionately known by his family and friends, was a keen sportsman from an early age and an outstanding all-round athlete. So, it was no surprise when he excelled in a workshop football competition in January 1909 and was quickly acquired by local amateur team Seedley Rangers and from there he subsequently moved to Weaste in Salford.

At 5ft 8in and 10st 6oz, Stephenson was built for speed and, after going on to prove a highly-talented outside back with the Weaste club, he was signed up by local rivals Swinton at the age of 21 on 17 September 1912, making his Northern Union debut on the wing on 29 March the following year. Things did not go quite according to plan, with Stephenson's side suffering a 23-10 home defeat to Oldham. But he did feature in the 16-2 success at Barrow and 11-2 home win over Warrington which followed, before he was part of a Swinton side that lost 15-5 at home to Rochdale in the final game of the season on 19 April 1913.

Having featured in four of the last five games of the campaign, Stephenson would have hoped to see his first-team career kick-on. Instead, however, he found his senior ambitions placed on hold the following season, although he remained firmly on the first-team books at the time war was declared.

An entry in the *National Roll of the Great War* states that he enlisted with the Rifle Brigade in November 1914 and embarked for France the following January, fighting at Neuve Chapelle, St Eloi, Hill 60, Ypres, Festubert and Loos, where he was wounded. When he re-joined his unit, he served at Vimy Ridge.[13] However other records appear to indicate he did not actually go to France until 1916.[14] They also show he was initially with the 1st Battalion, but by the time of the Battle of the Somme he was serving with the 2nd Battalion Rifle Brigade.

Stephenson's battalion was charged with the task of attacking at Ovillers-la-Boiselle, near to where the massive Lochnagar mine was detonated just before 7.30am. Exactly what happened to Stephenson is not known, although his unit war diary paints a very vivid picture of just how bad the situation must have been.

> The Battalion being in Reserve, left the assembly trenches at 7.30am and proceeded up to the communication trenches to the front line. The leading troops and about half the supporting troops were met with heavy machine gun, rifle and shrapnel fire and only succeeded in reaching the enemy trenches at [a] few points, whence they were soon driven back. The Battalion being blocked in the trenches came under intense shell fire from guns of all calibre. As it was decided to attempt no further infantry attack, A, B and C Coys were withdrawn to the support line whilst D Coy with details of the rest of the Brigade held the front line. Shortly before dark details of other Battalions were withdrawn and relieved by A Coy in the front line. The battalion was relieved ..... shortly after midnight and returned to

Bivouac on the Long Valley. Casualties, nearly all shell fire, consisted of 5 officers wounded ..... and 128 other ranks killed and wounded.[15]

One of those killed was 25-year-old Ernest Stephenson, whose body has no known final resting place. He is remembered on the Thiepval Memorial.

Sadly, however, Ernest was not the only member of the Stephenson family to be killed that day, with older brothers Edward and Harold, who were both members of the Salford Pals, also losing their lives. All three are remembered together on Pendleton St Thomas' War Memorial.

The news that the possibility all three died on 1 July was reported in the *Manchester Evening News* of 10 August. Under the headline 'Three Salford Brothers. One Killed and Two Missing' it said:

Private Edward Stephenson, Lancashire Fusiliers, whose relatives live at 4, Fern-street, Florin-street, Pendleton, killed on July 1, leaves a widow and six children. He was 36, and the eldest of three brothers who took part in the Somme fighting. The other two, Harold and Ernest, are reported missing. Edward, who was in the Salford 'Bantams', formerly worked for the Pendleton Co-operative Society. Ernest, who is in the Rifle Brigade, played wing three-quarter for Swinton, and worked at Seedley Bleach Works, while Harold was formerly employed at Messrs. Pykes' flour mill, Ordsall Lane, Salford.

Although an Army Chaplain wrote to his mother informing her that Ernest had been posted missing and this meant he had likely been killed but his body not found, she clung onto the vain hope that he was a prisoner and would one day return home.

Despite the fact almost 40,000 soldiers were injured rather than killed on 1 July, not all of them were to survive from the wounds they received. Rochdale's Great Britain forward Walter James 'Rattler' Roman was one of them.

The former Bridgwater and Somerset rugby union forward was one of the most highly-respected players in the 13-a-side code, having the honour of captaining Rochdale during their successful 1911 Lancashire Senior Cup-winning campaign, representing Wales and the West of England against the touring Australians at Bristol in 1911, England against Wales at St Helens in 1914 and then being picked for the Great Britain tour to Australia and New Zealand later that year.

Although Roman did not feature in the three Test matches against Australia or the one against New Zealand, he did play in seven of the representative games and scored one try in a 43-11 win over New Zealand side Taranaki.

It was while Great Britain were in Australia that war on Germany was declared. As a former soldier who had served in the Boer War at the turn of the 20th century and later in India, and therefore a Reservist, Roman along with Rochdale teammate and fellow tourist Jack Robinson, presented himself at the Victoria Barracks in Sydney requesting the earliest possible return to England to rejoin the Colours. That, however, turned out to be on the ship bringing back the squad in mid-August.

The *Rochdale Observer* of 30 September paints a vivid picture of what the Great Britain squad's return journey during wartime was like.

Lights were not exhibited on the Orient liner

Orontes on which they returned, and the boat was not stopped by any war vessel. Frequently, they were 'discovered' by searchlights from cruisers. Brief wireless messages showing the progress of the war were posted up on the ship each day. In the Red Sea they passed a troopship and saw a large number of Indian troops on deck.

Upon docking at Plymouth, Roman quickly travelled home to his adopted Rochdale, where he was a licensed victualler at the town's Beehive pub, to say farewell to his wife Henrietta who he married in 1911, and two children. The following day he left for Taunton to re-join the Somerset Light Infantry as a Corporal.

Born in Bridgwater on 1 July 1880, the son of George and Bessie, Roman was very quickly following in the footsteps of his grandfather and father, who were both county rugby union players and earned the nickname 'Rattler' for the nature of their bone-crunching tackles. It was a title the young Roman was also to earn with some justification.

After a highly-successful junior career playing in the three-quarters for his hometown club and being selected captain, he made his senior Bridgwater debut at the age of just 15, and less than two years later represented Somerset in County fixtures against Middlesex, Surrey and Glamorgan. Going on to play for England appeared a natural next step. Yet just as his union potential was at its highest, Roman took the decision to enlist with the 2nd Battalion of the Somerset Light Infantry in 1899, going on to see service in South Africa in the Boer War. He was then stationed in India and discharged in 1907, when he returned to Bridgwater and became a brickwork labourer.

Roman also re-joined Bridgwater, became captain and

represented Somerset on 16 further occasions, putting him back in the frame to earn England recognition. But despite impressing in England trials in the 1909-10 season, he was surprisingly overlooked by the selectors, which appears to have prompted his move into the professional ranks.

Roman was not short of Northern Union offers – powerfully built at around 15 stone, and in his prime, the successful club would be getting one of the biggest players around at the time – with Rochdale winning the race for his signature in January 1910 amidst rumours they had paid him a substantial signing fee of £200.

He made his Rochdale Northern Union debut as a forward in a game at Oldham on 22 January 1910 and almost immediately became a mainstay of the Hornets pack, going on to make 165 appearances, scoring 47 tries and kicking 15 goals. His final appearance was on 24 April 1915 in a 9-2 Challenge Cup defeat to St Helens during his time on leave.

But having served his country during the Boer War, few were surprised he immediately answered the call for the Great War, stating as soon as he returned from the 1914 Great Britain tour:

> I think our team one of the greatest combinations that ever left England ..... Our last match was a revelation of bulldog courage and British pluck..... [I] have now sterner work to face for King and country. I shall do my best in this great game, just as I always do in football.[16]

He went out to France at the beginning of January 1915. Before arriving on the Somme, Roman and his regiment were involved in heavy fighting around Ypres in Belgium and Armentieres in northern France, during which time he was promoted to Sergeant. It was also around the time of his promotion that he had a very lucky escape, as the *Hull Daily Mail* of 17 May 1915 recounted.

> Walter Roman has had a narrow escape. He was struck on the shoulder by a piece of spent shell but did not receive an injury.

But, unfortunately, Roman was then demoted to Private on 12 July the same year after being court-martialled for drunkenness, something not mentioned when a letter was received by the *Newcastle Journal* and printed on 21 August 1915 from Corporal Marks about his frontline friendship with Walter.

> Corporal H.J. Marks, the former Bristol Rugby three-quarter, writing from the front, says: 'I thought you might like to know of that great forward "Rattler" Roman, who together with me is serving in the 1st Somerset Light Infantry out here, and is well amongst the "Gott strafe England" merchants..... He looks better than ever and revels in the listening-post business. I pity the "Gott strafe" merchants if "Rattler" only mixes with them. I am of the opinion they won't stop when they catch sight of that good-hearted brawny athlete. When we have time we sit and think of the past games and chat of the best games we have ever taken part in, as well as speak of the scribes who used to mention "So-and-so failed to tackle". I can assure you that we shall not fail to tackle the "Gott strafe England" merchants.'[17]

Having seen so much action earlier in the conflict, the Somerset Light Infantry were among the most battle-hardened soldiers to advance on Beaumont Hamel shortly after the detonation of the huge Hawthorn mine at 7.20am on the morning of 1 July – Roman's 36th birthday. Yet that did not save them from suffering heavy casualties on the day totalling 26 officers and 438 other ranks,[18] with Roman among them.

Within moments of leaving the trenches, the experienced soldier and rugby player suffered shrapnel wounds to his left arm and leg (some newspaper reports mention both arms) in no man's land. From there he was fortunate to be picked up by a stretcher bearer named Private John Griffiths of the Royal Army Medical Corps, who revealed this fact in a piece about his role at the front to his local *Rochdale Observer* newspaper on 2 September 1916. Roman was evacuated back to England within days and admitted to Suffolk Hall Voluntary Aid Detachment Hospital in Cheltenham.

Initially, his health appeared to improve, but towards the end of the month his condition deteriorated and on 28 July he lost his fight for life when blood poisoning set in, with his wife believed to have travelled from Rochdale just too late to see her husband before he passed away. His death was announced the following day in a major piece in the *Rochdale Observer*. Under the headline 'Died from Wounds', it stated:

Lance-Corporal Walter Roman of the Somerset Light Infantry, a former captain of the Hornets club, who was seriously injured during the early days of the present advance, died yesterday morning at a hospital at Cheltenham. After being admitted to the institution for a time, his condition seemed to improve. Roman had been shot through both arms and the left leg. On Friday of last week, he was able to write a few lines to his wife, who lives at Rochdale. A few days later a nurse at the hospital wrote to Mrs Roman to the effect that her husband had seemed to be rather easier during the last few days, and that he was 'getting on nicely'. Later on Thursday night, however, a telephone message was received at Rochdale asking Mrs Roman to go to Cheltenham as her husband's condition was serious. She left Rochdale for that town yesterday morning, but it is doubtful whether she arrived at the hospital in time to see him alive. About one o'clock yesterday afternoon a telegram was received locally stating that he had died.

After his death, his body was brought back to Bridgwater, with his funeral service taking place at Holy Trinity parish church, where he had been a chorister as a child. An imposing funeral procession then followed for his interment at the Wembdon Road Cemetery. The Rochdale Hornets club sent representatives, and amongst the floral tributes were ones from the Hornets officials, players and the Sports Committee, as well as one from his customers at the Beehive pub in Rochdale.

Within weeks of his death, his widow relinquished her pub licence and returned to Bridgwater.

Well-respected: Durham-born Ben Lloyd of Leigh

courtesy of Mike Latham

The Battle of the Somme Continues

10

The first day of the Somme offensive on 1 July 1916 would be the first of a 141-day battle that would not end until 18 November 1916. During that time, more than three million men from both sides saw action, with over one million killed or wounded. That made it one of the bloodiest battles in the history of warfare.

The Northern Union lost six players on day one and, unsurprisingly, many more were to die before the battle drew to a close. Next to fall, on 3 July, was one of the sport's most colourful characters – Warrington legend George Thomas.

The highly-popular Welsh forward was a true Wire hero, making 385 appearances for the club and scoring 47 tries, 191 goals and seven drop goals, for a total points tally of 537. That included four Challenge Cup final appearances. Furthermore, he earned the distinction of becoming Warrington's first international player when he represented Wales against New Zealand in 1908. He also set a then club record for the points scored in a match with five tries and nine goals for a 33-point haul (38 points in the four-point try modern era) in a 78-6 victory over St Helens at Wilderspool on Easter Monday, 12 April 1909. Thomas's tally was also the highest number of points scored by a forward in the game. As a result, he is a deserved member of the Warrington Hall of Fame and was inducted in 2006.

But his rugby roots were in union. William George Thomas, to give him his full name, was born in Abercarn, Monmouthshire in Wales in 1881. Brought up in Pontnewydd (Thomas's nickname was Ponty in homage to that village), he soon began to impress on the rugby field for the Pontnewydd club before joining top side Newport. It was during that time that he began to catch the eye of Warrington, who moved quickly to secure his signature in August 1903. He came up north with his wife Ethel Mary Williams, who he married in Newport in 1901, and only child Osmond Clifford, also born that year.

Some Wilderspool committee members at the time had reservations about the new signing. At 5ft 8in tall and weighing around 13st, Thomas was hardly the biggest forward in the world, but his response to the criticism was 'good stuff lies in little room' and the immediate demonstration of his uncompromising, tough-tackling style soon helped turn opinions around.

His debut came within weeks of him putting pen to paper, as he helped his new club secure an 8-3 home win over Leigh. His Warrington career was under way. Within a season, he had helped Warrington reach the 1904 Challenge Cup final, where they were beaten 8-3 by Halifax at The Willows, Salford. The following year Thomas played a key role as the Wire went one better to beat Hull KR 6-0 in the final at Leeds's Headingley Stadium. In 1907, the Challenge

Cup was won again by Thomas and his teammates as they defeated Oldham 17-3 at Wheater's Field, Broughton, before, in his fourth final, Warrington lost 9-5 to Huddersfield in the 1913 final at Headingley.

His international debut with Wales against New Zealand in 1908 was quickly followed by his one and only Great Britain Test appearance against the same opposition later that year, while he made a second Welsh appearance in 1912. Thomas had been expected to earn a squad spot for the first Great Britain tour to Australia and New Zealand in 1910, but it was believed his outspoken views cost him a call. He was never one to keep quiet if he felt something in the rugby world was not right. In fact, when Warrington's first-team players went on strike over the non-payment of a £1 bonus in January 1914, it was Thomas who addressed a 4,000-plus Wilderspool crowd at the end of a second team game to explain exactly why the players reacted the way they did.

Despite his stance, Thomas remained a virtual ever-present throughout that 1913-14 campaign, with his final Warrington appearance coming in an 8-5 home defeat to Broughton Rangers on 12 September 1914.

By that stage, the proud Welshman had already decided to defend his nation's cause and he enlisted with the Prince of Wales's Volunteers (South Lancashire Regiment) in Warrington on 6 October 1914, posted to the 8th Battalion two days later. Even on that eventful day, the colourful Thomas was up to his old tricks, stating on his official papers that he was 30 years old (knocking a good three years off his age).

It was pretty clear from day one of his military service that his Army life was going to be as 'interesting' as his rugby life. Within weeks of joining up, and well before leaving these shores, Thomas was clashing with the military authorities, as his service records revealed.[1]

His first indiscretion came between Christmas and New Year 1915 when he was 'absent off all parades from Wednesday, 29-12-14 until Saturday, 2-1-15' for which he reverted from Lance Corporal to Private. Other blemishes on his record included more unauthorised absences, making an insubordinate answer to an officer, telling a falsehood to a NCO (non commissioned officer) and 'creating a disturbance in the barrack room,' all of which earned varying periods of detention.

After his 'lively' time preparing for war, Thomas went to France on 28 September 1915. With an enemy to face, his scrapes with authority diminished, although there was an award of 14 days Field Punishment Number 1 in February 1916. This type of punishment involved the soldier being tied to a fixed object for up to two hours per day. On 11 April 1916, he was transferred from 'B' Company to 'C' Company as preparations began to intensify ahead of the start of the Somme offensive, with Private Thomas writing a letter home at that time in which he made his feelings clear.

> I have had some trying times on the football field and our side usually came out on top, but as true as there is a drop of British blood runs through my veins I hope to give the Germans a sound thrashing. But if I fall, you can tell the boys I fell fighting like a hero should do for his King and country.[2]

There was, however, still one more chance for Thomas to have a brush with his superiors before the battle commenced, receiving seven days of Field Punishment Number 1 for 'using obscene language to a NCO'.[3]

Within days of this final outburst, Thomas was dead.

There is no reference to his death in the unit war diary, although a signals message to headquarters at the time confirmed the battalion was coming under frequent heavy artillery attack. But after surviving the initial assault on 1 July and his battalion moving to Aveluy Wood, south of Thiepval, an eyewitness account suggests Thomas was 'blown to pieces' after taking a direct hit from one of the barrage of German shells at 4am on the morning of the 3 July. He was 35 years old. He has no known grave and is remembered on the Thiepval Memorial.

The death of such a huge Warrington figure as Thomas was one which hit the area hard, with a major article in the *Nantwich Guardian* on 25 July summing up the mood.

Official news has been received that one of the best-known Warrington Rugby footballers, Private George Thomas ..... was killed in action on July 3rd. The first news received in Warrington of Thomas' death was contained in a letter which Sapper William Molyneax, of the Royal Engineers, wrote to his wife ..... Before enlisting Private Thomas was employed by the Richmond Gas Stove and Meter Co. Ltd., but previous to this was in the service of Messrs. Fletcher, Russell and Co., Ltd ..... George Thomas was certainly one of the most accomplished forwards who ever migrated North. We in Warrington knew his worth, and in his day he was one of the most dangerous men who ever put his head into a scrummage. What a rare leader he was to be sure! He possessed a certain amount of hypnotic influence over his comrades, and we could recall many matches where he was the life and soul of the attack ..... He was just a shade too loquacious, and there is no doubt that this told when the Selection Committee made up their team to visit the Antipodes [*in 1910*], ... Thomas gained International (Wales) and Lancashire County honours, and his death will be regretted by followers of the game throughout Lancashire.

Then, on 20 July, another well-respected Lancashire player perished – Leigh's Ben Lloyd. Although born in Durham, his birth was registered in the Wigan District in 1886 by his parents, Benjamin and Elizabeth Lloyd (née Carter). The Shropshire-born couple had married in Leigh and that is where they eventually settled, Benjamin Snr being a coal miner.

The Leigh winger was one of 10 children born to the couple, and after leaving school he gained employment at Messrs Ackers, Whitley and Co's Plank Lane Colliery. But as well as working as a miner, Lloyd was also a talented rugby league winger with Leigh Shamrocks. It was during this time that his ability was recognised by the professionals from Leigh, who signed him in 1909 and handed him his first-team debut in a 10-0 win over Huddersfield in front of a 10,000-plus crowd at Fartown on 27 September 1910.

Lloyd's debut proved to be one of the highlights of the win, with the *Leigh Chronicle and Weekly District Advertiser* of 30 September waxing lyrical over what they had seen.

Davies [*Lloyd's centre partner on the day*] got through a tremendous amount of work and played in his very best style, and was an excellent coach for the debutant, Lloyd, the ex-Shamrocks man. The latter has the makings of a permanent left-winger, and I especially noticed a wonderful side-step or hop, reminding one of Jack Fish, which he has cultivated. His defence too was good.

Lloyd then featured in the next two senior Northern Union fixtures against Wigan and Salford before dropping back down into the 'A' team. This was around the time that Lloyd and his wife Hannah, who he married in May 1909, lost their first child Gladys.[4] He then spent the following two seasons proving to be a mainstay of the reserves and making a highly-successful transition from the backs to the forwards. Such was his impact in the 'A' team pack that, by the 1913-14 campaign, he was back in the senior fold, making his return to Northern Union action at loose-forward in a 10-7 home triumph over Oldham on 13 December 1913, which brought to an end a five-game losing run for his club.

He then went on to make 15 appearances that season – half in the back row and half at prop – and scored one try in a 16-5 home win over Hunslet on 28 January 1914. But despite being well and truly back in the first-team fold, he had no hesitation in joining teammates Fred Coffey and Jack King in becoming among the first Leigh players to enlist with the South Lancashire Regiment on 20 January 1915.

Lloyd must have made a positive impression during his training with the 3rd South Lancashires, the home-based training battalion, as he was promoted to Lance Corporal in December 1915. He was posted to the 7th Battalion in France on 9 March 1916. His battalion also made a positive impression during the opening days of the Somme offensive, with their heroics helping in the capture of La Boisselle.

In fact, it was an operation that earned them a Special Order of the Day on 6 July from Brigadier General C.C. Onslow, the Commander of the 57th Infantry Brigade. It read:

The Brigadier wishes to congratulate all ranks on their magnificent performance in capturing the village of La Boisselle and maintaining their hold on the ground won.

This was a soldiers' battle, when the determination and grit of the individual comes so prominently to the fore. These qualities were shown to such an extent that the name of the Brigade will remain famous.

He takes this opportunity of expressing the gratitude and thanks of all ranks to the Lt Col Winser and the officers, N.C.Os, and men of the 7th South Lancashire Regiment, who came to support the Brigade at a critical time, and who not only helped to maintain the ground already gained but added largely to it by an attack carried out with the greatest of determination and maintained that also.[5]

Unfortunately, they had little time to bask in their glory, with several engagements taking place against the enemy ahead of the fateful day of 20 July when the 30-year-old Lloyd was to lose his life. The events leading up to his death were recorded in a diary written by Captain R.G. Garvin, and subsequently published.

At 7.00pm on the evening of Wednesday 19 July, the 7th South Lancs ..... left Hénencourt for trenches near Mametz Wood, where they were to relieve the 4th King's Liverpool Regiment, in readiness for the night attack of 22-23 July. The ten-mile night march was, according to Colonel

Winser, 'hellish': the roads leading to the front were congested and the guides who met them at Fricourt could not find the way. As dawn broke on Thursday 20th, the battalion found itself in the valley north of Caterpillar Wood, a few hundred yards from Mametz Wood. The valley offered the only suitable ground for forward gun batteries and it was packed with field artillery, which attracted heavy German shelling. Colonel Winser therefore moved his battalion to a ravine on the eastern edge of Mametz Wood, where they dug in at once. They were shelled by German 5.9-inch guns all of that day and the next, and suffered casualties.[6]

One of those casualties was, unfortunately, Ben Lloyd. He was killed by a shell. Notification of his death was given in the *Leigh Journal* under the heading 'Leigh Footballer Reported Killed'.

> It is reported by a Leigh soldier that a bomb, the fragments of which he himself was wounded, blew Lce.-Cpl/Ben Lloyd to pieces. The last-named is well known as the ex-Leigh Rugby F.C. player ..... He was 30 years of age.

It went on to report that his widow, Hannah, received a letter from Private Levi Pemberton, who was recovering in the Red Cross Hospital at East Grinstead, Sussex, from the injuries he suffered in the incident – which left little to the imagination:

> They were in a trench when the Germans commenced shelling. One dropped in the trench

and buried five of them. They could not find Lloyd after they got hit. He must have been blown to pieces. 'We were only wishing we were back in England at nine o'clock that morning.'

Lloyd is remembered on the Thiepval Memorial. In addition to his widow, he also left three young children – twins Benjamin and Henry, and daughter Ethel.

A day later, a second Northern Union star who had been part of the Great Britain tour to Australia and New Zealand in 1914 had also died. He was Huddersfield forward Fred Longstaff.

The 25-year-old was at the very top of his profession when he answered the call to enlist, having been a key member of Fartown's legendary 'Team of All Talents' which totally dominated British rugby league in the years leading up to the Great War and completed a clean sweep of the trophies in 1914-15. He also featured in the 23-5 opening Test triumph against Australia in Sydney on 27 June 1914. Playing at loose-forward, he kicked two goals in the game, but missed the second and third Tests through injury.

Longstaff did continue his Huddersfield career into the glittering 1914-15 season when he returned from the tour Down Under, but after being part of such a disjointed campaign due to the number of Northern Union players who had already joined up, the Great Britain international followed his rugby-playing colleagues' example by volunteering to fight for King and country. By then, Longstaff had worn the claret and gold on 135 occasions, scoring 15 tries and kicking 25 goals, and having won every domestic honour in the game. He had come a very long way from his junior days playing for Bradford parish church school and then Bradford club Victoria Rangers.

Born in Bradford on 18 September 1890 and baptised at Bradford Cathedral the following month, he was one of George and Sarah Jane Longstaff's (née Dennison) six children. It did not take him many years to show he was a rugby player with an incredible amount of talent. He was a star at school and he was a star at Victoria, and even during his fledgling junior days he was head and shoulders above all those around him.

It was not long before a host of Northern Union clubs were queueing up to secure the saw mill labourer's services, with Halifax winning that particular race. During his two seasons with the Calderdale club, his status continued to rise, and on 23 January 1912, the outstanding young forward made the short move to the Northern Union 'giants' at Fartown. It was a switch which was heralded by the *Leeds Mercury* under the headline 'Huddersfield's Capture.'

> .....the Huddersfield club have secured the services of Fred Longstaff, the well-known forward, who has shown great form with the Halifax club. Longstaff, who resides in Bradford, began his football career with the Victoria Rangers club, a prominent junior organisation in the Bradford district. He is twenty-one years of age, weighs 13st. 10lb., and stands 5ft. 8in. in height.[7]

Unsurprisingly, given his reputation in the game, it was a move that was soon reaping its rewards for Longstaff and his new club. By the end of that first season, he picked up his first winners medal as Huddersfield beat Wigan 13-5 in the League Championship final at Halifax's Thrum Hall on 4 May 1912 – he added one of the conversions on the day – and also tasted success in the Yorkshire League Championship. More trophies were collected during the following 1912-13 campaign, with Longstaff at the heart of a 29-2 League Championship final triumph over Wigan at Wakefield's Belle Vue and a 9-5 Challenge Cup final victory over Warrington at Headingley. The Yorkshire League title was also retained that year.

Then, the following season, Longstaff also got his hands on a Yorkshire Cup winners medal as the Fartowners beat Bradford Northern 19-3 at Halifax on 29 November 1913.

His efforts were now earning him representative honours as well, with two Yorkshire County calls in 1913 followed by an England appearance in a 16-12 triumph over Wales at St Helens on 14 February 1914. That England call proved to be one of the relatively limited highlights for the forward that year, with Huddersfield restricted to just a solitary Yorkshire League Championship success during what was seen as a disappointing season for such a star-studded side.

It proved a totally different story during the war-affected 1914-15 campaign, of course, as Longstaff and his teammates won all four cups available to confirm their status as the 'Team of All Talents'. But by that stage, Longstaff and many of his Huddersfield colleagues knew the time had come to answer the nation's call, sacrifice their Northern Union hero status and prepare for battle on the Western Front.

The Bradford-born star enlisted with the West Yorkshire Regiment and successfully completed his training before leaving English shores some time in early 1916. During those early months Longstaff and his 1/6th Battalion comrades spent most of their time in a holding role rather than taking on the enemy head-on in the frontline trenches.

There was also time for the Fartown legend to show off his exceptional rugby ability during this period, with a nostalgic account in the *Athletic News* of 10 March 1919 recalling what an impact Longstaff made in a representative rugby union match whilst he was on leave in early 1916.

> When Mr. R.F. Oakes's North of England military team played against a local side organised by Mr. T.H. Crumbie at Leicester in 1916, there was a conspicuous forward playing whose name was not recorded on the programme, and it was Longstaff. He was indeed brilliant in the game. There were few harder workers in Northern Union football than this Bradford lad. He first served Halifax, and then proceeded to Fartown to render assistance to the powerful Huddersfield team. He played a game peculiarly his own. He was a rare scrummager, a strong tackler, capital in the loose, and no forward could serve out passes better. Longstaff was faster than folk imagined, and was enormously strong for his height.

By the summer of 1916, however, Longstaff was on the Somme preparing for the 'Big Push'.

On 1 July his battalion moved up to their positions in Thiepval Wood with orders to attack the village of Thiepval. But against strong enemy resistance they made no progress and were forced to retire to their own trenches. They were relieved on 2 July and withdrew to trenches in Aveluy Wood and then back to billets at Martinsart.[8]

But their respite was short-lived, being told on 9 July that Longstaff and his battalion would have to relieve the

1/7th West Yorkshire Regiment in the Leipzig Salient, with the order that it had 'to be held at all costs' due to its strategic importance.[9] As soon as Longstaff and his comrades arrived, they came under heavy shelling, as well as a flamethrower attack on 15 July. Longstaff survived all this but was killed in action six days later on 21 July. The unit war diary in the lead-up to his death records daily shelling from 16 July.

News of the Fartown legend's demise started filtering through at the end of July 1916, with the *Huddersfield Daily Examiner* reporting that Arthur Bennett, the Huddersfield trainer, had received a letter conveying the sad news.

Almost a month later the *Halifax Courier* of 19 August 1916, in a piece headlined 'How Pte Longstaff Died,' outlined the exact circumstances. It read:

> More details are to hand concerning the death of Pte. Longstaff, the Halifax footballer, who was killed in action ..... Sec.-Lt. A.L. Vaughan, 6th West Yorkshire Regiment, writing on August 11, says:- 'It was during 'stand to' in the early morning that an odd shell landed on 'B' Co's headquarters. Longstaff with others inside. He and another man were killed instantaneously, and five others were wounded ..... A piece of shell caught his head, and he had absolutely no pain. I cannot say that I knew him very well, but from the very first, I, like everybody else, took a great liking to him. I am assured by his two closest friends – Sgt. Turner and Cpl. Duff – that the big good-hearted fellow was the pet of his company, and I know for a fact that his death has been a great blow to the battalion. He was buried in a little cemetery just behind the firing line by our

chaplain ..... Only yesterday a cross was placed
over his grave, which stands about 4ft. high, and
is painted white with black lettering, giving his
name and regiment.'

His grave lies in Blighty Valley Cemetery, Authuille,
alongside Frank Matthewman, another from the battalion
killed that day. Only days earlier Matthewman had written
home to his parents informing them of the death of his older
brother, Charles, in the flame-thrower attack. The family now
had a letter from the chaplain informing them of the
instantaneous death of the younger of the brothers.

As soon as the news of Longstaff's death reached home,
the tributes began to pour in, with countless tales of his rugby
league exploits and no-nonsense Yorkshire traits.

A typical example was recorded in the *Yorkshire Evening
Post* of 29 July 1916. Under the title 'Longstaff and Lloyd
George', the article said:

The death in action of Fred Longstaff, of the
Huddersfield football team, is one more painful
local reminder of the heavy price which civilised
mankind is paying in its struggle for freedom.
Longstaff, though he played for Halifax and
Huddersfield, was one of Bradford's rough
diamonds, but he has shown the stone to be of
the purest quality ..... As a typical Yorkshire lad,
a story about Longstaff may be re-told here as it
was told to mc a day or two ago. While in receipt
of wages as a professional with the Huddersfield
team, he was served with the usual income tax
form by the Inland Revenue authorities. He took
it to an official of the club, and asked what it

meant, and received the reply that if his income reached the stipulated sum, Lloyd George[10] required him to pay fifteen pence in the pound on the amount assessable. Longstaff waxed indignant, and exclaimed: 'Does Lloyd George think A'm bahn to be kicked all over t'cloise on Saturday afternooin and pay for 't? I'll give up laaking first.' He did give up laaking, but it was only to lay down his life for King and country.

And the final example of the 'true Yorkshireman' Longstaff has to be the tale the Huddersfield Rugby League Heritage group enjoy so much.

On Saturday, April 24, 1915, Fartown beat Leeds in the League Championship final at Wakefield by 35 points to 2. The previous evening Fred and (RFL Hall of Fame member) Harold Wagstaff were walking along New Street in Huddersfield town centre when a local tailor approached them. He offered Waggy the best suit in his shop if his team beat Leeds the next day. Fred told the tailor – 'You fellows always think about the backs and never the forwards, what do I get if we win?' Thereupon the tailor said that if Fred scored a try then he could have one as well. During the game, Waggy was put through by Bert Ganley, which left him with only the full-back to beat. As he approached him, he heard a voice on his shoulder shouting 'suit suit suit', Waggy turned and popped the ball in to Fred's hands for him to touch down under the posts.[11]

Fred Longstaff got his suit but had very little time and opportunity to wear it.

Further Deaths on the Somme – NU's Devastating Blows

11

Within the opening month of the Battle of the Somme, the impact back in England was devastating. Almost everyone knew someone who had been killed, and it was affecting all walks of life. Like every other section of society, the Northern Union family had been hit hard, with the loss of high-profile Great Britain internationals Fred Longstaff and Walter Roman striking a major hammer blow. And on 15 August 1916, another tourist's name had been added to the list in the shape of Leeds's Samuel William Jarman.

Known throughout the rugby league world as Billy Jarman, the 29-year-old Leeds-born utility player was another who was idolised throughout the game. He was a star for Leeds and a star for Great Britain, having played in two of the three Tests against Australia on the 1914 summer tour Down Under. Significantly, he was at full-back in the 23-5 first Test triumph over the Kangaroos on 27 June and then appeared at loose-forward in the 12-7 second Test defeat two days later. Only a handful of players have played in the forwards and backs for Great Britain.

Unfortunately, he picked up an injury during the second Test, which forced his withdrawal and meant he missed the famous 14-6 'Rorke's Drift'[1] third Test triumph on 4 August as the tourists took the Ashes series 2-1. He did return to play in a couple of the games against representative sides during the New Zealand leg of the tour but twisted an ankle and was ruled out of Great Britain's 16-13 Test triumph over the hosts.

But it was while Jarman was on tour that he knew his rugby league career was about to go on hold and he could very soon be fighting with the British Army against the Germans. Having served as a professional soldier with the Scots Guards for three years between 1905 and 1908, Jarman was a Reservist when war was declared, meaning he had to report for duty at the earliest opportunity.

Within a short time of the Great Britain squad arriving back in England, the Leeds legend was bidding his family farewell to rejoin his old regiment. Here he embarked on a period of intense rehabilitation on an injured knee he picked up acting about on the boat back from Australia – known as a bit of a team joker he had been attempting a handspring. As the *Yorkshire Evening Post* of 26 September 1914 described it:

> .....in endeavouring to contribute to the enjoyment of his fellow passengers, [*he*] was jerked off his balance by the roll of the ship and sprained his left knee.

Jarman was always confident he would be fit for action before war came to an end, and said as much in an interview he gave to the *Athletic News* on 28 September 1914, revealing:

I am hoping to gain as good honours there [*on the battlefield*] as we have done in Australia, and my prayer is that I come safely back to my wife and children and to take part again in the sport I dearly love.

Regrettably, of course, that would not be the case, with Jarman dying on the battlefield and leaving his widow Jane Hannah, who he married in 1909, and three children Samuel William, Lillian and Jinnie. His fourth child, Walter, was born in February 1916.

Samuel William Jarman was born in Leeds in around early 1887 and baptised at St Matthias, Burley on 6 February that year, the son of Samuel and Martha Jarman. After beginning his working life as a trainee pork butcher, Jarman's sense of adventure took him down the military path, something his father had done before him with the Grenadier Guards. Jarman chose another Guards Regiment – the Scots. Within months of enlisting with them in November 1905, he was underlining his sporting prowess in a wide range of disciplines, including rugby union which he had learned prior to enlisting. Whilst with the regiment Private Jarman represented them at Army Association Football. He also participated in the light and heavyweight tug-of-war teams and represented the battalion at cricket. His real achievement, though, was to win the heavyweight boxing championship of the Scots Guards in around 1907 – a title which he held upon leaving them in October 1908. Now the sports-gifted and sturdily-built Jarman, who weighed in at 13st and stood at 5ft 8½ inches, chose to pursue a life as a professional rugby player with hometown club Leeds.

Having been such a regimental sports star, he had little

trouble adapting to the professional 13-a-side rugby code and, after a successful Headingley trial period, the 21-year-old Jarman made a Northern Union tryscoring debut in a home defeat to Wakefield Trinity on 28 December 1908. It was to be the first of his 148 appearances in the blue and amber, during which time he crossed for 35 tries and kicked four goals for a total points tally of 113. Arguably his biggest highlight during his domestic career came in the 1909-10 Challenge Cup final when he helped Leeds lift the famous trophy for the very first time after the first draw in the showpiece finale. Jarman played hooker as Leeds drew 7-7 with Hull in front of a 19,413 final crowd at Fartown on Saturday, 16 April 1910. But for the replay two days later, again played in Huddersfield, Jarman switched to the second row to help his side storm to a 26-12 triumph in front of an 11,608 crowd.

Having established himself as an accomplished forward, it then came as a major surprise when he was switched to centre the following season, although any fears were immediately allayed as he produced another tryscoring match-winning display to sink Bramley in a crucial league game to underline his new status as a quality utility player. His confidence was also growing all the time, and he proved almost unstoppable during the 1911-12 campaign, having opened the season by scoring the only hat trick of his career in a 16-13 victory over Hull.

Jarman maintained that exceptional form during the next two seasons, making him an automatic choice for that 1914 Great Britain tour to Australia and New Zealand. Had he not suffered his tour injuries he would doubtless have been in the thick of it far earlier. It was not until 1916 that Private Jarman linked up with the 2nd Battalion Scots Guards on the Western Front.

Ironically, he died during what was regarded as a relatively 'quiet' period during the Somme offensive. In fact, his battalion spent some time in Belgium before returning to northern France on 28 July. They then slowly made their way back to the Somme front line, where they faced a hostile welcome from German shells as they took up their position in Wolfe Trench, as the entry of 14 and 15 August in Jarman's battalion's unit war diary revealed:

> A shell fell amongst the Headquarters Detachment as they were coming in and killed 3 men and wounded 4 men ..... Headquarters were shelled with 5.9" shells at 6.20pm ..... During the night the front line was shelled with a minenwerfer and was blown in in four places in Wolfe Trench.....[2]

Jarman was one of those killed by the shells, with the Leeds and Great Britain star having no known grave, so his name is remembered on the Thiepval Memorial.

Newspaper reports of his death were soon coming in. The *Wigan Observer and District Advertiser* of 26 August 1916 gave their assessment of Jarman's ability as a player. Under the headline 'Jarman, of Leeds, Killed,' it said:

> S.W. Jarman, the well-known Leeds Northern Union player, and the utility man for his side, has been killed at the Front ..... His strength and energy, and his swarthy complexion, caused him always to be noticed. It was probably because of all-round worth more than on account of particular skill in scrummage work that he was chosen for the Colonial tour. For the Headingley

organisation he had figured at full-back, in all three-quarter back positions and, of course, forward, and he had hoped that some day he might have the chance to complete the process of variation by playing at half-back, not as a makeshift but as a chosen performer, However, it was not to be.

Tragically, as with Wakefield's Arthur Clarence Cockcroft, who died in the First World War and then had his nephew of exactly the same name killed in the Second World War, it was a similar story for Samuel William Jarman, although this time the family tie was even closer. Just 25 years after the Northern Union star lost his life in northern France, his son, Gunner Samuel William Jarman of the 234 Light Anti-Aircraft Regiment Royal Artillery lost his life on 17 December 1941.

Jarman senior was the only senior professional player to die in August 1916. But by the third day of September two more had been killed – Batley's Walter Johnson and Warrington's Alex Brown.

The Hunslet-born Johnson was tipped to have a big future in the game, with Batley delighted to have secured the forward's services from the Lane End United club on 9 September 1913. By that time, he was already a well-known figure in the South Leeds area where he had grown up. Born in the spring of 1891 to parents John and Sarah Ann Johnson (née West), the young Walter proved to be an outstanding all-round sportsman, both during his schooldays and on the Hunslet junior sporting club scene.

After completing his education, Johnson was employed as a coal hewer. On 19 October 1912 he married Margaret Thompson Scaife at St Mary the Virgin Church, Hunslet. The following year, their son Fred was born.

It was also around that time that Johnson's rugby ability caught the eye of Batley, who made their move and snatched the top 22-year-old prospect from under the nose of hometown club Hunslet. At first, Johnson needed to play the waiting game in his Mount Pleasant career, failing to break into the first team during the 1913-14 season. But in the 1914-15 campaign, it was a totally different story. He made his debut in a 23-7 League defeat at Hull KR on 12 September 1914 and then went on to make 23 further appearances - he scored one try in a 24-5 victory at York on 4 November – alternating between prop, second row and loose forward.

Unfortunately, the First World War made sure he would never fulfil his great potential. Arriving in France on 27 December 1915, Rifleman Johnson of the 1st/8th Battalion Prince of Wales's Own (West Yorkshire Regiment), better known as the Leeds Rifles, lost his life at the age of 25 on the Somme.

It seems likely Johnson perished during an attack on the enemy at Aveluy on the morning of 3 September, as the battalion's unit war diary explains:

> At 5.10 we attacked the enemy but were unable to hold and consolidate, Casualties, 9 officers and 294 other ranks.[3]

Johnson is yet another man with no known grave and is remembered on the Thiepval Memorial.

News of his death was given in the *Batley News* of 23 September 1916 under the heading 'Batley Footballer Gone.'

> Batley football enthusiasts will regret to hear that Walter Johnson, who played as a forward with the Batley team two seasons ago, and a portion of the

preceding winter, is amongst the West Yorkshires
who have been killed in recent fighting. Nothing
had been heard of Johnson for some time at Mount
Pleasant, the explanation being of course, that he
was 'otherwise engaged'. He was employed at
Messrs. Charlesworth's Fanny Pit, Leeds.....

Warrington's Alex Brown was another with the rugby league
world at his feet. Alexander Thomson Brown (Thomson
being his mother's maiden name) was born in Pendleton in
1893 to James and Eleanor Brown, and baptised at St Paul's,
Paddington, on 8 June 1893. He joined Warrington from
Salford club Weaste on 26 November 1912.

Although still a teenager, Brown wasted little time
making a positive impression with the Wilderspool club,
being handed his Northern Union debut at stand-off on 14
December in an 8-0 defeat at Broughton Rangers. That was
to be the first of his three senior starts that season, with his
second on Christmas Day in a 4-0 home triumph over Leigh
and a third on 15 February 1913 when Warrington lost 15-12
at Wakefield Trinity.

He then found himself relegated to the reserves for the
rest of the campaign and then the start of the 1913-14 season,
before re-appearing in the Northern Union during a
Warrington players' strike at Hull on 17 January 1914, when
a significantly-weakened Wire side was thrashed 51-8. On top
of that, Brown suffered a broken collar bone during the game,
which immediately brought a premature end to his season –
with the injury recorded in the *Liverpool Evening Express* on
the day. The report began:

Warrington were accompanied by several
hundreds of excursionists..... There was an

attendance of about 6,000 present, when Hull lost
the toss and started against the breeze. The nippy
Warrington forwards surprised their opponents
by their dash and speed. They were a lively set in
the opening stages, and carried play to the home
line, where Rogers' smart work saved the
situation. After ten minutes' play, Brown,
Warrington's right back, sustained a damaged
collar-bone and left the field.

It was the last time he would be seen on the Northern Union
stage.

After being ruled out for the rest of the campaign and
then struggling to get back to match fitness for the start of the
1914-15 season, Brown volunteered in Salford on 5 September
1914 as a rifleman with the King's Royal Rifle Corps. After
completing his training, he arrived in France on 21 July 1915
serving with the 10th Battalion. At the start of 1916 his battalion
were sent to Belgium, where Brown was wounded, according
to the Daily Casualty List which appeared on 17 July 1916.

Within a month, Brown and his battalion were back in
France and involved in the Somme offensive – with the
Warrington player killed during an attack on the village of
Guillemont. It proved a bloody affair, with the total casualties
at the close of the battalion's actions on 5 September reported
in the unit war diary as 10 officers and 263 other ranks. The
diary also revealed there were errors in the orders given to
the advancing troops and a general lack of communication.[4]

It was at some point during the first day of the attack,
3 September, that Brown lost his life at the age of 23. He is yet
one more with no known grave, so is commemorated on the
Thiepval Memorial.

News of his death, along with a little more detail about

how he perished, appeared in the *Salford Reporter* of 30 September:

> Rifleman Alec [*sic*] Brown, King's Royal Rifles, who was at one time a playing member of the Weaste Rugby Football Club but latterly half-back for Warrington, was killed in action on September 3. He was killed whilst going over the parapet with a bombing party, which he volunteered to join. Brown enlisted on September 5, 1914, and after training at Winchester and Aldershot went on active service in July 1915, his parents, who reside at 19 Melrose-street, Pendleton, not having seen him since. He was 23 years of age and formerly worked for Messrs Garner, Telford, Hardman and Co,[5] Cobden-street, Pendleton.

Another player who was relatively new to the Northern Union scene and just embarking on a highly-promising career was Swinton forward John Daley. Having signed from the local Swinton St Mary's amateur club for a fee of £5 on 2 September 1913, the 22-year-old made his senior debut at prop in an 11-7 defeat at Runcorn on 22 November the same year. He may have been relatively young for a front-row forward, but his physical presence ensured he quickly established himself as a mainstay of the Swinton pack, going on to make 34 appearances before joining up.

Raised in Pendlebury by parents John and Margaret Ann Daley, the young Jack – as he was also known – was a powerful man, standing 5ft 10in tall and weighing over 13 stone. As a result, he was not only a no-nonsense forward but also a respected middleweight wrestler. That tough background made him ideally suited for a life as a coalminer at the Sandhole Colliery in Linnyshaw. But even though at the start of 1915 he had a steady job down the mines and was a Swinton Northern Union regular, he enlisted with the Grenadier Guards in the February.

That immediately brought a halt to his blossoming rugby league career, although he did make one final senior appearance at loose forward while on leave in a 5-0 Challenge Cup defeat to St Helens on 13 March. And that appearance made big news, with the *Manchester Evening News* match preview of 11 March majoring on the fact Daley would be having a run-out:

> Swinton will have a strong team for their Cup tie encounter against St Helens at Chorley Road on Saturday. Jack Bailey and Daley have been granted permission by the officer commanding the Grenadier Guards, London, to play in the match....., and Worsley and Smith, two other recruits who are training in the district, will also appear in the home front rank.

But by the autumn of 1915 Daley had completed his full training and was on his way to France to join the 3rd Battalion Grenadier Guards, arriving overseas on 9 December 1915. The Guards spent much of the first half of 1916 serving in Belgium, not being involved in the first day of the Battle of the Somme on 1 July. They only made the move to northern France towards the end of July 1916 entraining at Esquelbecq at midnight on 29/30 July. They then arrived at billets at Le Souich the following day. It was now time to prepare for the major attack which would claim Daley's life – Flers-Courcelette and the first use of tanks, on 15 September 1916. Details of the operation are recorded in the unit war diary.

The Battalion marched off by companies at 9.00pm to take up position. This operation was favoured by a fine clear night with a moon. Companies moved up via Trones Wood, Guillemont and Ginchy. The assembly place of the Brigade was clear of the village as the enemy had proved to be very quick in putting down a barrage on it ..... This Battalion was the right front battalion and was formed up in 4 waves, all men in single rank and companies in columns of half companies. This formation was in accordance with the training carried out. The Battalion reached the assembly point without difficulty or interruption, only 1 man being slightly wounded.[6]

The diary reports prior to zero hour on 15 September 'the "tanks" which were allotted to the Division could be heard making their way up in rear of us'.[7] It also recorded the numbers of killed, wounded or missing when roll call was taken at the end of 15 September 1916: 413 officers and men. This was to prove the largest single day's loss for this battalion in the entire war. One of those killed was Lt Raymond Asquith, son of Prime Minister Herbert Asquith. Another casualty was Jack Daley.

Involved in that same assault was Jack's brother, Andrew, serving as a Private with the King's Own Yorkshire Light Infantry. Having heard Jack was missing, he went searching for him, but with no joy.

Reports revealing this information first appeared in the *Swinton and Pendlebury Journal* of 13 October under the headline 'Swinton Footballer Reported Missing'.

Much anxiety is being felt by the wife and parents of Pte. Jack Daley, the well-known Swinton F.C. forward. He has not been heard of since the 15th September, and any news regarding him would be welcomed at 2, Watson-St., Swinton. It appears that he went into battle with his regiment, the Grenadier Guards, and was not seen again. Pte. Hy. Thomas....., of the same regiment, has written to say that Daley did not answer the roll call, and his comrades reported him as missing.

Daley's body was never found and his death was officially confirmed by the Army Council in July 1917, with his name remembered on the Thiepval Memorial. The official date of death recorded by the Commonwealth War Graves Commission is 14 September 1916. He left a widow, Jessie, who he married in 1915.

A further Northern Union name on the Thiepval memorial is Runcorn's William Newall, who died on 15 September 1916. He was born in Latchford in 1888 and baptised at the local church of St James' on 28 June 1888, one of 12 children born to painter William Newall and his wife Sarah Ann (née Howard).

In his junior rugby playing days, Newall proved a star with his local Latchford amateur club and earned a trial with Warrington's 'A' team in the Lancashire Combination League. But nothing came of that, and the iron moulder instead joined Runcorn in September 1912. He made his senior debut in the three-quarters in the 1912-13 season – his first start was in a 13-7 home defeat to Warrington on 28 September – and went on to make 14 Northern Union appearances during that first campaign. He also made one appearance in the 1913-14 season, at scrum-half, which proved to be an ill-fated occasion as Runcorn were on the receiving end of a 37-0 hiding at Hunslet on 11 October 1913.

After that, Newall was unable to force his way back into the first-team reckoning, although he remained on the club's books hoping to get another chance. Unfortunately, that never came. Newall enlisted in Warrington in the early months of the war. He was assigned to the 9th Battalion, Rifle Brigade – formed as part of Kitchener's New Army. In the Somme offensive the 9th Battalion Rifle Brigade were involved in some of the fiercest fighting during the battles of Delville Wood and Flers-Courcelette. Like Daley, this latter battle was the one to claim Newall's life.

Unfortunately, Newall is another of whom nothing is known about the way he died. His death was recorded in the *Runcorn Examiner* of 7 October 1916, saying:

> Mr and Mrs Wm. Newall, 18, Miller-street, Latchford, have been officially informed that their son, Rifleman William Newall (better known as Dawley) was killed in action on September 15th. Rifleman Newall, who was twenty-eight years of age, was well-known as a footballer, having played in the local works' competitions and also for the Warrington and Runcorn teams. Before enlisting two years ago, he was employed as a moulder by Messrs. Richmond and Co., Ltd. He had been at the Front twelve months. As a boy he attended St James' School. His brother George, of the Rifle Brigade, has been wounded twice, and another brother, Ike, is in training with the R.A.M.C.

A Rugby League Family's Double Tragedy

12

In September 1915, the West family from the West Country were mourning the loss of Rochdale Hornets' three-quarter Tom West, who had been killed in action in France.

On 15 November 1916, the family were again in mourning after the death of Oldham forward Arthur Douglas West, again on the battlefields of northern France.

Tom and Arthur were cousins from Bath. But they were also outstanding rugby players who had made their names playing for their hometown club and their county of Somerset in the 15-a-side code.

However, when it came to the reasons for their switch to the 13-a-side code and a career in the Northern Union, the circumstances could not have been more pronounced. While Tom had decided to move north in late 1908 on his own terms after a successful career in club rugby union which culminated in him becoming Bath captain, it was a completely different story for the far younger Arthur.

The Greatest Sacrifice

The son of James and Elizabeth West, Arthur was born in Bath in 1893. After leaving St Michael's School he was employed as a porter by Messrs. Richard King and Son, Milsom Street. He was clearly an outstanding rugby union prospect, having made his county debut with Somerset while still a teenager. The Bath youngster looked capable of going on to achieve big things in the game. But everything fell apart as the 19-year-old was preparing to play for Somerset against the touring South Africans on 3 October 1912. On the day of the game, it was announced in the *Gloucestershire Echo* that:

> The Somerset Rugby Union have found it necessary to suspend A. West, the well-known Bath forward, who was chosen for the Somerset v South African match today. It is alleged that he has committed an act of professionalism.

It was then revealed in the *Pall Mall Gazette* five days later that West had been temporarily suspended by a Somerset Rugby Union Emergency Committee to investigate the matter, and went on to give details of what the 'professional' charge had been.

> It is stated that last Thursday week West's fare to Bridgwater, for the Somerset County Trial match, had been paid by the treasurer of the Bath club; that the treasurer of the County Union, not being aware of this, also paid him the money for the journey, and that West declined to return the fare. The meeting ..... found [West] guilty of professionalism under Rugby Union Rule No2, part 1, section a, sub-section d – receiving 'expenses in excess of the amount actually disbursed on account of

178

reasonable hotel or travelling expenses.' He was formally suspended, and ordered to be reported to the English Rugby Union. Now, it is declared, he will proceed to Rochdale to aid the Hornets.

West immediately denied the rumours about a potential move to Rochdale – where he would, of course, have linked up with his older cousin Tom – with local newspaper reports stating in mid-October he had returned to Bath. That, however, all changed on 1 November when the *Gloucestershire Echo* reported the formal decision of the English Rugby Union:

> A.D. West, the Bath forward, who has been under the ban of the Somersetshire Rugby Union for professionalism, has now been expelled from all Rugby Union football clubs.

West's universal union ban now made a switch to the Northern Union even more likely, although it was not until the first week of January 1913 that he was given the all-clear to pursue a career in the professional game, with the confirmation coming via the *Yorkshire Post and Leeds Intelligencer* of 8 January. It announced:

> An emergency meeting of the Cup Committee was held last evening at the Grosvenor Hotel, Manchester, when the principal business was the consideration of an application to play under Northern Union rules by Arthur Douglas West, of Bath, who had been suspended by the English Rugby Union for an offence against the professional laws. West appeared in person and his application was granted.

It was also revealed the same day in the *Manchester Courier and Lancashire General Advertiser* that West had signed for Oldham.

> The Oldham officials have at last made a move in the direction of strengthening their front rank. This department has not been too strong, and the club have been accused of not introducing new blood. Yesterday, Arthur West, late of Bath, who recently suffered suspension by the English Rugby Union, was signed on. West stands 5ft. 9½in., and has youth on his side, being only 19 years of age. It is not expected he will appear in the match with Runcorn on Saturday.....

Not turning out against Runcorn did prove the case, but it was not long before West was proving his worth in the Oldham team, quickly establishing himself in the senior side and going on to make 45 appearances and crossing for five tries, including a two-try haul in a big 35-3 home triumph over Runcorn on 2 January 1915. By that stage, West had become a regular starter in Oldham's second row, and he even played the final four fixtures of the 1914-15 season at prop.

But even though his Oldham career was starting to flourish, it did not prevent him from enlisting, signing up for the 10th Manchesters, where he quickly rose to the rank of Sergeant. He still had time to make the odd Oldham appearance while on leave, however, with the *Bath Chronicle and Weekly Gazette* of 15 January 1916 still keeping a keen eye on his rugby fortunes. They reported:

> A.D. West, the Bath Rugby forward ..... who

migrated to the Northern Union, is now a
Sergeant in the Army. Being home on leave, on
Saturday last, he played for Oldham against
Rochdale Hornets, and is commended in the
'Athletic News' for his capital forward game.
Sergeant A.D. West is a cousin of the late Tom
West, killed in France some months ago.

It was soon after this appearance that West went to the front,
with the 1st Battalion of the King's Liverpool Regiment. He
was soon involved in some heavy fighting in the Somme
region, although he did not lose his life until 15 November
during the Battle of the Ancre – just three days before the
official end of the 141-day Battle of the Somme.

In the hours leading up to his death, West's battalion's
objective was to breach a stronghold of German trenches,
known as the Quadrilateral,[1] at the northern flank of
Beaumont Hamel. The assault commenced on 13 November
in boggy, muddy conditions – the attack had been postponed
several times from 16 October because of the bad weather. A
large amount of rain and slush had accumulated in no man's
land, which was described in a large part as an 'insurpassable
morass,' and the troops were subject to heavy German
machine gun fire and shelling. By the time they were relieved
on the morning of 16 November the casualty count according
to the unit war diary was 2 officers killed and 8 wounded
with a further 245 other ranks either killed, missing or
wounded.[2] Nothing is recorded about how West fell, and his
siblings – his parents now being dead – were informed in
early December 1916 that he had been posted missing some
time between 13 and 15 November. His body was recovered
after the war and reburied in Tilloy British Cemetery.

Yet even though the 23-year-old may have been the last

Northern Union player to die before the end of 1916, five others involved in the top-flight competition also lost their lives in those final few months. They were Hunslet's Thomas Henry Tillotson, who was killed on 16 September; Bradford's Harold James Ruck, who fell on 26 September; Batley's James William Debney, who died on 29 September; Leeds' Jimmy Sanders, on 13 October; and Bramley's Tom Wagstaff, whose death was on 18 October.

In the case of Tillotson, followers from two very different sports were mourning the loss of their man. Not only was the 26-year-old a rugby league player who had competed in the Northern Union and was a senior member of Hunslet's first-team squad, he had also been one of the county's top swimmers as a junior and played water polo to boot. In fact, before making a name for himself at hometown club Hunslet, Tillotson was hitting most of his sporting headlines for excellence in the pool, where at the age of 12 he was being tipped to become a national champion. He went on to win 12 first prizes in swimming competitions and was a prominent figure at the Holbeck Swimming Galas.

Unfortunately, he never fulfilled that potential, possibly because he was also devoting his attention to the oval-ball game, and clearly proving a pretty decent exponent of that, too, hence the fact he signed for the South Leeds club from Burley Lawn at the age of 18.

That would clearly have been a thrill for the Tillotson family, who had such strong ties with the locality.

Thomas's parents, John William and Sarah Ann Tillotson brought their family up in the area. They had in total 11 children, three of whom had died before the 1911 census. Thomas was born in around early 1890. He continued the Hunslet links, marrying Gertrude Elizabeth Little on 16 November 1912 at St Peter's parish church, Hunslet Moor.

Their son, Jack Richmond Tillotson, was born in May 1913 in Hunslet.

And it was in Hunslet where Tillotson excelled as a swimmer, leading to a *Yorkshire Evening Post* article of 3 October 1902 hailing him as a future Great Britain star. The big headlines barked out: 'The Best Boy Swimmer in Leeds. A Prodigy in the Water'. The story read:

> A swimming prodigy has been found in Leeds. Thomas Henry Tillotson, aged 12, is a Cockburn schoolboy, and leader of the team which has this season won both the Leeds School Board Cup and the Yorkshire Schoolboys' Squadron Championship. He is a lad with a perfect swimmer's physique – light bones, an abnormally large chest, thick round limbs, and a fair muscular development ..... He is a long way the finest boy swimmer Leeds has ever produced, and within the next two years his admirers will be very disappointed if he does not win the Schoolboys' Championship of Great Britain ..... His best times are 30 yards in 21sec, and 50 yards in 36sec. A youth of 18 or 20 who can swim 50 yards in 40 seconds is considered an expert, but this twelve-year-old prodigy could give such a youth four or five seconds start ..... Great things are expected of him.

But over the next few years, rugby began to have the bigger pull over the outstanding young athlete. Within weeks of signing from the Burley club as a teenager in 1908, Tillotson was making his Northern Union debut, going on to make six appearances that year. The following campaign he featured

12 times and scored one try, while three further senior starts were recorded the year after that. At the same time as playing rugby league, he also played water polo competitively, representing the Selby club for three seasons. In May 1913 he resumed his water polo career with Holbeck, after a break of five years, in the newly-resurrected Leeds Swimming and Life Saving Association League.

This coincided with the senior starts for Hunslet drying up. Having said that, Tillotson did remain on Hunslet's first-team books, regularly featuring for the reserves and standing by to return to the Northern Union fold when required. In fact, in 1913, he played alongside the up-and-coming George Wishart in Hunslet's second team, before the Scotsman broke into the senior side and then lost his life in the early months of the war.

Unfortunately, just under two years after Wishart had sacrificed his life, Tillotson suffered a similar fate. He enlisted with the Coldstream Guards in Leeds in February 1915 and went out to France in November 1915, serving the 2nd Battalion. A brief summary of his military life is recorded on the *National Roll of the Great War 1914-18*. It states that after volunteering, Guardsman Tillotson was drafted to the Western Front and:

> There he took an important part with his unit in many engagements and fought with distinction at Ginchy, where he was unhappily killed in September 1916.....[3]

The Commonwealth War Graves Commission records his death as taking place on 16 September – yet another casualty of Flers-Courcelette. Confirmation of his death was relayed home, with the family notice published in the *Leeds Mercury* on 5 October, stating he was killed in action between 14 and 16 of September. Thomas Henry Tillotson is remembered on the Thiepval Memorial, one more man with no known grave.

While two sports were mourning the loss of Tillotson, two areas of England nearly 200 miles apart were feeling the impact of the death of 28-year-old Bradford Northern forward Harold Ruck. There were those in his adopted West Yorkshire and the rest of his family back in his home town of Stroud, Gloucestershire.

Ruck was no stranger to Army life, having served with the Grenadier Guards before signing for Northern on 22 July 1913. But even though their new Painswick-born recruit had signed from the Army rather than a club, Bradford never felt their move was a gamble. Before re-joining the Grenadier Guards as a Reservist at the outbreak of war, Ruck had proved a very competent rugby union player with Stroud and then went on to be a star of the Guards' 15-a-side representative team. And the strict discipline of a life in the Army, as well as on the rugby field, was probably what Ruck needed to make sure he travelled down the right path towards adulthood.

Born in 1889 and baptised in the parish of Slad, he was the son of William Francis and Clara Ruck. By all accounts, the young Ruck was a 'lively' teenager, who found himself in a minor scrape with the Stroud authorities as he was growing up. The incident occurred in May 1902 when he and a number of other boys were charged with 'obstructing Russell Street in Stroud, by standing on the pavement.'[4] The miscreants were all fined one shilling inclusive. In another incident later that year the 14-year-old Ruck suffered injuries to his ear and side whilst working on a winding machine at Fromehall Mills. These necessitated treatment at Stroud hospital.

But youthful scrapes aside, Ruck was growing up quickly on the rugby field as an up-and-coming player. At 6ft tall and over 14 stones, he proved a difficult opponent to handle. He continued to shine as a rugby forward after enlisting with the Guards, being based at Wellington Barracks, St James Park, Westminster in 1911 with the 3rd Battalion. It was with them that he went on to play a starring role for the Army against the Navy.

That was enough to convince the West Yorkshire club that this was the man for them and, just over a month after putting pen to paper, the 25-year-old made his Northern Union debut in Bradford's 12-0 home opening-day defeat to Barrow on 3 September 1913. Although it was a far from convincing start to the season for the club, Bradford's new second-rower was hardly to blame, and he went on to feature in 38 of his side's 39 first-team fixtures in the 1913-14 campaign and crossed for one try in a 9-4 Yorkshire Cup victory at York on 1 November. That success over York helped Bradford reach the county cup final, where they were beaten 19-3 by Huddersfield on 29 November. It was clear, however, that Northern had unearthed a major talent.

But that exciting potential remained unfulfilled because of the outbreak of war. Having served with the Grenadier Guards and being on the Army Reserve, Private Ruck immediately re-joined his regiment. He made the trip overseas, posted to the 1st Battalion in March 1915. Having survived for 18 months, the now Lance Sergeant Ruck's luck unfortunately ran out on the second day of the Battle of Morval in September 1916, which was part of the Somme offensive.

The Guards enjoyed some initial success during this part of the campaign by capturing their first-day objectives in front of the heavily-defended village of Lesboeufs. The unit war diary of 26 September claimed the attack had left the 'Huns thoroughly demoralised.'[5] However, the attack had come at a high price, with many killed in the bid to take the enemy trenches, with Ruck one of dozens to perish that day. He is buried at Caterpillar Valley Cemetery, Longueval. He left a widow, Edith Eliza (née Hayward) who he married in Stonehouse, Gloucestershire in February 1913.

Tragically, as his family were learning of his death, his parents were still coming to terms with the loss of his brother Francis, who was killed in France on 20 February 1916 while serving with the 1st Battalion Gloucestershire Regiment. He is commemorated on the Arras Memorial.

While Ruck was relatively new to the Northern Union scene, it was a different story for Batley's James Debney, who had been a regular with the Heavy Woollen club for five seasons before the war intervened – and turning out in virtually every position during that time. For instance, in the 1913-14 season alone, he is down on teamsheets appearing at full-back, wing, stand-off, prop, hooker and second row!

On top of that, he also shared the goalkicking duties during that 13-14 campaign, landing a total of 15, while also crossing for six tries in his 24 appearances. That 48-point tally made him the club's top points scorer that season, finishing ahead of fellow First World War victim Jack Tindall on 41 points with 13 tries and a goal. Debney had also been a notable figure the previous year, having played a starring role in Batley's 13-5 triumph over the Australasian Tourists in front of a 5,000 Mount Pleasant crowd on 27 January 1912. According to the reports of the day, his finest moment came in the closing stages to wrap up the contest, when he broke clear of the Australian defence and cross-kicked for Tom Williams to gather and score. It was easy to see why he was so valuable to the 'Gallant Youths.'

The son of Joseph and Alice Debney (née Williams), he was born in 1890 and baptised at St Thomas' parish church, Purston-cum-South-Featherstone on 6 October that year. Debney grew up in a very strong rugby-playing area but moved to Mount Pleasant from the Darfield club in Barnsley in August 1909. This was because his family moved to Darfield from Featherstone some time after 1905. Despite still being in his teens, the coalminer very quickly became a key member of the Batley side, playing an active role in the squad both on and off the field – as reflected in the 1911 census[6], which was conducted on 2 April. Rather than showing that many of the Batley players at that particular moment were living at their home addresses, the census states they were all in Morecambe, presumably on a 'team bonding' trip. Batley had a free Northern Union weekend that weekend, and many squad members clearly took full advantage.

But despite Debney putting his heart and soul into the Batley cause, he became one of the club's first players to enlist, attesting with the 6th Battalion York and Lancaster Regiment on 24 August 1914. And his surviving service records showed he was in excellent health when he answered the nation's call.

His medical report stated he was 5ft 6in tall and weighed 164lbs. He had a 39in chest, boasted *'very good'* physical development and had a pulse rate of 76. He also had perfect vision. But there was one negative in his military history account – he had *'a few carious teeth.'* In other words, he was suffering from tooth decay. This was a condition that the records stated was a slight defect *'but not sufficient to cause rejection'* from the Army.[7]

After successfully completing his medical, Debney joined up with his new comrades to train to be a soldier. Yet rather than initially preparing for battle against the Germans on the Western Front, the 6th York and Lancasters found themselves training to fight the Turkish Ottoman Empire as part of the ill-fated Dardanelles campaign. It was an eventful sailing from Liverpool, in which the alarm was raised as they dodged a threatened submarine attack off Ireland's south coast. Debney and his regiment arrived in Gallipoli – at Suvla Bay – on 6 August 1915, by which time the British were pinned down by their brave and resilient adversary. As a result, the Batley player and his colleagues were eventually evacuated from the area on the night of 19/20 December 1915 and arrived in Egypt in early February 1916.

From there, the battalion moved on to northern France, where they arrived for the start of the Battle of the Somme. But it was not until 29 September that Debney was to finally lose his life in what was to prove a successful attack resulting in the capture of most of the German-held Hessian Trench in the Battle of Thiepval Ridge. At what stage of the day Debney fell is not recorded in the unit war diary. His body was recovered after the war and identified by a piece of his disc. He was given a permanent final resting place at A.I.F. Burial Ground, Flers.

When his death was announced on 21 October 1916, the *Batley News* devoted a major piece about it. The main headline read: 'Another Footballer Killed', while under two separate subheads it added: 'The Fourth "Gallant Youth" to Lay Down His Life, and Debney Goes Down in an Attack on a German Trench.' The report read:

> Another Batley footballer has laid down his life for King and Country – James William Debney – one of the finest forwards who ever played for a Northern Union Club. Poor Johnson was killed a few weeks ago, so with the late Jack Tindall and

Bob Randerson no fewer than four members of Batley's first team have made the Great Sacrifice.

The report then added that official confirmation of his death had been sent in a letter from his mother to Mr W. Kershaw Newsome, the secretary of the Batley Cricket, Athletic and Football Club. Included in that correspondence was a letter sent to Mrs Debney from Lieut-Colonel G.H. Wedgwood which read:

> Dear Mrs Debney – I am sorry to have to inform you that your son, No 11477 Pte. J.W. Debney was killed by a shell on Sept 29th 1916. The Battalion was attacking a German trench at the time, and your son fell with many others of the Regiment. The trench was taken and held, so your son's death was not in vain.

The *Batley News* piece then concluded:

> Debney's career as a member of Batley Football Club commenced in 1909. He took part in two matches with the 'A' team and was given his first trial with the premier team against Hunslet on September 11th, 1909. He proved a most versatile player and filled every position from forward to full back with success. In February 1915, whilst in training, Debney assisted the 'Gallant Youths' in the first round of the Northern Union Cup at Bradford ..... Little did anyone think that that would be the last match in which he and Walter Johnson would wear the Batley colours.

Although just 24-years-old when he enlisted with the 15th Battalion Prince of Wales's Own (West Yorkshire Regiment), James Henry Stacey Sanders was already something of a 'veteran' of the Leeds team, having made his Northern Union debut while still a teenager at scrum half in an 11-8 home win over Halifax at Headingley on 4 September 1909. He then went on to make a further 182 appearances, scoring 28 tries and kicking three goals in the process, before the Great War brought a halt to his career.

Born in Newport, Gwent, on 29 December 1889 to Peter and Emily Sanders, he was an outstanding all-round athlete and an exceptional rugby union player from an early age, having represented Wales against England in a schoolboy international in 1902. Within two years of earning those schoolboy honours, he was starring for the Pill Harriers Extras rugby club, progressing into the first team by the age of 16.

Just two years later he was being courted by Leeds, with a deal being struck which went down well in the *Yorkshire Evening Post* of 28 June 1909 – even if they did not know how to spell his namely correctly! It read:

> The Leeds Northern Union Football Club have made an important capture for next season in securing the signature of J. Saunders, Pill Harriers, half-back. He will be the first Welsh school-boy international to figure in Northern Union football. He played a leading part in assisting his club to win the Monmouthshire League last season, and represented his county against Glamorgan, showing fine football against Owen, the Welsh international. Saunders is 19, built on sturdy lines, and should prove an ideal partner to Reg. Jones.

His decision to sign for the start of the 1909-10 season brought instant results, with the diminutive half-back (he was around 5ft 5in tall) impressing in his first trial, as reported in the *Leeds Mercury* of 18 August 1909.

> There was a good attendance of spectators at Headingley yesterday evening to witness Leeds at practice. Sides were played, and though some of the play was naturally rather ragged, the men worked hard, and there were a number of clever efforts, both individually and combined. The 'star artiste' was the Welshman Sanders, who partnered Reg. Jones at the base of the scrimmage. Nippy, and possessed of a fair turn of speed, he gave and took the ball well, and some of his bursts were very smart. Though a trifle short, Sanders is well and sturdily built, and if he can reproduce his practice form in the more important contests he should prove a decidedly useful man for Leeds.

That clearly proved the case. Sanders made his Northern Union debut in a win over Halifax on 4 September 1909, and also helped Leeds reach the Challenge Cup final for the first time during that season, although he suffered a shoulder injury after 15 minutes in the 7-7 draw against Hull at Fartown, which the *Athletic News* felt was crucial in Leeds not winning the first time around. The publication said:

> Sanders was smart during the brief period he was on the field, but Leeds' 12 men heroically hung on.

Two days later, and with Sanders absent as he recovered from his knock which had required hospital treatment, Leeds claimed the trophy for the first time as they stormed to a 26-12 replay win.

The half-back then returned to become a regular fixture in the senior side, scoring two tries in a game on three occasions, against Huddersfield, Keighley and Bramley. He also kicked a goal in Leeds' club record 102-0 home rout of Coventry during the 1912-13 season.

Sanders was also one of the players who featured regularly in the disrupted 1914-15 campaign after war was declared, playing 36 of the 38 games that season. His last appearance came in the heavy 35-2 play-off final defeat to Huddersfield at Wakefield on 24 April 1915.

Employed as a warehouseman, it was two months later that Sanders enlisted with the West Yorkshire Regiment in Colsterdale, North Yorkshire, a fact championed by the *Yorkshire Evening Post* of 25 June 1915.

> 'Jimmy' Sanders, the well-known Leeds Northern Union footballer, enlisted to-day in the Leeds 'Pals' Battalion. A Welshman, who came north six or seven seasons ago, Sanders has rendered yeoman service for Leeds as a half-back.
>
> Other footballers who have been attested in the Leeds 'Pals' Battalion to-day are: Colin Crumpton, the old Leeds forward; J.W. Fairburn and F. Langstaffe, of York; and J.G. Hitchen, a Leeds Association player who was in the Amateur International junior team last year.

Private Sanders did not remain with the Leeds 'Pals'. At some point he transferred to the West Yorkshire Regiment's 1st Battalion and went to France during 1916. Having survived the initial onslaught on the Somme, Sanders' luck ran out during the Battle of Le Transloy. In what was a complicated attack involving two Infantry Brigades of the 6th Division, the West Yorkshires were tasked with attacking Cloudy and Mild trenches. Prior to the attack the West Yorkshires were bombarded by their own misdirected guns as well as the German artillery. On leaving their trenches they were met with intense machine-gun and rifle fire and the Germans had reinforced with fresh troops, anticipating the attack. An extract from *The West Yorkshire Regiment in the War* puts it into perspective just how tough the conditions were on the eve of his death.

> At 3-55 p.m., 6th Divisional Headquarters received a report, forwarded by Headquarters, 18th Infantry Brigade, from the O.C., 1st West Yorkshires: 'Impossible to advance against concentrated machine-gun and rifle fire. Hold part of Cloudy Trench on my right, otherwise in original position. Fire of every description very heavy at present.'[8]

They were ordered to consolidate, but it was at a cost. Two officers were wounded and 24 other ranks were killed, 71 wounded and 10 missing.

The unit war diary then takes up the exact story on the day of Sanders' death on 13 October. The entry went:

> Trenches – Very heavy shelling – The Battalion was relieved by 2nd D[*urham*] L[*ight*] I[*nfantry*]. Relief completed by 11pm. On relief the Battalion

proceeded to bivouacs at Trones Wood. Casualties: 6 Killed, 22 Wounded, 2 Missing.[9]

Sanders was one of those casualties. Fears the popular half-back may have lost his life began to filter through towards the end of the month, with the *Leeds Mercury* of 26 October reporting:

> According to news received in Leeds, there is reason to fear that 'Jimmy' Sanders ..... has been killed in action ..... He went to the front some months ago as a machine-gunner.

And it was confirmed in the *Yorkshire Evening Post* on 31 October:

> The news published ..... on Friday that it was believed that Jimmy Sanders, the Leeds footballer, had been killed in action, turns out to be only too true. Official confirmation has now been received from the War Office ..... He joined a local reserve battalion eighteen months ago.

Tributes were paid to Sanders over the next few months, with the *Evening Post* leading the way with an article under the headline 'Sanders, the Humourist' on 11 November. It stated:

> Those in touch with the Leeds Northern Union's team know how exceedingly droll was their little half-back 'Jimmy' Sanders, unhappily killed in action a month ago. As ..... the club's secretary ..... writes in the official programme, Sanders could always see the humorous side of everything.

Having seen in a programme that J.R. Brooksby had been made a lance-corporal, he promptly wrote 'No wonder we are advancing in France.' A few weeks ago he met F. Godward and A. Sykes, who were going into the trenches as he was coming out. 'I only just managed to shout to them, but I noticed Godward was hugging the bag with the rations in it. What brainwork!' Sanders added, 'I have been in it thick and thin just lately, and have been over the top twice and back, a winner on each occasion. It was quite amusing to see Germans running towards us with their hands up, flapping them like seals, giving their famous war cry, "Kamerade!"'

The 26-year-old was another who had no known grave and is remembered on the Thiepval Memorial.

It was five days later that Tom Wagstaff fell. Although the forward was playing for Bramley when he answered his nation's call, he would have known Sanders well, with both men having signed for Leeds in 1909. In the case of Wagstaff, he made his Leeds debut a month after Sanders in a home game against Wakefield on 16 October 1909.

That was to be the first of his 54 senior appearances for the Headingley club, during which time he crossed for a couple of tries. He then made the move across to Halifax on 23 July 1912, but failed to make his mark at Thrum Hall and signed for Bramley on 13 August 1914. It was a move which proved far more beneficial.

Wagstaff made his debut at prop in a 7-0 Northern Union home defeat to former club Halifax a month later, on 5 September, and then started in the front row in the next five games before switching to hooker for the rest of the season.

That was for 27 consecutive games. His final appearance came on 17 April 1915 in a 16-5 away derby defeat to Hunslet.

It was then that Wagstaff turned his attention to the war effort. Born in Normanton on 17 August 1887, the son of John and Mary Wagstaff, he had previously been with the local Territorials, the 4th King's Own Yorkshire Light Infantry. However, when he attested in his home town on 10 June 1915, it was with the Queen's Own Cameron Highlanders. He underwent his training with the 3rd (Reserve) Battalion, which was a training unit of the Special Reserve. Standing 5ft 9¼in tall, he gave his occupation as a 'coal and clay merchant and professional footballer.'[10]

Wagstaff arrived in France on 1 October 1915 to join the 5th Battalion. They were involved in heavy fighting during the Somme offensive, including the Battle of Albert, the Battle of Bazentin (when the Division captured Longueval) and the Battle of Delville Wood. But it was on the final day of the Battle of Le Transloy on 18 October 1916 that Wagstaff lost his life at the age of 29.

The main objective was to take the Butte de Warlencourt German stronghold – an ancient burial ground mound which gave the enemy an excellent view of the British front line and an ideal artillery observation point. Many Allied troops would die in the attempt to seize it, with Wagstaff just one of them. He fell in the battalion's bid to capture German frontline trenches, part of the advance towards the Butte.

Zero hour for the attack was 3.40am on 18 October. During the course of the day, Wagstaff's battalion's unit war diary reported that, despite counter-attacks, their objective was taken. The battalion were relieved at midnight and withdrew to the reserve line, but without Wagstaff who was a casualty of the attack. The only consolation for his family was he is one of those with a named grave, and he is now buried in Warlencourt British Cemetery.

His death was officially announced in the *Leeds Mercury* on 13 November 1916, under the headline 'Bramley Footballer Killed.' Incorrectly stating he was a Corporal, when he was in fact a Private, it said:

> Corporal Tom Wagstaff, of the Cameron Highlanders, has been killed in action. He was the centre man of the Bramley club's pack before the war, and was a sterling scrimmager, who did much to improve Bramley's forward play.

First Months of 1917 – Flower of Scotland

13

The winter of 1916 on the Western Front proved to be quiet, especially when considering the appalling loss of life which had taken place during the Battle of the Somme. The bitterly-cold weather put an end to any major offensives on 18 November, while the German front became almost silent. Little did the Allies realise at the time, but the Germans were struggling to hold their lines and had withdrawn a number of miles to their rear to build the Hindenberg Line, which would strengthen their defences and shorten the front.

As a result, the number of soldiers losing their lives at that time fell dramatically, with just a couple from the Northern Union dying at the start of 1917. And one, in fact, passed away without leaving British shores on 16 January. That player was Oldham's William Boyd Jardine.

The Jedburgh-born forward was another who had made a name for himself playing rugby union, where he shone for Jed Forest. And it is highly likely he had his older brother Adam – he was five years William's senior – to thank for securing a professional Northern Union contract with the Roughyeds.

Before signing Billy – as he was affectionally known – it was Adam who caught the attention of the Oldham committee. Signing the older Jardine proved a smart move for the Lancastrians, with Adam on the club's books between the 1903-04 and 1907-08 seasons, making 67 appearances and scoring three tries in the process.

Oldham's club officials clearly felt there was profit to be made in investing in the Jardine stock and in the 1908-09 campaign they secured the signature of Billy, who by that time had earned a reputation as one of the best forwards in Scotland. Not surprisingly, it was a capture that went down well in the red rose county, as the *Manchester Courier and Lancashire General Advertiser* of 29 July 1908 confirmed.

> The Oldham club has secured the signature of William Boyd Jardine, captain of Jed Forest Club, Scotland. He is a forward, stands 5ft. 8in. in height, and is 21 years of age. Three years ago he played in the Rest of Cities' match, which is practically the Scottish international trial match. He is stated to be one of the finest forwards in Scotland.

At the same time, the *Jedburgh Gazette* made their report clear how much their local club would miss one of their star players.

> Wm. B. Jardine, a prominent forward in the Jed-Forest team, and who six weeks ago was elected captain of the first fifteen for the coming season,

has signed on for Oldham, and leaves Jedburgh
about a fortnight hence. He has had many offers
before this, and refused, and is parting from Jed-
Forest with reluctance ..... Jardine ..... is a fine type
of player, with all-round qualifications that are by
no means common. Jed-Forest will miss him
much.

When Jardine put pen to paper, Oldham were one of the
strongest clubs in the Northern Union competition, having
been crowned League Champions in 1904-05, claiming the
Lancashire County Cup two seasons later and then the
Lancashire League the year after that. But even though
Jardine was joining such a star-studded side, he was soon
establishing himself as one of the most valuable players at
the Watersheddings. During his first season, he helped
Oldham finish third in the Championship and was then
influential in taking his new club to the Championship final,
where they were beaten 7-3 by Wigan, with Jardine scoring
his side's only try of the game.

It got even better the following season as he played a
leading role in helping Oldham complete a Championship,
Lancashire Cup and Lancashire League treble. After that, he
was instrumental in helping them retain the Champions title
in 1910-11 and winning the Lancashire Cup again in 1912-13.
It meant that by the time Jardine joined up, he had chalked
up 164 senior appearances and scored 26 tries and 60 goals,
claiming some illustrious rugby league winner's medals
along the way.

After such a successful Oldham career, it could not
have been easy for the 29-year-old to turn his back on the club
and enlist with the 10th (Reserve) Battalion, Manchester
Regiment on 29 September 1914, although by that stage his

appearances in the Roughyeds senior side were becoming far less frequent. Having said that, he featured at prop for much of the 1914-15 campaign, being allowed to turn out regularly in the Northern Union whilst on leave. Playing those games were clearly at the Army's blessing as he was appointed Acting Corporal on 2 July 1915.

It was not long after that, however, that Jardine was struck down by a serious chest problem from which he would never recover. He picked up the illness after catching a chill during the final stages of his military training in the UK and was eventually discharged from the Army on 20 October 1915, after being deemed unfit for service,[1] although there were high hopes at that time he would make a full recovery. The *Jedburgh Gazette* of 26 November 1915 reported:

> W.B. Jardine ..... is at present in hospital at Hawick. Jardine was serving with the Manchester Regiment, and he contracted a chest trouble, but is well on the way to complete recovery ..... Many Jedburgh friends will earnestly hope that his restoration to good health may be completed soon.

But on 18 January 1917, the *Dundee Courier* announced the illness had taken his life.

> The death has taken place at Jedburgh of W.B. Jardine ..... Deceased, who was 31, had not been in good health for some time. He was a magnificent footballer, and on numerous occasions was chosen to play for Lancashire.

The *Jedburgh Gazette* the following day then revealed Jardine died at the home of his brother-in-law, Sam L Davison, of 87 Castlegate, Jedburgh. This was all confirmed in Jardine's death certificate. As well as confirming the location of his death at 6.45 in the morning of 16 January 1917, it also stated Jardine was 31, single, a tweed finisher by trade and had died of Phthisis pulmonalis (more commonly known as tuberculosis). He had suffered with the condition for 'about one year three months'.[2]

A 2 February report in the *Jedburgh Gazette* then paid a full tribute to their famous son. It included the following high praise:

> His early football work was soon stamped as 'class'. A finely-built youth, endowed with speed and brain, he was great with the ball at his feet, and likewise a sure carrier. He was recognised as a master of goalkicking in Scotland ..... He played his 'trials' for Scotland and, had he but stayed, a 'cap' and a thistle badge would certainly have been his. We, with our amateur pride, sincerely regretted his going, but we always read with pride his doings with Oldham.

Having died at home, Jardine was buried at Jedburgh (Castlewood) Cemetery.

Sadly, the loss of Billy was only a third of the tragedy for the Jardine family, one thankfully his parents, John and Margaret Jardine (her maiden name was, incidentally, Boyd), did not have to endure, both already deceased by the time Billy passed away. Two of his brothers also died as a result of the conflict, including Adam. A Lance Corporal in the 10th Battalion, Queen's Own (Royal West Kent Regiment), he was the second Jardine brother to be killed, losing his life on 31

July 1917 during an attack on Ridge Wood when he was picked off by a sniper. He was 37 years old and remembered on the Menin Gate at Ypres. Then, on 24 February 1919, the 42-year-old Walter Boyd Jardine died of pneumonia following influenza. A Gunner in the Royal Garrison Artillery, he had been transferred to the 487th Agricultural Company of the Labour Corps and was based at Ripon. He was one of millions to lose his life in the flu pandemic in the wake of the Great War.

Another former union convert from 'up north' who died early in 1917 was Wakefield Trinity captain William Lindsay Beattie, who was killed in France on 27 January at the age of 26.

Top prop Beattie was one of the biggest stars of the game when he answered the call to arms. Born in Maxwelltown, Kirkcudbrightshire, Scotland in 1889, Beattie grew up alongside his parents, William and Margaret, and his five sisters. Being the only boy in the house must have been tough for the young Beattie, who would have enjoyed the release of being able to hone his talents on the rugby field. This he did with considerable success at his local rugby team, before moving to the Blackhill club in Consett, County Durham where he had employment as an insurance clerk, and then catching the eye of Wakefield, who formally registered the 21-year-old on 3 October 1911.

It was not long before the strapping 5ft 11in Beattie had quickly established himself as a mainstay of the Trinity pack and went on to make 90 first-team appearances. Arguably his finest hours came in the 1913-14 season when he led Wakefield all the way to the Challenge Cup final as Wakefield captain – although it was his heroics in the thrilling 9-8 second-round home win over Leeds on 14 March 1914 that became the stuff of legend. In front of a 12,000 crowd, Trinity found themselves 8-7 down with just five minutes remaining. The home side were then, as the *Wakefield Trinity Heritage* site recalls, awarded a penalty seven yards inside their own half. But Beattie stepped up and, showing nerves of steel, managed to slot the ball straight between the posts to send the Wakefield fans into ecstasy.

Trinity then went on to beat Wigan 9-6 in the next round and Broughton Rangers 5-0 in a semi-final replay to set up a final showdown with Hull, who took the honours 6-0 on 18 April in front of a 19,000 crowd at Halifax's Thrum Hall.

It was efforts such as this that earned Beattie selection for Great Britain's summer tour to Australia and New Zealand, although he declined due to business reasons. He had a successful career working as a cashier at the Wakefield branch of the Prudential Assurance Company. But he did not decline the opportunity to join the Army when war was declared, being among those first to enlist on 5 September 1914 as a Private in the 1/4th King's Own Yorkshire Light Infantry. He was very soon being used as a recruitment 'tool' by the military, as the *Yorkshire Evening Post* of 24 October 1914 explained in its match report of Wakefield's home game against Keighley:

> The military authorities attended the match at Belle Vue, to-day, between Wakefield Trinity and Keighley, arrangements having been made for recruiting speeches to be delivered to the crowd at the conclusion of the game. Unfortunately, there was a very meagre attendance of spectators, only about 1,000 being present at the start. Additional interest was lent to the event owing to the fact that Beattie and E. Parkin, who had

> joined the 4th Battalion KOYLI, who are training
> at Gainsborough and who were on leave, were
> included in the Wakefield team.....

How successful the recruitment drive proved is unknown, but it was certainly a successful day for Trinity, who thrashed Keighley 57-0, with Beattie chipping in with a try and two goals. There were also two tries that day for winger Arthur Cockcroft, who was to fall on the Somme in 1916.

Besides training in Gainsborough, the now Lance Corporal Beattie[3] and his battalion also spent time in York, and it was while he was there that the Scotsman was granted a commission as a temporary 2nd Lieutenant in the Border Regiment with effect from 15 March 1915. It was reported in the *Huddersfield Daily Examiner* of 25 March 1915, under the headline 'Commission for Wakefield Footballer'.

> The well-known Wakefield Trinity forward, W.L.
> Beattie, who for some time has been training at
> York with the 4th Battalion King's Own Yorkshire
> Light Infantry, has received a notification that he
> has been given a commission in the Border Regt
> ..... Beattie had recently arranged with the
> Wakefield Club to allow him to appear with the
> York team when his military duties in that city
> allowed him to do so.

This, and a second promotion to Temporary Lieutenant which followed with effect from 15 August 1915, were both officially announced in the *London Gazette*.[4]

Upon completing his training, he joined the 6th Battalion Border Regiment on 11 October 1915 in Gallipoli to face the Turks. Their unit war diary notes his arrival.[5] As already described, the Gallipoli campaign between the spring and autumn of 1915 proved to be a complete disaster, with the Allies suffering a miserable time in the searing heat and failing to make any sort of breakthrough against their brave foe. But at first, Beattie seemed to be enjoying the harsh and unforgiving surroundings, as reported in the *Leeds Mercury* of 17 November 1915. It published a letter to his former employers, at the Wakefield branch of the Prudential Assurance Company.

> I am not allowed to say where I am, and, to be candid, I have not much of an idea myself. It is somewhere in Gallipoli, and I am certain it is in the neighbourhood of some person or persons who apparently do not appreciate our company, for they keep shooting at us with rifles. To-day I am supposed to be resting, which means lying somewhere behind the firing line. I live in Shaftesbury-avenue, a name given to the path some months ago by the men who first landed. If you saw the whole country you would think it impossible for men to make advances, and I have come to the conclusion that the troops who dealt with the question up to now must have been supermen. In the days when I was a private I used to 'love' plum and apple jam, and thought I had seen the last of it when I was commissioned, but it has turned up once again – the same old tin and the same old label, but with one word altered: plum and apple is now called apricot. This morning four of our officers went down to the sea for a swim. One old Turkish gentleman (from some unknown region), who probably did

not believe in infidels bathing in Oriental waters, commenced sniping. Fortunately for all of us, his shooting was as bad as my swimming, so everything went on gaily.

But by the time the letter was published, Beattie was already dangerously ill, as reported to his mother in a series of telegrams at the end of October.[6] On 21 October 1915 the unit war diary noted he was transferred to the 35th Field Ambulance.[7] By the end of the month he was in a hospital in Alexandria, with confirmation he was suffering from acute dysentery. Lucky to survive, Beattie was invalided back home from Alexandria on board the 'Dover Castle' at the end of November 1915. It took some time for him to make a full recovery, spending his time in England with the 10th (Reserve Battalion) before being posted to France to join the 1st Battalion on 21 July 1916.

For a short time the battalion was pulled back to Flanders, before returning to France once more in October 1916. Back in France, Beattie spent time with the Brigade Pioneers and Army School as well as with his battalion. He was to lose his life on 27 January 1917.

His battalion, along with the 1st Royal Inniskilling Fusiliers, had orders to attack a section of the enemy position south of Le Transloy, known as Landwehr Trench. Although the battalion's unit war diary recorded fierce resistance encountered throughout the day, the attack proved a success, with the objectives taken and many prisoners rounded up. As a result, by mid-afternoon the diary entry stated:

All objectives gained and consolidation proceeding very slowly owing to hardness of ground. Following received from Commander-in-

Chief: 'Congratulate the 29th Div[ision] warmly and in particular the 1st Border Reg[imen]t and 1/R[oyal] Inniskilling Fusiliers on the success of their operations carried out this morning. In forwarding this message the army commander wishes to add his congratulations to the 29th Div[ision] in their most successful enterprise.'[8]

But despite the success of the operation, the diary's final entry at the end of the day showed the objectives had been achieved at a cost. Amongst those to fall was William Lindsay Beattie.

His death was reported in the *Dumfries and Galloway Standard* on 3 February 1917 under the headline 'Dumfries Officer Killed', and said:

Mrs Beattie, 8 Carnegie Street, Dumfries, received a telegram on Thursday evening stating that her son, Lieutenant (Temporary Captain) William Lindsay Beattie, of the Border Regiment, was killed in action on 27th January. Lieut. Beattie was the only son of the late Mr W. Beattie, clogger.....

Then on 10 February, the *Dumfries and Galloway Standard* revealed much more about the nature of his death, via a letter to Beattie's mother from Lieut-Colonel F.G. Morris of the Border Regiment. It read:

I knew your son very well, and I know what he was to you and you to him, which makes the writing of this letter very difficult and painful. In your great grief you must still consider yourself a proud woman for having produced such a son;

you will always have the right to that. He was one of the most capable officers in any battalion, and I placed him in command of a company above the heads of many of his senior officers as a reward for excellent work, and to show the great confidence I had in him. To ease your pain a little, I can tell you he died a most gallant death. Some of his men were very young and inexperienced soldiers, and four of them had been knocked over. Many more were coming on to suffer the same fate when he rushed to the front to stop them, and at once was killed stone dead. By this heroic action he saved the lives of many of his men. It will be a very long time before I shall see a young officer of his merit and great courage ..... We have had him buried with four other officers, and a cross will be put up. I will let you know where later on.

In April 1917 his mother received confirmation of his burial, on the west side of the Western Road from Morval to Lesboeufs. He is now laid to rest at Quarry Cemetery, Montauban. His mother was also sent home personal effects consisting of an officer's advance book, cheque book, metal mirror in a case, a note wallet, snapshots, charm and a piece of heather.

A very fitting tribute was also paid to Beattie in a column in the *Yorkshire Evening Post* on 24 February 1917 by the Rev. Harold Ewbank, a rugby union man, but in war an Army Chaplain with the Border Regiment.

One of the saddest losses to football since the war began is the death of Lieutenant W.L. Beattie, who used to play with Wakefield Trinity. He went over the top with the battalion on January 27 in a magnificently successful attack. Seeing that his line of men were not quite correct, he went ahead to straighten things out, and was hit by a shell which killed him at once. No man will be more missed by everyone; he was a real, good-hearted, cheery giant whose popularity spread far beyond the regiment. He was as straight as a die; always merry, always kind. In football he was absolutely 'it' as a forward, a beautiful dribbler, a ferocious tackler, a hard worker, a safe catch, and a fast runner.

Keighley's Harry Bairstow left a wife and two young children

courtesy of Bradford Telegraph & Argus

1917 - Arras Brings More Bloodshed

14

Despite the Somme offensive failing to break the stalemate on the Western Front, the Allies continued to seek ways of striking a decisive blow. In late 1916, Haig and Joffre once again met at French headquarters at Chantilly to draw up plans for their 1917 assaults.

But before those plans could be formulated, the French government moved in to replace Joffre with General Robert Nivelle. The new man was convinced he knew exactly what tactics would be required to break through the German lines and signal the beginning of the end of the enemy's challenge. It would prove to be a disaster, with the French Army again suffering appalling losses and leading to a near mutiny of its soldiers, which was only avoided by Nivelle's sacking and the appointment of Philippe Pétain on 17 May 1917.

Many within the British ranks, including Haig, feared all along that the Nivelle Offensive would be a recipe for disaster. But with new Prime Minister David Lloyd George –

who took over from Asquith in December 1916 – desperate to find a way to end the bloodshed, he was persuaded by the charismatic English-speaking Nivelle to back his plans.

Britain's role in the offensive would be to provide a diversion to the start of the French attacks on the Chemin des Dames ridge on 16 April. That diversion was the Battle of Arras, which began on 9 April 1917 and initially brought huge success. In fact, on that first day, the British enjoyed their most successful 24 hours since the start of trench warfare.

Unfortunately, just like with so many of the earlier offensives, the assault eventually ground to halt. The initial successes were soon to be forgotten, with the daily losses of 4,076 in a battle which lasted until 16 May, higher than those at the Somme and worse than at Passchendaele later in 1917.

And during the course of this bloody five-week campaign, a number of Northern Union players were involved – and lost their lives. In fact, by the end of the opening day, Batley's Joseph Child had fallen.

The utility back, who was born in Leeds on 10 December 1889 and baptised at St Mark's Church, Woodhouse Lane the following month, had already endured tragedy in his short life. In March 1896 his father Samuel and younger sister Hilda died within days of each other, their burials again recorded at St Mark's.

His mother, Maria, remarried in 1898, her new husband being Harry Skelton, with the family still living in the Leeds area. By that stage, Child was showing some promise as a rugby player and in 1909 signed for Batley from the Leeds Institute at the age of 19. And, according to the 21 August 1909 *Leeds Mercury* in their preview of Batley's 1909-10 Northern Union campaign, they felt the young Child looked a good bet.

The [*Batley*] management consider themselves fortunate in having secured the services of Child, a young player from the Leeds Institute, as a capable understudy for 'Wattie' Davies at full-back. He played exceedingly well against Leeds, at Headingley, at the back end of last season, and so far as one is able to judge he will show improved form this year.

Over the next few years, Child became a Mount Pleasant regular and featured alongside fellow fallen Great War comrade James Debney in that Batley team which beat the Australasian Tourists 13-5 on 27 January 1912, with the Leeds-born centre landing a first-half drop goal. But soon after that, Child suffered a serious knee injury which threatened to end his career prematurely. Fortunately, that did not prove the case, with the *Leeds Mercury* of 8 January 1914 announcing:

J. Child, the Batley player, who has been out of harness for a considerable time owing to knee trouble, is to resume activity on Saturday, when he will assist the Mount Pleasant Reserves against Methley.

Child was unable to regain his first-team spot before the end of the 1913-14 season, but did return to make three senior centre appearances in the first half of the following campaign. He then got the nod to start at full-back in a home game against Salford on 16 January 1915 in place of the rested first-choice No1 Jimmy Lyons in what was to prove to be his last Batley appearance – when the *Batley News* of 23 January provided a scathing no-holds-barred account of the way he had played.

> Childe [*sic*], who on first joining the Club, gave promise of developing into a great custodian, made a poor show with the wind at his back, though perhaps no worse than one or two other members of the team. Time after time the ball was kicked so hard from midfield that it went sailing down into the Warwick Road region. More senseless kicking it would be difficult to imagine.

Batley did at least win the game 11-3.

Child, who was employed by Messrs Samuel Kirk and Sons, dyers, Woodhouse Lane, enlisted in Leeds initially with the West Yorkshires but transferred to the Royal Scots (Lothian Regiment). Little is known about Private Child's time training and then his involvement overseas – or the exact nature of his death on that fateful 9 April whilst serving with their 9th Battalion. But it was clear he was part of a well-executed attack that achieved all its initial objectives.

Yet despite the successes, the diary entry of 12 April showed it had come at a high price, with casualties amongst other ranks on the 9th being 69 killed, 138 wounded and 27 missing.[1] Joseph Child was one of those killed. His death was reported in the *Yorkshire Post and Leeds Intelligencer* on 1 May 1917.

> Pte. Joe Child, of the Royal Scots, late West Yorkshires, a well-known Batley football player, was killed in action on April 9. He was the eldest son of Mr. and Mrs. H. Skelton, of the North-West Ward Liberal Club, Woodhouse, Leeds. He

played three-quarters and full-back for the Batley
Club for seven seasons, and later assisted Hunslet
for a season.

He is buried at Nine Elms Military Cemetery, Thelus, Pas de
Calais.

Two days later, on 11 April 1917, a second Northern
Union player from West Yorkshire fell in the sizeable shape
of Keighley forward Harry Bairstow. He died of his wounds
at a Casualty Clearing Station and is buried at the Aubigny
Communal Cemetery, nine miles north-west of Arras.

The Bradford-born Bairstow spent his life living,
working and playing rugby in the locality, moving up the
road to Baildon after his marriage to Ethel Taylor on
Christmas Eve 1912. However, when he enlisted in Bradford
in November 1915, it was with the Seaforth Highlanders
(Ross-Shire Buffs, the Duke of Albany's) he ended up serving.
He left behind his wife and two young children.

By the time Bairstow left these shores he was certainly
a relatively well-known figure around the area, with a large
number of acquaintances. As well as being a Northern Union
forward, he was known for his auctioneer and valuing
business work with the firm of Haley and Bairstow.
Additionally, his wife's grandfather was Mr Joseph Taylor,
who was highly respected in business and social circles
throughout the Bradford and Baildon area. However, it was
in the world of rugby league where Bairstow came to the fore.

Born in around 1884, it appears Bairstow was the son
of Harrison Paxman Ward and his wife Hannah. Harrison
Ward died in 1890 and the same year Hannah married
Richard Bairstow. Harry originally signed for Bradford
Northern from Bradford Rugby Union. However, after failing
to make the decisive breakthrough, he made the move to

Keighley in October 1911 – and was immediately making a positive impression. His debut came in a convincing 24-8 home triumph over Bramley on 9 October 1911, with the *Athletic News* impressed by what they saw:

> The recent unconvincing displays by the Keighley forwards had caused the committee to search for men of better physique, and they tried two strapping and speedy men in Bairstow, late of Bradford, and Buckle, who has appeared with Stanningley. Both men pleased the crowd immensely, and they undoubtedly strengthened the pack, for Narey and Duggan, the home backs, were far oftener in possession than the opposing pair.

The *Athletic News* was also full of praise for the goalkicking forward in its match report of 30 October 1911, when Keighley beat Wakefield 23-5 at Lawkholme Lane.

> The best of the forwards were Bairstow and Waite (Keighley) and Crosland and Anton (Wakefield).

Yet despite such a positive beginning, Bairstow was unable to go on and command a regular starting spot. He was in and out of the side for the rest of the season and then made just one appearance at prop during the 1912-13 campaign. The unfortunate Bairstow was frozen out throughout the following season, but returned to the fold for the first half of the 1914-15 campaign, making four appearances at loose forward and another at prop, before his attentions started to turn to the war.

As for his military service as a Private with the Seaforth

Highlanders, according to his obituary in the *Shipley Times and Express*, he was engaged for eight months teaching musketry. He left for France around December 1916 and was at the base for a few months before volunteering to go down the line, where he served with the 4th Battalion Seaforth Highlanders. The same report also indicates he was promoted to Sergeant, but there is nothing in surviving records to corroborate this.

It is impossible to know exactly when Bairstow suffered the injuries that would cost him his life. But there is a strong possibility it was right at the start of the major Arras offensive, probably during the Battle of the Scarpe – and there is also a chance he fought alongside Batley's Joseph Child, given that his unit war diary described how his battalion had worked with Bairstow's to capture their objective trench on 9 April.

The news of Bairstow's death was recorded in the *Bradford Telegraph and Argus* of 20 April 1917 and sheds more light on him as a person and a sportsman. This report also refers to him as Sergeant Bairstow and says he was:

> .....one of the best known men in Bradford sporting circles, and played football for the Bradford Northern and Keighley Northern Union Clubs. He always played as an amateur, and rendered valuable service to both clubs. He was also well known on the running track and assisted Bradford Northern to win many team races. In business he was an auctioneer, and was associated for many years with the firm of Haley and Bairstow. He was a genial, good natured fellow, and did much to encourage sport in Bradford. The news of his death will be greatly regretted by a host of his friends in Bradford.....

It appears that after his death his widow renamed the family home *'Seaforth Cottage'* in honour of her husband's regiment.

Then, on 20 April, Swinton full-back George Crabtree lost his life at the age of 23.

Born in Salford in 1893 to parents John Henry and Ellen Crabtree (née Fitzpatrick), his talents were spotted by Swinton when playing for the Mandleberg's works team – the company produced waterproof garments – in a works competition organised by the professional club.

His performances in that competition immediately caught Swinton's eye and he signed for them on 17 September 1912. He had to wait until the following April to make his senior Northern Union debut, although the newspapers of the day were not entirely convinced by Crabtree's potential. In fact, in the *Wigan Observer and District Advertiser* of 8 April 1913, they were downright scathing as Swinton fell to a narrow 5-3 defeat to their hosts in Cherry and White:

> Of the home backs, Crabtree is lacking in experience ..... Crabtree, the Swinton full back, was extremely weak, and often let his side down through his slowness.

For a 19-year-old just starting out in the game, such stinging criticism could have had a detrimental effect. But far from going into his shell, Crabtree clearly produced a positive reaction, putting in a strong pre-season and starting the opening seven games of the 1913-14 campaign at full-back. His Swinton club started the season equally strongly, winning four of their opening six Northern Union fixtures, with Crabtree serving well as the last line of defence.

Unfortunately, after a heavy 24-2 Lancashire Cup defeat

at Widnes on 18 October 1913, the young No1 lost his place in the side, only to re-emerge once more that season in a demoralising 36-0 defeat at Wigan on 13 December. That setback at Central Park was to bring an abrupt halt to his Northern Union career, and he remained on the first-team fringes until he answered the call and enlisted with the Lancashire Fusiliers in 1915.

Private Crabtree entered active service some time in 1916. He lost his life the following April, serving with the 3/5th Battalion Lancashire Fusiliers as the Battle of Arras was starting to lose its momentum. His death occurred during what was a relatively 'quiet' spell for his battalion. There is no unit war diary entry for the day on which he died, but the previous day's entry places the battalion in the Givenchy Left Sub Sector:

> .....in support in Village Line at Windy Corner (Map La Bassee.....). Enemy artillery fire much increased.[2]

It would appear Crabtree was killed by one of those shells, with the battalion's typed list of casualties for the month of April 1917, showing '202431 Pte Crabtree. G.' was one of two men killed on 20.4.17. The list finished off by indicating five of the deceased for that month were buried at Brown's Cemetery, Gorre.[3] One of those five was George Crabtree, whose body remains there today. The news of his death appeared in the *Salford Reporter* of 12 May and stated:

> Private George Wilfred Crabtree, Lancashire Fusiliers, killed in action in France on April 20, was 23 years of age. He enlisted in the Army nearly two years ago and had been on active

service fifteen months. In civil life he lived at 48, Gill street, Pendleton, and was employed at Messrs. Mandelberg's Works, Pendleton.

On 23 April, three days after Crabtree's death, Leeds forward Leonard Leckenby also fell. The York-born forward was a player many believed had huge potential, with Leeds winning the race to secure his signature on 15 October 1912, when he was aged 21. By that stage, Leckenby was already a big name in York rugby circles.

Born in York on 7 October 1891 to parents Thomas and Agnes Leckenby, he was the second of their four children. His siblings were Gordon, Stanley and Alice. Leckenby received his education across a number of the city's schools. He attended the Practising School, then the Model School, where pupils were said to receive *'superior instruction,'* followed by Brook Street Board, Cherry Street Boys School and, according to newspapers, Haxby Road Council School. It was during his schooldays that he began to develop into a talented rugby player.

He first shot to prominence with York Groves United – where he was a teammate of another Leeds signing in Albert Dennis – before moving to York Leeman Wanderers. Both were well-respected rugby clubs in the city. Leckenby was described as being quick for a forward, standing 5ft 9in tall and weighing 13st 6lbs, according to the *Leeds Mercury* of 9 October 1912. He was also as strong as an ox, having been a successful competitive weightlifter before deciding to focus all his athletic attention on rugby.

When he signed for Leeds, according to the club's Leeds World War 1 Heritage Project he was described as:

A well-built young player with plenty of dash

and determination with a fancy for the wing three-quarter position, where he had shown in junior football that he was no mean performer in that department of the game, being a splendid kicker who takes the ball very well.[4]

Within four days of putting pen to paper, Leckenby made his Leeds debut at prop in a narrow 3-2 defeat at Hull FC. The match was recorded in the *Yorkshire Post and Leeds Intelligencer* on 21 October 1912, and although Leckenby was not singled out, the general rule was that it had been a good contest.

> About 10,000 spectators saw this match on the Boulevard, and a spirited tussle it proved from first to last.

That was the first of his four senior appearances in the 1912-13 season – he did not register a try during those games – and the following season he failed to feature in the senior side, having to bide his time in the 'A' team hoping to get the Northern Union call.

The year before making his move to Headingley, Leckenby was employed as a footman. However, prior to enlisting, in February 1916, he was employed in the starch room at Rowntrees, the famous York confectioners. According to newspaper reports he enlisted with the Seaforth Highlanders in February 1916, where he spent time as a drill instructor, rising to the rank of Sergeant, before moving to the front to join the 8th Battalion in late 1916.

On the day Leckenby lost his life, the 15th Division, of which the 8th Seaforths were part, were involved in a battle to take Guemappe from the enemy. Zero hour was just before 5am, and in the face of heavy machine gun fire in which many casualties were suffered, they were forced to use shell holes for cover in the move towards the village. They eventually entered the village at just after 9am, to find the Germans had evacuated it. They continued to be subjected to heavy shell, machine gun and rifle fire and attempts to consolidate east of the village failed. It was at some stage during this attack that Leckenby fell.

His body was, however, recovered and he is buried at the Guemappe British Cemetery, Wancourt. His parents went to visit his grave shortly after the war, and when his headstone was erected by the Imperial War Graves Commission (forerunner of the Commonwealth War Grave Commission), his family were one of those who paid for an inscription to be included. A maximum of 66 letters, less spaces in between words, was allowed, at a charge of 3½d per letter, with Sergeant Leckenby's reading: 'Sleep on dear son while the day dawns and the shadows flee away'.

The announcement of his death appeared in the *Yorkshire Herald* of 19 May and included details of how he died under the headline 'Well-known York Footballer Killed'.

> Mr. and Mrs. T. Leckenby, 41 Walmgate, York, have received official intelligence of the death in action of their second son, Sergeant Leonard Leckenby. The deceased, who was 25 years of age and unmarried, joined the Seaforth Highlanders, at York in Feb. 1916 ..... Capt. J.F. Lyles, who has written sympathising with the deceased's parents, stated that Leckenby was a sergeant in whom he could place the utmost reliance. He died a gallant death. Corpl. Joseph Staveley has also written to Mr and Mrs Leckenby:- 'It is with deep regret that I have to inform you of the death

of your son Leonard during a charge of the German lines on April 23rd. I can assure you that he suffered no pain, death being instantaneous. I was close to him when he met his death.'

Jack Harrison's valour at Arras earned the Hull man a VC

courtesy of Bernard Shooman

1917 – The Bravest of the Brave. Arras and its Aftermath

15

There were countless acts of bravery throughout the First World War. And the heroic efforts of the British during the Battle of Arras were shining examples. Between the 9 April and 16 May offensive, an impressive 25 Victoria Crosses (VC) were awarded – out of a total of 628 during the entire 1914-18 conflict. The VC, which is the highest military honour for bravery and valour, is awarded for gallantry 'in the face of the enemy.'

Rugby league can lay claim to three of the 628 awarded during the Great War. They are Jack Harrison, Thomas Bryan and Thomas Steele.

Of the three, Harrison was the only one to die during his incredible act of bravery during the Arras campaign, with his VC being awarded posthumously. And unlike Bryan and Steele, who had brief spells within the professional ranks, Hull FC winger Harrison was one of the Northern Union's superstars when he went off to fight, having scored a try in the Black and Whites' 6-0 Challenge Cup final triumph over Wakefield Trinity at Halifax on 18 April 1914.

Then, the following season (1914-15), he crossed for a total of 52 tries, which remains a Hull club record for tries in a season to this day. His biggest one-game try haul during that campaign was a massive six in the 51-3 destruction of Wakefield on 17 April 1915. Those statistics meant that in the three seasons he played for his hometown club, he amassed an amazing 106 tries in just 116 Hull appearances.

As someone who was a Hull lad through and through, his legendary status around the city was guaranteed, even before he made the ultimate sacrifice and was awarded his VC. He was described at the time as one of the most brilliant players in the north of England. Another observer, in the *Hull Daily Mail* of 15 June 1917, described how:

> .....his natural swerve, combined with a fine turn of speed, enabled him to make tries where others less brilliant would have failed. His modest nature on the field was noticed by everyone and even after a brilliant and successful scoring effort he was almost too embarrassed to face the applause.....

Born in Hull on 12 November 1890 to parents John and Charlotte Harrison (née Carr), John 'Jack' Harrison was soon proving a star pupil at Craven Street School, where he excelled both academically and physically, winning the school's first ever medal for all-round excellence in outdoor sports. He initially favoured football, playing centre-forward for the Central Higher Grade AFC and proving a prolific goal scorer. After leaving school, he studied to become a teacher at St John's College, York. During his time at the college he continued to excel on the sporting field in a wide range of disciplines, before qualifying as a teacher and earning a posting to Lime Street School in Hull in 1912.

His rugby exploits while he was at college were not missed by the local York Northern Union club, who were keen to secure his services and handed him a first-team debut as an amateur in the 1911-12 season, where he went on to make five appearances and score three tries.

As soon as he returned to Hull to begin his teaching career, he cut his ties with York – the split was somewhat acrimonious – and immediately became one of the hottest properties in the game, with the *Hull Daily Mail* of 3 August 1912 announcing Hull had signed him for the Black and Whites. The report said:

> The question 'Will John Harrison sign on for Hull or Rovers?' was answered this morning when information was made known that the Hull F.C. had succeeded in adding the ex-York wing three-quarter to their list of this season's 'captures'. Both Hull and Rovers have been anxious to secure the young athlete's services, and Messrs Arthur J. Boynton (Hull president) and Mr. A. Charlesworth, the popular secretary, were entitled to express their satisfaction. 'Jack' Harrison's cleverness as a N.U. wing three-quarter is known throughout the leading clubs in the League, and I am not betraying a secret when I inform our readers that not just Hull and Rovers, but Wigan, Oldham, Leeds and others have vainly endeavoured to obtain Harrison's signature to a professional form.

Having put pen to paper, teetotaller and non-smoker Harrison made his senior Hull FC debut on 5 September 1912 in a 9-3 win over former club York at the Boulevard. Playing alongside fellow new signing Billy Batten, Harrison's career soon began to flourish, and in the 1913-14 season he made 28 appearances and crossed for 23 tries, with a highlight clearly being his Challenge Cup final try.

After marrying Lilian Ellis on 1 September 1914, he made his first Hull 1914-15 appearance in a 26-0 opening-day home League win over Keighley two days later, when he raced over for a hat-trick of tries. It was a taste of things to come during his record-breaking season. In June 1915 Lilian gave birth to a son, John 'Jackie' Harrison. Just over four months later, Harrison enlisted in the Inns of Court Officer Training Corps, on 4 November 1915.

Once he completed his training, he was commissioned as a temporary 2nd Lieutenant in the East Yorkshire Regiment on 5 August 1916 and posted in September to France to join the 11th Battalion. It was not long before Harrison was seeing action in the front line and proving himself to be a natural leader. For his actions on 25 February 1917, he was awarded the Military Cross for leading his 'B' Company patrol, consisting of one platoon, proceeding from Hair Alley near Hébuterne to the German fourth line. He reached his objective before withdrawing, in the process capturing a German machine gun as well as a prisoner, with a loss of six other ranks either killed, wounded or missing.[1] His citation in the *London Gazette* of 17 April 1917 reads:

> For conspicuous gallantry and devotion to duty. He handled his platoon with great courage and skill, reached his objective under the most trying conditions, and captured a prisoner. He set a splendid example throughout.[2]

A couple of months later, the exchanges became even more intense with the start of the Battle of Arras, and Harrison was once again in the thick of the action. The British suffered heavy casualties right from the start, with the Allies making initial gains and the Germans then counter-attacking strongly. As a result, it soon became clear a decisive breakthrough was highly unlikely, although attempts continued to be made in a bid to force the issue. One such attempt was on 3 May and the Third Battle of the Scarpe, with Harrison and his men ordered to capture Oppy Wood as part of the assault.

The attack commenced before break of day but, as the unit war diary described, the lack of daylight, the darkness of the woods, the smoke and dust caused by the hostile enemy barrage and the Allies' own creeping barrage all combined to make it impossible to see. By the time the barrage had lifted off the German front line, the enemy had time to get machine guns in place and were firing from the wood and trees, as well as the front trench. The East Yorkshires came under terrific fire but attacked again and again. One of those who refused to give up was Hull hero Harrison who did everything in his power to save his men, displaying conspicuous bravery and self-sacrifice as the citation for his VC, which was recorded in the 12 June *London Gazette*, made clear:

> T/2nd Lt. John Harrison, M.C., E. York. R. For most conspicuous bravery and self-sacrifice in an attack. Owing to darkness and to smoke from the enemy barrage, and from our own, and to the fact that our objective was in a dark wood, it was impossible to see when our barrage had lifted off the enemy front line. Nevertheless, 2nd Lt. Harrison led his company against the enemy

trench under heavy rifle and machine-gun fire, but was repulsed. Reorganising his command as best he could in No Man's Land, he again attacked in darkness under terrific fire, but with no success. Then, turning round, this gallant officer single-handed made a dash at the machine gun, hoping to knock out the gun and so save the lives of many of his company. His self-sacrifice and absolute disregard of danger was an inspiring example to all. (he is reported missing believed killed.)[3]

Harrison's colleagues were unable to bury him and subsequently his body was never re-discovered and identified, although it is possible his remains lie in the Orchard Dump cemetery at Arleux-en-Gohelle. The cemetery contains a large number of unidentified soldiers who were exhumed from battlefield graves straight after the war. It means John 'Jack' Harrison VC MC is officially remembered on the Arras Memorial.

Initial newspaper reports that filtered back to England suggested Harrison was 'missing' rather than killed, although the *Hull Daily Mail* of 9 May 1917 was preparing its readers for the worst. The piece said:

Second-Lieutenant 'Jack' Harrison ..... is reported as having been wounded and missing since May 3rd ... Although it is not officially reported, several of his men say that he was killed, while others state he was wounded in the knee and dragged into the enemy trenches a prisoner of war. His Lieutenant-Colonel writes:- 'He was a splendid officer, and his loss to the battalion is great. He was loved by all his men.'

The news of his death was not officially confirmed until mid-December 1917 – some six months after the announcement of Harrison's VC award. The proud news of his VC appeared locally under the banner *Hull Daily Mail* headline of 15 June 1917: 'Sec.-Lieut. "Jack" Harrison, V.C. Another Honour for Hull,' and read:

> Another V.C. honour has come to Hull. This one has been awarded to Second-Lieut. 'Jack' Harrison, of the East Yorks. who is a familiar figure to thousands who have seen him playing for Hull at the Boulevard..... The intimation was conveyed officially in the 'London Gazette' .....
> Mrs Harrison ..... showed the 'Mail' a telegram offering her congratulations, and giving the intimation that her husband had been awarded the Victoria Cross. It was exactly six weeks since he was reported wounded and missing, but she still had hope he was alive and was a prisoner of war. There is a little son, aged two, also called Jack after his father. He was as blithe as a cricket in the room, and his mother said he was just like his father.

The paper also reported Harrison had written a letter to Lillian the day before he died, saying:

> We are having a glorious time as far as weather is concerned. It seems just like a lovely summer's day to-day, whilst the nights have been fine, clear, and moonlight [*sic*]. I am afraid though that the Old Hun can see us through its brilliance. It

reminds one very much of Barnsfather's cartoon about 'her' saying: 'I wonder if this lovely moon is shining on him too?' whilst he is saying, 'This blinking moon will be the death of me!' as he is crawling about in No Man's Land. Ha, ha! You can't help but smile when you know the life on this side.

Tributes from comrades poured in to Lilian, describing how well-loved her husband was. These are typified by one from the Chaplain, Rev. R.T. Newcombe:

Before the battle he came to holy communion in the trench, and on the afternoon he talked about you and the boy to me. Everybody loved Jack. He was so straight, so true, so brave, and his men simply worshipped him.....

His widow and young son were presented with his VC by King George V at Buckingham Palace in March 1918. When she died in December 1977, her husband's medals were bequeathed to the East Yorkshire regimental museum in Beverley, which is now part of the Prince of Wales Own Regiment of Yorkshire Museum in Tower Street, York.

After her husband's death, a fund was raised in Hull to provide for the education of their son. A fund was also established by the directors of Hull FC to raise £500 for a cot for Hull Royal Infirmary in his memory. The appeal was a success with the *Hull Daily Mail* of 26 July 1919 announcing:

The secretary of the Infirmary desires to acknowledge receipt of £500 from the Hull Northern Union Football Club, with the aid of public subscriptions for the endowment of a cot in the children's ward of the Institution, to be known as the 'Lieut. Jack Harrison, V.C., M.C., Memorial Cot,' .....It is very appropriate that the memory of a man who rendered such heroic services to his country should be thus perpetuated in the Children's Ward of the Institution.

Sadly, Jack's son was also to lose his life serving his country. Captain Harrison served as an officer in the Duke of Wellington's West Riding Regiment during the Second World War and was killed in the defence of Dunkirk on 1 June 1940.

Of rugby league's other two VCs, Thomas Bryan was also to be honoured for his act of bravery during the Battle of Arras. Bryan was born in Stourbridge, Worcestershire on 21 January 1882, with the family moving to Castleford to find work in the Yorkshire collieries when he was still an infant. When he was older, Bryan followed his father into the mines at Askern Colliery, but he also played rugby league for Castleford in the 1906-07 season, before the club was forced to withdraw from the Northern Union due to financial reasons.

At the outbreak of war, he joined the 25th (Service) Battalion (2nd Tyneside Irish) Northumberland Fusiliers where he was promoted to Lance Corporal. And it was while he held that rank as a 35-year-old, he was awarded his VC for his actions at Arras on 9 April 1917, as recorded in the *London Gazette* of 8 June 1917:

No. 22040 L//Cpl. Thomas Bryan, North'd Fus.... Although wounded, this Non-commissioned Officer, went forward alone, with a view to silencing a machine gun which was inflicting

> much damage. He worked up most skilfully
> along a communication trench, approached the
> gun from behind, disabled it and killed two of the
> team as they were abandoning the gun ...... the
> results obtained by Lance-Corporal Bryan's
> action were very far-reaching.[4]

After the war, Bryan lived in Bentley, Doncaster, where he died at the age of 63 in 1945.

Thomas Steele played three matches in the Northern Union for Broughton Rangers and had a successful amateur career with local club Healey Street in the Greater Manchester area. Upon joining the Seaforth Highlanders, he rose to the rank of Sergeant and was awarded the VC for his actions during the Mesopotamia campaign, on 22 February 1917 at Sanna-I-Yat.[5] Steele's VC citation read as follows:

> At a critical moment when a strong enemy
> counter-attack had temporarily regained some of
> the captured trenches, Sjt. Steele rushed forward
> and assisted a comrade to carry a machine gun
> into position. He kept the gun in action till
> relieved, being mainly instrumental in keeping
> the remainder of the line intact. Some hours later
> another strong attack enabled the enemy to
> reoccupy a portion of the captured trenches.
> Again Sjt. Steele showed the greatest bravery, and
> by personal valour and example was able to rally
> troops who were wavering. He encouraged them
> to remain in their trenches and led a number of
> them forward, thus greatly helping re-establish
> our line. On this occasion he was severely
> wounded.....[6]

Steele was 26 years old at the time, and died in his hometown of Springhead, a suburb of Saddleworth in the Oldham area of Lancashire, in 1978 at the age of 87.

As well as Harrison, current Northern Union colleague Howell Rees was also killed during the Battle of Arras, losing his life on 8 May. The diminutive Welshman learned his trade in the 15-a-side union code before making the move to Yorkshire to sign for Keighley, via Millom. At 5ft 1¼in and around eight stones, the young half-back was hardly the biggest in the world, but he had shown during his rugby-playing days in Wales that he had what it takes to be a useful Northern Union competitor.

Born in Aberdare in around 1886 to parents David and Mary Rees, the young Howell quickly overcame a lack of height to emerge as a midfield playmaker with a big heart, rising up through the junior Union ranks to sign for Treorchy. But even though he had grown up in strong 15-a-side code country, he was attracted to the 13-a-side game and signed for Mid-Rhondda, who were competing in the Welsh League.

It was relatively early in his Mid-Rhondda career that Rees was part of the team that faced the might of top Northern Union club Hull during a brief tour in late November 1908. Rees and his Welsh colleagues were easily beaten on the day, with the *Hull Daily Mail* of 30 November stating:

> Another great weakness of the visitors was the incapability of the forwards ..... Under such circumstances the Welshmen could not hope to gain possession very often. The consequence was that the greater part of their game was spent in running after the home backs, who led them a pretty dance.

But, interestingly, despite the visiting backs being starved of possession, the report then went on to say:

> The pick of the remaining backs was perhaps Jack Rees, the right centre, and Howell Rees, the auburn-haired half-back.....

The performance of the 22-year-old must have created the right sort of impression, with the half-back involved in the Welsh League XIII's 15-13 victory over Australia at Ebbw Vale on 16 January 1909. Rees continued to thrive as a rugby league player and by 1911 he had made the move to Cumberland, joining the Millom club, and working at Millom Ironworks.

By this time, his prowess was starting to attract the interest of top flight Northern Union clubs, the Welshman's registration for Keighley submitted on 29 October 1912. That came 10 days after making his Northern Union debut at stand-off in an 18-8 triumph at Bramley. Rees then went on to start the next 23 games in the No6 shirt, during which time he crossed for a couple of tries and, after finishing the season in the side that was beaten 11-7 at York, he would have been hopeful of maintaining his strong Northern Union start.

Instead, however, he was restricted to the odd first-team game here and there – just three senior appearances were forthcoming in 1913-14 – and was forced to play a waiting game for much of that time in the Keighley Zingari feeder side, where he was often 'head and shoulders' above his teammates. This was made apparent in the *Keighley News* of 3 October 1914.

> Before an attendance of between 500 and 600 at Lawkholme on Saturday last, Keighley Zingari

defeated Brighouse Rangers in the Halifax and
District League by one goal three tries (eleven
points) to one goal ..... Rees did some fine work
in the scrimmage half position, but his partner
Bailey was not always aware of his tricky moves,
with the result that possible points were lost.

Rees did, however, make one final Keighley Northern Union
appearance at scrum half in a 0-0 draw at home to Bramley
on 12 December 1914. But due to the demands being placed
on players, both on the fighting and domestic front, because
of the conflict, Keighley were forced to close down their
operations temporarily and Rees signed for Bradford
Northern in October 1915. The half-back remained there until
the end of the season.

Whilst at Bradford, Rees attested under the Derby
Scheme on 11 December 1915, and was placed on the Army
Reserve. Now working as a surface grinder, he was in a
badged occupation. However, in June 1916 he appeared before
the Keighley Tribunal. Here he made public his desire, as a
proud Welshman, to serve with a Welsh regiment on the
battlefields. The *Leeds Mercury* of 6 June 1916 reported his plea:

At the Keighley Tribunal, yesterday, Howell Rees,
the Keighley half-back, although badged, said he
was willing to serve, and at once, but being a
Welshman, he wished to join either the Royal
Welsh Fusiliers or the South Wales Borderers, or
some other Welsh unit. The tribunal agreed to
forward his request to the proper quarter.....

Rees did not get his wish. On 8 June 1916 he was assigned
initially to the 23rd Battalion, Durham Light Infantry, and

subsequently in August 1916 to the 3rd Battalion – both home-based depot and training units. His posting came at an eventful time for Rees, who just over a month later, on 15 July, married Bertha Speight from East Bierley at Tong parish church. Obviously keen to spend time with his new bride, Rees made the mistake of overstaying his leave pass and not returning until 17 July, which was punished by forfeiting two days' pay and being confined to barracks for a week.[7]

Whilst training, Rees proved to be handy with a rifle and, according to his half-brother Henry James, he was awarded a Military Bronze Medal for crack shooting. Sniper Rees, as the *Rhondda Leader* of 9 June 1917 described him, went to France on 14 October 1916 to serve with the Durham Light Infantry's 10th Battalion. He was soon preparing for the start of the Arras offensive the following April.

Despite surviving the initial Arras onslaught, Rees was killed by a shell which burst near him – his battalion were based at Wancourt at the time - with reports later emerging, in the *Yorkshire Evening Post* of 30 May 1917, that it also claimed the life of 10th Battalion Durham Light Infantry colleague and ex-Hull FC star Harry Wallace, who had played for the Black and Whites between 1906 and 1910 and made one England appearance in 1908.

In fact, when Rees turned out for Mid-Rhondda in their game at Hull in 1908, the *Hull Daily Mail* stated the star of the day had been Wallace, reporting:

> There are few half-backs who can provide such a fund of entertainment as Wallace, when his forwards treat him liberally. He was given abundance of opportunities in this match, and the mercurial manner in which he danced his way in and out of the opposing backs was a treat.....

The reports of the two men's deaths began to filter back to England towards the end of May, with the news on Rees appearing in the *Keighley News* on the 26th. Under the headline 'A Footballer Killed', it said:

> Private Howell Rees, of the Durham Light Infantry, who has been killed in action, was a well-known football player, obtaining an international cap in 1906 and 1907 when he was with a Treorchy club in Glamorganshire. He played with Millom and Keighley, and in the seasons 1915-16 was with Bradford Northern ..... he rendered splendid service with the Zingari, notably in the season they won the Halifax Charity Cup. He was a tricky little half back.

Howell Rees has no known grave and is remembered on the Arras Memorial. His widow received his personal effects of letters, photos, a wallet, diary and cards. Bertha subsequently remarried in September 1921.

Even though the Battle of Arras officially came to an end on 16 May, the fighting still continued, with casualties being taken by both sides on a daily basis. This was the case with Leeds' Welsh winger Arthur Llewellyn, who lost his life on 1 June at the age of 24.

Like so many other Northern Union players to lay down their lives, Llewellyn was just beginning to establish himself in the game when he answered the call to arms. The Leeds club spent much of 1913 looking for a winger with genuine pace, capable of terrorising opposition defences, and that search took them to Wales. They had already recruited centre Joseph Hopkins from Abertillery, one of the Leeds players who died on the first day of the Battle of the Somme. While completing the Hopkins deal, the exploits of exciting wing prospect Llewellyn caught their eye.

Llewellyn, born in 1893, grew up in Abertillery, the son of Thomas and Sarah Llewellyn. He proved a renowned sprinter as well as a talented rugby union player, with his achievements proudly recorded by the *Leeds Rhinos Players' Association*. These included winning nine major prizes as a schoolboy sprinter, feats which alerted Abertillery Rugby Union Club to his raw talent, with the leading Welsh club quickly preparing him for a first-team career. In fact, it was not long at all before he was underlining his rugby potential, making 15 senior appearances in his first season and earning a reputation for having 'a capable place kick as well as a consistent try getter.'[8]

By this stage, he still had not abandoned his competitive sprinting ties, and in his second season he competed in the prestigious Cambrian Dash at the Mid-Rhondda Athletic Grounds in Tonypandy, an event which, according to *Abertillery Online*,[9] attracted professional sprinters from all over the world. He also won two major 80-yard races at other meetings. Those sprinting appointments meant Llewellyn was not always on first-team duty with Abertillery, and in one destructive spell for the second team he scored 51 points in just four matches.

He also put in a highly-significant performance back in the senior side to help Abertillery defeat Gloucester, which was the final proof for Leeds that this was their man. Llewellyn put pen to paper on 20 January 1914 and made the move north, in a deal heralded by the *Yorkshire Evening Post* the same day. Under the headline 'A Young Speedy Player from Wales', it proclaimed:

> Announcement is made to-day of the capture of
> a new Welsh three-quarter by the Leeds Club.
> The newcomer is A. Llewellyn, who hails from
> Abertillery, from which club, it will be
> remembered, came Hopkins, also of the Leeds
> Club. Llewellyn is a young player, and is likely to
> prove as fast as any man in the Leeds team. He is
> 5ft 7½ and weighs 10st 10lb. Llewellyn is to be
> played with Hopkins against Bramley on
> Saturday.

His debut could not have gone much better, with the flying
Welsh winger scoring a try in an 18-7 Northern Union home
win over their Leeds rivals on 24 January. Also playing that
day were his centre partner Hopkins, as well as two more
Leeds men who lost their lives in 1916 in Billy Jarman and
Jimmy Sanders. The *Yorkshire Evening Post* match report of 26
January admitted Llewellyn had very little to do on the day,
but was clearly a player with a great deal of potential:

> Leeds had no difficulty in winning their home
> match with Bramley and, allowing for the
> weakness of the opposition, the debut of the two
> new Welsh three-quarters, Hopkins and Llewellyn,
> was distinctly creditable to the players concerned.

That was to be one of four first-team appearances for
Llewellyn that season, while he also featured in a 25-2 home
triumph over Bramley on 31 October in the following
campaign, in which he kicked three goals. But shortly after
that, he returned to his native Wales and enlisted with the
Lancers in Cardiff, although it seems he soon switched to the
Rifle Brigade.

He arrived in France on 23 June 1915. It was not long after that that Llewellyn was sampling life in the front-line trenches, from where he wrote to a friend back in Leeds describing one of his trench raid 'adventures'. The letter appeared in the *Leeds Mercury* on 28 July 1915 under the headline 'Spying on the Enemy'. The article stated Trooper Llewellyn was in the 9th Lancers[10] and quoted his letter to a friend:

We soon discovered that we had a series of snipers' posts about forty yards from our trenches, so we set about to destroy them. My captain, my chum and myself went out as it got dark with a few bombs to pay our respect to the enemy. We crept quietly out past the sniper's dug-out, fixed bayonets and then wormed to the back. Fortunately for him, the sniper was out, but we got a quantity of ammunition for souvenirs. Disappointed of our sport, we crept on. I thought we were spotted as a light went up and machine guns opened fire. It soon got quiet again, much to our relief. We still crept on, and got right up to the enemy's barbed wire. There stood the German sentry singing softly to himself, little dreaming that three lads in khaki were watching every movement. We could easily have thrown our bombs, but getting back was the thing, and no purpose would have been served by attack, so we made our way home. We greatly enjoyed our trip and learned a lot about the German ways of doing things in the night. I will tell you of my first taste of shell fire. We were up to our necks in mud and feeling fed up of it all. It was awfully quiet as we took breakfast. Then it suddenly started to rain shells. I was a bit afraid at first, I will admit, but I got used to it after an hour. It's awful to see your chums falling by your side not knowing when your turn will come, but you even get used to that.

According to the *Leeds Rhinos Players' Association*, Llewellyn later went out to the Greek port of Salonika in late 1915, where the British and French had sent troops to provide support from the south for retreating ally Serbia, who were on the back foot in their fight against Germany, Austria-Hungary and Bulgaria. Yet even though Llewellyn and his comrades had escaped the bloodshed on the Western Front, the fighting was just as intense in southern Greece, with the Leeds player injured during one exchange and going on to suffer enteric fever, a disease of the intestines. He was then shipped back to England and hospitalised in Manchester.[11]

It took Llewellyn a significant time to get back to full fitness, but once he did, he was posted to Northern France, by which stage he was serving with the 13th Battalion Rifle Brigade. He was heavily involved during the Arras offensive, with Llewellyn and his battalion at the very heart of the action in the 2nd phase of the Battle of Arras on 23 May, as the unit war diary explained.

> 1 hour before Zero (4.45am) the Battalion formed up 2 Co[*mpan*]ys in Front Line and 1 Co[*mpan*]y being in Reserve with the 4 L[*ewis*] Guns of 'A' Co[*mpan*]y. At Zero hour the Batt[*alio*]n moved forward in Artillery formation ..... Very soon after the Battalion started, the enemy put down a heavy barrage of 5.9" H[*igh*] E[*xplosive*] shells. Casualties

were very heavy going through the barrage but the men continued to advance without a halt. Just before reaching the enemy's wire we came upon what appeared to be assembly trenches. The first wave had halted in these, the officers leading it having been either killed or wounded. The second wave of the leading Co[*mpan*]y joined the first and together pushed on through the enemy's wire into the Black Line which they at once began to consolidate.[12]

The diary then reported the Germans spent the rest of the morning shelling the Black Line, and by this stage many in Llewellyn's battalion were dug in on a road just outside the village of Gavrelle, which proved a dangerous place to be.

At 12.30 pm ..... We found the enemy were holding the high ground in the neighbourhood of the Cross Roads in some strength and more of the enemy were coming in. The 13th KRRC, who were dug in on the road, were completely enfiladed from the Cross Roads and had had casualties from Rifle fire and the situation was certainly unsatisfactory.[13]

At some point during the day's fighting, Llewellyn was injured, with his name appearing on a very long casualty list for the 23rd. But his wounds could not have been too serious as the Leeds man was back at the front within days. However, by the end of 1 June he was dead, with the unit war diary entry for the day pointing to the fact he must have been killed by a shell.

The Battalion in the trenches 2000 y[ard]s S. of
Monchy-Le-Preux. Enemy artillery very active on
our front line causing 6 casualties.[14]

His death was announced on 23 June in several newspapers
of the day, with the *Hull Daily Mail* typical in reporting:

The death in action is announced of Private
Arthur Llewellyn, of the Leeds Northern Union
football team. Llewellyn ..... joined the Leeds club
the season before the commencement of the war,
playing in the second, and occasionally in the first
team. He was regarded as a very promising three-
quarter back.

The reports added that second lieutenant Eric Thomas, a
former teammate of Llewellyn's at Abertillery, had also fallen
at the same time.

Like Harrison and Rees who had died a short time
earlier, Llewellyn has no known grave and he is remembered
on the Arras Memorial.

But there was at least some comfort for the family of
Huddersfield centre Theodore Marshall, who is buried in his
hometown of Elland. Like fellow Northern Union fallen
Ernest Swinton, George Thom and Walter Roman, the 22-
year-old Marshall was injured while fighting in France, was
brought back to England and ultimately died of the wounds
he received. In his case it was on 1 August 1917.

Born on 6 November 1894 to parents Joseph and Sarah
Marshall (née Farrar), Theodore was one of their nine
children. Joseph supported his family by working as a delver
at a stone quarry. Connected with St Michael's Church,
Elland Lower Edge, being a member of their choir, it was

clear from an early age that Marshall was a very gifted all-round athlete, and whilst still a teenager he was proving to be the star of the Elland Free Wanderers team. The talented three-quarter was soon attracting the attention of a number of Northern Union clubs, with the mighty Huddersfield winning the race to secure his signature on 30 June 1914. He was only 19 at the time.

However, it was never going to be easy for Marshall to make a first-team breakthrough, with the 'Prince of Centres' Harold Wagstaff and top Australian Albert Rosenfeld occupying the positions he craved. But with Wagstaff having toured Australia and New Zealand with Great Britain for the 1914 summer tour and not arriving back until the 1914-15 season had got under way, Marshall was handed the chance to step into the Northern Union fold after impressing in the pre-season trial games. Those included a club practice match at Fartown in August 1914, with Marshall part of a Reds team that won the contest with a lot to spare, as the *Huddersfield Daily Examiner* on the 24 August explained.

> The teams [*Reds and Blues*] consisted mainly of local district players, together with a few of last year's second team ..... The Reds were the better side and won by 8 tries 4 goals – 32 points to 3. The proceeds, as arranged previous to the outbreak of the war, were in aid of the District League Fund.

It was enough to put Marshall in pole position for a senior start. As a result, the rising star featured in the first five games of the season – when Huddersfield's 'Team of All Talents' would walk away with all four major trophies on offer – as Fartown opened with two wins, two draws and a defeat. His debut was an 18-0 away win at Keighley on 5 September

1914. The narrow 13-12 home defeat to Warrington two days later must have come as a disappointment, but at least Marshall was on the tryscoring sheet for the first and only time.

He was also earning praise for his performances in the *Huddersfield Daily Examiner*, with the paper acknowledging the youngster showed some neat touches in the 15-8 home success over Halifax on 19 September, although the report did add later in its post-match review:

> Marshall is not fast enough to make up for his lack of inches, but he has quite an idea of a centre's duties, though why he waits for the ball to bounce when he could catch it with ease is one of those puzzles that is so difficult to solve.

Yet even if Marshall had been 100% faultless in his opening games, he was always going to make way for the RFL Hall of Fame legend Wagstaff when he returned to the Northern Union competition at the start of October. The Elland ace would have been well aware of that fact. Marshall still remained on Huddersfield's senior books, however, hoping to get back into the club's star-studded line-up.

But on 24 January 1916, he enlisted for Army service in Bradford, joined the Cameron Highlanders and put his rugby career, and employment as a warper at Ashbrow Mills, on hold and waved goodbye to his family and friends at Lower Edge Working Man's Club. When Marshall arrived in France in July 1916, he was almost immediately thrust into the thick of the action, suffering a bad head wound in an explosion in September, before returning to the front around Christmas.

Four months later, during the Battle of Arras, whilst with the 7th Battalion, he picked up another head wound from which he would never recover – with a major account appearing in the *Halifax Courier* on 11 August 1917.

> The death took place at St Luke's Hospital, Bradford, on Wednesday, from severe wounds received in action, of Pte. Theodore Marshall, of the Camerons Regiment, whose parents reside at 105, Lower Edge, Elland. On April 28 last, he was struck by a sniper's bullet which passed clean through his head, and which had the effect of paralysing one side. He was conveyed to Bradford, arriving at St Luke's on May 19. This was the soldier's second wounding, for in September 1916 he was buried as a result of an explosion and had to be dug out. At that time he was badly wounded about the head. After being in hospital, and a short stay at home, he rejoined his regiment in Dec[*ember*] 1916 and continued in the firing line until he received the wound which proved fatal. The body was brought from Bradford to Elland, and was interred at the local cemetery on Saturday. Prior to the burial a short service was conducted at the house by the Rev. H.N. Pobjoy, and at St Mary's Church, Elland, by the Rev M.A. Maddocks, ... Among the floral tributes were wreaths from the Huddersfield Football Club (decorated with the club's colours), the Lower Edge Working Men's Club and the workpeople of Ashbrow Mills. Three other brothers are with the forces in France.

Sadly, the Marshall family were to lose another son to the war before the year was out. Albert, eight years Theodore's senior, died on 16 December 1917 and is buried in Belgium.

S/18732 PRIVATE
T. WAGSTAFF
CAMERON HIGHLANDERS
18TH OCTOBER 1916

Thomas Wagstaff
(Bramley),
Warlencourt British
Cemetery
Jane Roberts

John Linton Ewart pictured with the Halifax team of 1914

Andrew Hardcaste

Jimmy Flanagan (St Helens)
Saints Heritage Society

Jimmy Flanagan's grandson holds his
grandad's jersey and cap   *Saints Heritage Society*

Leonard Leckenby (Leeds)
*Leeds Rhinos Foundation
Heritage Committee*

Lewis Bradley (Wigan)
Mike Latham

Mark Kay, *front,* with the Hunslet side of 1914   *Pat Benatmane*

Phil Thomas (Hull KR)
Michael Turner

R.Topping (Leigh)
Mike Latham

"Paddy" O'Neill Killed.

Followers of Northern Union Football will be especially sorry to hear of the death of Gunner Patrick O'Neill, of the R.G.A., which took place on September 27th. Captain D. Seed, of his battery, writing to Mrs. O'Neill, at 10, Brunswick-st., Leigh, says: "Everyone of this battery speaks of his sorrow for you. Your husband was a great favourite, and will be deeply missed. It was during a heavy bombardment that your husband was struck. He volunteered to guide a rationing party to the battery, and just as he completed his work, a piece of shell bursting very near struck him. We brought him in, but he passed away in two or three minutes. Your husband and I have been together for two and a half years, and I cannot tell you how sorry I am for you. He was a brave soldier."

Gnr. PATRICK O'NEILL.

"Paddy" O'Neill played for Leigh for a number of years, and was a great leader of the forward line. Fearless, strong, and clever, he had a hand in many a victory and took his share in the winning of the League Championship in 1905-6. His forte was at forward, but he played many a good game on emergency at half and three-quarter back. Gunner O'Neill left his old club for Dewsbury and assisted them to beat Oldham in the final for the Northern Union Cup in 1912. He was thus a holder of the Cup and League Championship Medals. He joined the Army in May, 1915, and went to France 12 months later. When home on furlough he, on September 30th last year, played for Leigh and assisted them to defeat Broughton Rangers. Gunner O'Neill worked as a collier at the Nook Pit, Tyldesley, before enlisting. He leaves a widow and two children.

News of the death of Paddy O'Neill (Dewsbury) and his obituary, *below*
Mike Latham

A stunning period photograph of Robert Randerson's family. Randerson is pictured *second right*

Patricia Blackledge

Thomas Henry Tillotson, *right*, (Hunslet) was a champion swimmer as a schoolboy and regularly featured in the newspapers. This image appeared in the *Yorkshire Evening Post* on 3 October 1902

Yorkshire Post Newspapers

Stanley Young (Warrington)

Warrington Wolves

Thomas Owen Jones (Oldham)
Michael Turner

Thomas West (Rochdale)
Rochdale Rugby League Heritage

Walter Roman (Rochdale)
Rochdale Rugby League Heritage

William Boyd Jardine (Oldham)
Michael Turner

Theodore Marshall
(Huddersfield)
Paul Marshall

Killing Fields of Flanders: "I Did Not Know It Was Like This"

16

In 1916 and the first half of 1917, the vast majority of the British Western Front action had centred around the Somme offensive and Battle of Arras respectively. There had been sporadic activity in Belgium between the Allies and Germans throughout that time. But it was in the second half of 1917 when the Belgian front erupted into life in dramatic fashion.

Haig had been keen to attack the Germans in the Flanders area, and felt the time was now right. His plan was to break the German lines around Ypres, occupy the surrounding areas and advance onto the railhead at Roselare. From there the Allies would push on towards the Flemish coast and attack the Channel ports of Ostend and Zeebrugge, from where the Germans had been launching their destructive U-boat raids which they hoped would starve Britain out of the war. An Allied sea raid was also planned to take place at the same time.

The idea was sound, particularly as eastern-front ally

Russia was on the point of collapse following their revolution, and Haig feared the soon-to-be-bolstered German Western Front force may mount a summer attack against the demoralised French Army, who had come so close to mutiny in the wake of the doomed Nivelle Spring Offensive. The British needed to act to prevent this from happening and keep the French in the war.

Unfortunately, the execution failed to live up to the expectation, with the torrential rain, combined with the destruction of drainage systems, turning the hellish battlefields into a muddy mess, sucking the life out of the offensive and banging the final nail into the Allies' coffin.

The preparatory attack could not have gone much better, with the Battle of Messines softening up the German defences with the successful detonation of 19 deep mines on 7 June. At that stage, and with the Germans on the backfoot, the British troops should have pushed straight on. Instead, they waited until 31 July and the Third Battle of Ypres (or Passchendaele as it also became known) to get their full offensive under way – giving the enemy plenty of time to strengthen their defences. The Allies' chance to strike a decisive early blow had gone, meaning that by the time the battle drew to a close on 12 November – just six days after capturing the day one objective of the village of Passchendaele itself – British casualties were around a sickening 450,000 for a gain of just five miles.

Yet unlike the Battle of the Somme 12 months earlier when the Northern Union suffered a heavy loss of life, there were far fewer professional rugby league player deaths during this Belgium offensive – with the first coming during the initial Battle of Messines engagement. That man was 31-year-old Runcorn veteran Peter Okell.[1]

Born in Runcorn in 1885, the son of general labourer

William Okell and his wife Annie, Okell's life revolved around his home town, in terms of work, family and sport. Like his father, he too was a labourer when he married Harriet Jones at Runcorn parish church in December 1907. By that stage they had a one-year-old daughter, Alice. The couple went on to have Peter, James, Martha and Nellie. In 1910 Okell, displaying his credentials as a solid citizen, took a carving knife, fork and sharpening steels to the police. He found them hidden at his workplace at Haslehurst's Yard. They had been stolen from the Mersey Mission to the Seaman's Church and Institute and his evidence contributed to two men being committed for trial at the Cheshire Quarter Sessions.

Okell also remained loyal to hometown club Runcorn, signing for them in 1907 and going on to make 32 senior appearances and scoring three tries. His value to the side was underlined in the 1911-12 campaign when his versatility shone through as he appeared on the wing, centre, stand-off and scrum half, with his 11th and final performance of the season coming in a 21-0 defeat at Bradford Northern on 8 April 1912.

That also proved to be his last Northern Union appearance for his hometown club, although he remained on their first-team books at the outbreak of war, ready to offer his senior services whenever they may have been required. Unfortunately, that never came again in the Northern Union competition, with Okell finally joining the Cheshire Regiment in January 1917, and leaving behind his wife and young family.

After completing his training, he joined the 13th Battalion on the Western Front where he was to take part in the Battle of Messines. By 10 June, he was dead – just a month after arriving overseas. Okell lost his life as the Cheshires made their assault, which commenced at 3.10am on 7 June

1917 when the mines were detonated. Confirmation of his death came in the *Runcorn Guardian* of 22 June, with the date he was killed given as the 9th rather than 10th of June, the latter being recorded by the Commonwealth War Graves Commission. It said:

> Mrs Okell, 1 Mill-court, Mill-street, Runcorn, has received news that her husband, Private Peter Okell, was killed on June 9th. The news was conveyed to her in a letter from a friend as follows:- 'You can tell Jack Findlow and Mrs. Findlow next door that their nephew, Davison, out of Speakman-street, joined the same battalion as I am in on the 4th day of June, and so did Peter Okell. We have had a big battle here and Davison has come out of it quite safe, and I am sorry to tell you that Peter Okell got killed with a shell on the 9th. Probably this will be the first news of his death. Kindly break the news to his relations as easy as possible, and please give them my sincere sympathy over their sad loss. Peter Okell's last words to me were: 'I did not know it was like this.' Private Okell was 31 years of age and enlisted only in January of the present year and was drafted out to the front a month ago. Prior to enlisting he was employed by the Salt Union Ltd. He was a local footballer, playing in the first and second teams.

Okell has no known grave and is remembered on the Menin Gate in Ypres.

The Northern Union did not have to wait long before suffering its first fatality at the start of the Third Battle of

Ypres either, with Hunslet half-back Mark Kay[2] dying on 31 July 1917.

By the time he fell at the age of 26, Kay had proved himself a distinguished soldier, being awarded the French Croix de Guerre 1914-18 for his actions while serving with the 6th Battalion Queen's Own Cameron Highlanders. The Croix de Guerre was created to recognise both French and Allied soldiers, either as individuals or at unit level, for their courage during the conflict. Kay was awarded the honour in the early months of 1917, with the news broadcast in the *Yorkshire Evening Post* of 5 March. It proclaimed:

> Hunslet Football Club players and supporters will be pleased to hear of the honour which has been conferred on that sturdy little player, Mark Kay, who is in the Cameron Highlanders. He has been awarded the Croix de Guerre by the French Government for conspicuous bravery in carrying despatches under fire from the trenches.

No doubt Kay was chosen to take messages (despatches) from one location to another due to his outstanding running ability. Although the half-back made a name for himself as a Northern Union player, he was also well known around the Leeds area for his sprinting ability, which meant he regularly competed in athletics meetings in the city whilst still a teenager. In 1910 and 1911, for instance, his name cropped up in the *Yorkshire Post and Leeds Intelligencer* for winning heats at 'Pedestrianism' events staged at the New Peacock Grounds, Leeds, always described as being well attended.

Kay's natural pace clearly proved a useful asset in his bid to pursue a professional rugby league career, with hometown club Hunslet snapping him up from Bramley

Albion on 20 January 1914 at the age of 22. He did not manage to force his way into the first team straight away, but made the first of his three 1914-15 senior appearances at scrum-half in a 12-4 home win over Batley on 19 September 1914. This was followed by a second start in the No7 shirt in a 13-3 home triumph over Widnes in which he crossed for a debut try on 6 March 1915.

It was a display that obviously made an impression on the *Yorkshire Evening Post* that day, with the player's exploits worthy of a headline – 'Kay goes over with two players on his shoulders'. The report described how Kay's unexpected starting place arose, as well as his try and overall contribution:

> The Hunslet committee had intended playing Fred Smith, their International half-back, this afternoon, in their home match against Widnes, but he is still laid aside with rheumatics, and Kay therefore partnered Fearn at half-back ..... Ashall and Kay interchanged passes, and after Guerin had taken part in the exchanges the forwards, with another rare burst, got past the opposition. Pratt got the ball, and after a powerful run he passed to Kay, who practically hurled himself over the line with a couple of opponents on his shoulders. He grounded the ball and scored a try ..... Noon and Kelly were a pair of good half-backs for Widnes, but they received the assiduous attention of Kay and Fearn, who acted in perfect concert.

A third start for Kay was recorded in a narrow 5-2 defeat at Rochdale a fortnight later, while he also turned out for the club in a friendly fixture while on leave the following year.

And it is clear Kay would have played far more frequently during his breakthrough season had he not enlisted in Leeds early in the war with the Cameron Highlanders, giving his place of birth as Glasgow. It appears, however, that Kay actually grew up in and around the Hunslet and Beeston area, the son of Mark and Ellen Kay.

That aside, there was no doubt he served the Camerons with distinction. After completing his training, he arrived in France on 1 December 1915, and was among those to survive both the Somme offensive and the Battle of Arras. But his final fateful battle would be in Belgium on the opening day of the Passchendaele campaign, in the Battle of Pilkem Ridge. In the area of the assault involving the Camerons, the 45th Brigade of which they were part were tasked with the final stage of a three-stage attack, capturing the so-called Green Line.

At 4am that morning, the 6th Camerons moved to their positions where they dug in at about 7.30am awaiting instructions to move, which they did two hours later once the leading brigades had apparently taken their objectives. However, this proved not the case and the Camerons came under heavy machine gun fire from Beck House and Iberian Farm which they had to deal with before moving to their Green Line objective, which they reached by 11.35am. They then consolidated, at which point they suffered the blow of losing their Commanding Officer. Even without orders, they retained their grip on the Green Line. Patrols were sent out, in accordance with Operation Orders, but they never returned. By the afternoon they came under a heavy enemy counter-attack which left them unprotected on both flanks as the battalions on either side fell back. With ammunition running out, the Camerons too were forced to pull back behind the Green Line where they spent the night in waterlogged conditions, it proving impossible to relieve them. So ended 31 July 1917.

The total number of casualties amongst other ranks over the course of 31 July and the following day, 1 August, according to their unit war diary was 279 killed, wounded or missing.[3] That figure included the 26-year-old Kay, whose body was amongst those lost on the battlefield and he is, therefore, remembered on the Menin Gate.

The news was reported home by the *Leeds Mercury* of 22 August 1917:

> Pte. M. Kaye [*sic*], who was well known in Hunslet as a footballer and a professional runner, and who, prior to enlisting in the Cameron Highlanders, resided in Ladypit-grove, Hunslet, Leeds, has been killed in action. He had previously been awarded the Croix de Guerre.

After the loss of Kay, it was not until 20 September that the second senior star was lost in battle – Oldham's Thomas Owen Jones who, like the Hunslet man, also excelled in sprinting. With a name like that, it was no great surprise that Jones was another talented player to hail from Wales. And it was certainly regarded as something of a coup when his capture by Oldham was announced, which the *Manchester Courier and Lancashire General Advertiser* of 11 December 1913, made clear.

> Oldham Northern Union club have signed on T.O. Jones and G. Evans, the left wing and centre-threequarter of the Neath club. Jones played for Neath and also Glamorgan County, and was selected for the Welsh trial game last Saturday.

The match, however, was cancelled owing to the railway strike. He is regarded as the fastest man playing Rugby football, either Northern Union or Rugby Union.

It was clearly that pace which gave him a head start as a rugby winger, first with hometown club Treorchy (where he was born to parents Thomas and Catherine Jones in 1887, one of their 11 children) and then Neath, where he started to hit the headlines and was regarded as a potential Welsh international.

Had there been no rail strike and Jones impressed in the trial, it is possible he could have gone on to prove the pundits right and star for his country in the 15-a-side code. Indeed, there was some bitterness at his defection, with the *Yorkshire Evening Post* of 27 December 1913 reporting one Cardiff writer's view that this was no spur-of-the-moment move:

> I do not blame T.O. Jones and George Evans for going North, with all that means. But I cannot compliment them upon leaving their enthusiastic club officials and colleagues in the Neath team in the dark, as to their intentions. It was no sudden resolve – a determination such as this never is. However, I wish them well. While I prefer to think of Rugby players as amateurs, my opinion is not of the ultra-purist, to whom all who play for pay are unclean beings.

Instead, Oldham had capitalised on the industrial action and lured Jones north, with their new man officially registered on 23 December 1913, after he had first turned out for Oldham in the Northern Union as a trialist winger in a 9-3 home defeat to Leeds on 15 December. Then on Christmas Day, 10 days later, he was celebrating his first Oldham victory in the 11-0 home success over Swinton, and his professional rugby league career was well and truly under way. Jones followed up in game No3 with his first try in a 5-3 win at Warrington and then crossed twice a day later in a 10-2 triumph over Leeds at Headingley. In no time at all the Welsh flyer had established himself in the senior Watersheddings side, going on to make a total of 46 appearances, scoring 19 tries and one goal in the process.

Yet, interestingly, during that time there appears to have been doubt cast over whether Jones was, in fact, the fastest man in rugby. In the *Leeds Mercury* match report of Huddersfield's 28-8 win over Oldham at the Watersheddings on 20 March 1915, it stated:

> T.O. Jones, who has a reputation as a sprinter, was time after time beaten in speed by his vis-à-vis, Rosenfeld, even when the latter had to give him yards start.

That pronouncement would certainly have sent shock waves throughout the athletics world, with Jones involved in several high-profile sprint events, where he was regarded as one of the quickest around. In fact, in the highly-respected £100 Stadium Sprint at Cardiff on 27 July 1914, Jones had come third to Bingley's Seymour in the 100 yards race.

It was exactly a month after that 1915 Northern Union clash with Huddersfield that Jones enlisted with the 15th Battalion Welsh Regiment at Southport, on 20 April 1915. The 5ft 5¼in wingman's occupation at the time was recorded as a collier. His attestation form also indicated previous service with the 10th Manchesters.[4] He made his final Oldham Northern Union appearance in a heavy 28-5 defeat at Hull four days later and then began to focus all his attention on his military training, part of which was with the regiment's 3rd Battalion where he was appointed Lance-Corporal (unpaid) in October 1915. He eventually embarked for France from Folkestone on 3 April 1916 to join the 9th Battalion. It was a moment the *Western Mail* felt worthy of mention:

> Lance-corporal T.O. Jones, Treorky, the well-known Welsh sprinter, has left for the front. He played brilliant games for the Treorky and Neath Rugby clubs, and latterly was a member of the Oldham (Northern Union) team.

Jones spent well over a year in the field – he was promoted to Corporal in November 1916 and twice evacuated during that time due to illness – before his battalion began preparing to take part in the massive Belgian offensive. And at some time during a costly attack on 20 September 1917, Jones lost his life, with his unit war diary describing what a bad day it had been:

> On night of 19/20 the Battalion moved to its Assembly position. A very wet night and assembly was carried out with some difficulty. At 5.40am [*on the 20th*] the Battalion attacked. Heavy M[*achine*] G[*un*] fire was encountered from Hollebeke Chateau ..... Casualties were heavy mostly due to M[*achine*] G[*un*] fire ..... O[*ther*] R[*anks*] casualties were 35 killed, 204 wounded and 40 missing.[5]

Thirty-year-old Corporal Thomas Owen Jones has no known grave and is remembered on the Tyne Cot War Memorial. The news of his death was confirmed in the *Liverpool Echo* on 4 October, under the heading 'Northern Footballers Killed' – when the death of a second Northern Union star was also announced. It stated:

> The deaths, killed in action, are announced of two well-known Northern Union players. One was T.O. Jones, the well-known Welsh sprinter and Oldham three-quarter ..... The other is Patrick O'Neill, the well-known Leigh forward, who, after playing for the Mather-lane club and Lancashire, assisted Dewsbury to win the Northern Union Cup.

This was the proof that one of the most respected props in the game had lost his life on 27 September – exactly a week after Jones – at the age of 35.

'Paddy' O'Neill was a huge Northern Union hero, both in his home town of Leigh and in the Heavy Woollen area of West Yorkshire, where he played a key role in helping Dewsbury beat Oldham 8-5 in the 1912 Challenge Cup final in front of a crowd of 15,271 at Headingley on 27 April. That was to prove to be Dewsbury's only major senior domestic success – apart from during the Wartime Emergency League – until they won the League Championship in the 1972-73 season, with former Sky Sports TV pundit Mike 'Stevo' Stephenson the inspiration.

But it was at Leigh where the rugged forward first made his name in the game, establishing himself as one of the most feared and respected front-rowers in the Northern Union. Born in Elswick, Northumberland, in 1882, he was the son of Irish-born James O'Neill and his wife Phoebe (née Barlow). James was a collier and his work took him to the coalmining areas of the country, but it was in Leigh that the family settled.

After school, the young O'Neill almost inevitably followed his father down the mine, eventually gaining employment at the Nook Pit at Tyldesley. By that stage, O'Neill had also made a name for himself as a no-nonsense front-row forward and made his senior Leigh debut against Batley in March 1903 at the age of 20. He went on to impress in the club's 1905-06 Championship-winning side. During that highly-successful season he featured in 37 of Leigh's 38 games, including their Lancashire Cup final replay defeat to Wigan.

In all, he made 211 appearances for the club, which also included Mather Lane victories over the touring New Zealand side in 1907 and the Australians a year later. O'Neill also played for Lancashire during that time. Yet even though he was a relative 'veteran' of the game at the age of 28 when he signed for Dewsbury in April 1911, the news still came as something of a shock to the Leigh faithful when O'Neill and teammate William Smith made the move across the Pennines, in a deal announced in the *Yorkshire Post and Leeds Intelligencer* of 4 April. Under the headline 'Dewsbury Secure Two Leigh Forwards', it read:

> William Smith and Patrick O'Neill, ex-Lancashire forward players, and who for some time have been playing with the Leigh Club, have signed on with the Dewsbury Club for next season. Smith, who is 28 years of age and scales 12st 8lb., is regarded by many as the fastest forward in Lancashire, and O'Neill, who is the same age and

> weighs 13st 12lb., has a good reputation. Smith,
> who is a tee-totaller and non-smoker, was born at
> Darfield near Barnsley, and O'Neill is a native of
> Elswick, Newcastle-on-Tyne.

Even though O'Neill continued to live and work in Leigh and travelled to Dewsbury by train to play and train, it did not take him long to establish himself as the club's inspirational pack leader. Within a season, O'Neill was holding the Challenge Cup aloft in the famous red, amber and black of Dewsbury, as winger Billy Rhodes scored twice to bring the trophy to Crown Flatt for the very first time. His legendary status in that part of the world was secured. 1912 also proved a memorable year on the personal front, with O'Neill marrying Ellen Blear and their son, James Stanley, born in October.

Whilst he was in the twilight of his Northern Union career by the outbreak of war, O'Neill remained a regular in Dewsbury's 1913-14 side – switching from the front row to the second row – and then featured in the opening games of the 1914-15 campaign. But those appearances began to dry up at the start of 1915, and in the spring of that year he enlisted, moving to France the following year as a Gunner with the 147th Heavy Battery, Royal Garrison Artillery (RGA). He did, however, get back to play one final game for Leigh during his time on leave on 30 September 1916, when he helped the club secure a 14-0 Wartime Emergency League victory over Broughton Rangers. O'Neill was named the man-of-the-match and was cheered off a field he would never be seen on again.

After seeing action on the French front, O'Neill and his battery moved to Belgium to be a part of the Ypres offensive. His role was a dangerous one. Although out of the frontline, those working with the Heavy Batteries behind the trenches were a prime target for the German shells. O'Neill and his RGA colleagues were equipped with the heavy guns used to neutralise enemy artillery and take out key strategic German military targets. They were obviously something the enemy needed to destroy – with one bombardment ending O'Neill's life, as a letter sent home to Ellen by an Officer in her husband's battery made clear. In the letter, published in the *Leigh Journal*, Captain D Seed wrote:

> Everyone of this battery speaks of his sorrow for you. Your husband was a great favourite, and will be deeply missed. It was during a heavy bombardment that your husband was struck. He volunteered to guide a rationing party to the battery, and just as he completed his work a piece of shell bursting very near struck him. We brought him in, but he passed away in two or three minutes. Your husband and I have been together for the last two and a half years, and I cannot tell you how sorry I am for you. He was a very brave soldier.

In addition to his widow Ellen, he left two children. O'Neill was laid to rest at Belgium Battery Corner Cemetery, near Ypres.

O'Neill was held in incredibly high esteem in Leigh and when the club won the Challenge Cup in 1921, his son Stanley was Leigh's final mascot. Stanley later worked the scoreboard at Mather Lane and became good friends with Leigh legend Tommy Sale. Following the death of his father, Paddy's brother James, who also played for Leigh, made sure he took Stanley under his wing.[6]

John Linton Ewart of Halifax

courtesy of Andrew Hardcastle

1918 Spring Offensive – Last Throw of the German Dice

17

At the start of 1918, the dynamic on the Western Front changed significantly. In April 1917, America declared war on Germany, while seven months later Russia surrendered to the Central Powers in the midst of the Bolshevik Revolution. It meant that in the early weeks of 1918, over half-a-million battle-hardened German troops were able to leave the Eastern Front and move to the Western Front to take on the British and the French.

At this stage, the Americans had not arrived in Europe in force. Like the British in 1914, the US entered the war with a relatively small Army that could only be increased through intense training. As a result, the bulk of the US Army – around the two-million mark – would not be in place until the summer of 1918 at the earliest. And the Germans knew it.

They knew their only realistic chance of winning the war was to force the Allies to surrender before the Americans arrived – and with over 500,000 victorious soldiers leaving the

Russian front, the Germans knew the spring of 1918 was the time to strike. This would be the German Spring Offensive.

Military chief Erich Ludendorff was fully aware this was effectively the German's last throw of the Great War dice – and so everything they had was fired into the fray. The main objective was to attack the British front around the Somme area and then push on to the British-occupied Channel ports. The Germans were convinced that if this objective was achieved and the British were beaten, the French would be forced to surrender.

Codenamed Operation Michael – with Operations Georgette (an attack on the Belgium front), and Gneisenau and Blucher-Yorck (to engage the French) to follow – the Spring Offensive began with a devastating bombardment of the British Somme frontline in the early hours of 21 March and then an attack by German stormtroopers deep into their enemy's territory.

The gains made by the Germans on that opening day were huge, as were the British losses, with more than 38,000 casualties suffered. The death toll was over 8,000, making it the second worst day in British military history behind the first day of the Battle of the Somme. Among those immediately in the firing line were the 5th (Service) Battalion, Queen's Own Cameron Highlanders, who included Halifax winger John Linton Ewart within their ranks. He died on 21 March.

The Scottish-born Ewart was a relative newcomer to the Halifax ranks, having signed for the club from Selkirk Rugby Union Club on 13 April 1914, just a day before the end of his new team's final game of the 1913-14 season, a 10-9 away win at Bradford, although the 22-year-old did not feature.

It was Ewart's pace that had caught the attention of the West Yorkshire club, with their new recruit having earned a reputation as a top sprinter. Just like Northern Union colleagues Mark Kay and Thomas Owen Jones who had fallen in Belgium in the autumn of 1917, Linton competed regularly in athletics meetings and earned some extra 'pocket money' in the process.

But unlike Kay and Jones who competed under their own names, it was a different story for Ewart, as an article in the *Southern Reporter* of 22 May 1913 explained.

> LOCAL PED'S SUCCESS – E. Oliver, Selkirk, in winning last Saturday's 130 yards handicap at Powderhall Grounds, Edinburgh, off 14 yards, put up a very fine performance. He is better known in rugby circles as J.L. Ewart, his speed having been of great value during the past season to the local team. Oliver beat a hot favourite in the final in J.S. Mather, Edinburgh.....

The same publication then reported two months later:

> ....and another honour has been added to the sheaf by E. Oliver (J.L. Ewart, Dunsdale Haugh) winning the handicap sprint at Jedforest Games. The value of the prize was £10.....

Ewart kept up his athletic interest when he moved south of the border, the *Southern Reporter* of 3 September 1914 adding:

> Last Saturday week at the athletic sports held under the auspices of Halifax Cricket and Football Clubs, J.L. Ewart, late of Selkirk Rugby Club, won first prize in the 120 yards handicap. The first prize was £4. Ewart ran from scratch and gave starts up to twelve yards.

Then, just a few days later, Ewart was focusing all of his attention on his professional rugby career, with the winger featuring for Halifax in their opening four 1914-15 Northern Union fixtures. He made a winning debut in a 7-0 victory at Bramley on 5 September and then crossed for his first try in a big 28-3 home triumph over Keighley 21 days later. After that, however, the Northern Union appearances began to dry up and he had to wait until Boxing Day 1914 to make one final outing in a 12-3 defeat at Rochdale. That marked the end of his Northern Union career.

By 2 January, Ewart had returned north of the border and enlisted in Edinburgh with the Queen's Own Cameron Highlanders – no doubt to the pride of his parents Robert and Elizabeth Linton Ewart, who raised John in Selkirk after his birth on 17 October 1891. On his enlistment papers the 5ft 6¾in Ewart gave his occupation as Professional Footballer.[1] His attestation papers also indicate he had done previous service with the King's Own Scottish Borderers.

After completing his training as a signaller with the 3rd Battalion, Ewart arrived in France on 13 September 1915 to join the 1st Battalion. It came only days after he reverted to Private from the rank of Lance Corporal at his own request. The following month he was sharing some of his thoughts on life in the frontline with the readers of the *Southern Reporter* on 28 October 1915 in an article under the title 'Tales From the Firing Line'. The report said:

> Below we publish further extracts from the letters sent by Selkirk soldiers at the front to Mr John Buchan, Hon. Secretary, in acknowledgement of parcels of comforts recently despatched by the Selkirk Sailors and Soldiers' Comforts

Committee. The letters prove the necessity for continuing this good work, and we hope further ways and means will be devised for keeping the fund adequately large for the periodic despatch of further parcels: – 'The contents were grand, and came at a time most appropriate – just as we came out of the trenches, after doing 9 days and having rather a rough passage ..... JOHN L EWART, Signallers, 1st Cameron Highlanders.'

That '*rough passage*' may have been Ewart's description of the Battle of Loos, in which the Camerons were involved – and it was, unfortunately, a taste of things to come. Between then and his death in the spring of 1918, Ewart was also involved during the Third Battle of Ypres and the last phase of the Cambrai operations in November 1917, when the British used tanks in large numbers for the very first time. And during his time at the front Ewart suffered several injuries. One, a laceration to the left knee joint and abscesses, was serious enough for him to be evacuated back to England in February 1916 and put him out of action until mid-November 1916, meaning he did not take part in the Battle of the Somme.

By 1917 he was with the 5th Battalion of the Cameron Highlanders, and still serving with them at the start of the German Spring Offensive the following March. It proved one battle too many for Ewart and many others in his battalion as they were struck down by the enemy's deadly hammer blow while attempting to defend their sector on the Somme. On the day Ewart died, 21 March, the unit war diary explained his battalion was charged with the task of holding the line, west of Gouzeaucourt.

4.40am – The enemy started a very heavy

> bombardment with gas shells and H[*igh*] E[*xplosives*]. The former ceased about 10am, but the latter did not diminish until 5pm. The BLACK WATCH withdrew from the front system after dark and the YELLOW LINE became the OUTPOST LINE. Batt[*alio*]n HQ moved to Gouzecourt [*sic*] Wood.[2]

It was during this massive bombardment that Ewart was lost. He has no known grave and is remembered on the Pozieres Memorial. His death was announced in the *Halifax Courier* on 13 April, which stated:

> News has been received that Jock Ewart, one of the Halifax three-quarter backs, was killed in action on March 21. He was a popular member of the Halifax team during the season after the war broke out and joined the Army in 1915 ..... He was about 23 years of age and his home was in Selkirk. His Halifax friends and numerous admirers will be sorry to hear of his death.

Within days of the Spring Offensive getting under way, the Germans had made the biggest gains of the entire war, with the British spending the next month desperately defending their lines in a bid to protect their approaches to the Channel ports and the vital rail junction supply lines at Amiens. It was ultimately to prove a successful defence, although it was achieved at a very high cost to human life. By the time the balance of power shifted back towards the Allies, several more highly prominent Northern Union stars had lost their lives, starting with St Helens' Hubert Sydney 'Jum' Turtill on 9 April. The vastly-experienced full-back was arguably one of rugby league's biggest names when he went off to fight, having the rare distinction of being a New Zealand dual rugby international – despite the fact he was actually English. Born in Mile End Old Town, London, on 1 February 1880, tragedy struck the Turtill family within weeks of Hubert's birth, with his father Arthur Charles dying at the age of just 32. That left his mother, Alice Eliza, to bring up Hubert and his older brothers Astley William and Tyrell James and older sister Ethel Margaret on her own.

It was clearly tough, with the 1881 census – a year after her husband's death – showing Astley in Essex with an aunt, Tyrell and Ethel lodging with relatives in Worlingham, Suffolk and Hubert living with the Powditch family in Southwold, Suffolk. And these sad circumstances may well have been the reason the children made a fresh start in New Zealand, where their maternal grandparents had settled.

According to some reports, it was during the long sea voyage south that three-year-old Hubert earned the nickname 'Jum', which was short for Jumbo – a common name for an elephant – due to his chubby appearance at the time. But despite his unathletic look as a young child, he began to shed his 'puppy fat' and took up the sport of rugby union.

He was soon excelling as a full-back in the 15-a-side code with Christchurch Albion, initially with two seasons at second grade. By 1902 he was firmly establishing himself in the seniors and getting his representative cap for Canterbury. The talented Turtill very quickly earned representative honours with the South Island, and in 1905 made his one and only New Zealand All Blacks appearance in a 14-3 victory over Australia at Dunedin on 2 September.

He had hoped that would be enough to earn him selection for the All Blacks tour to Australia in 1907, but he was overlooked and turned his back on rugby union – as many players in that part of the world were doing at that time. In an almost identical scenario to that which occurred in the creation of the Northern Union in 1895 and the split from the Rugby Football Union, there was considerable discontent among many New Zealanders that the Union authorities were not prepared to compensate players for a loss of earnings from having to take time off work to play.

As a result, Turtill and a number of other highly-talented New Zealand players accepted Albert Henry Baskerville's invitation to become members of their nation's first professional rugby league team for a 1907 tour to Australia – where they played as league players for the first time under the tag of the New Zealand 'All Golds' in a move which led to the 13-a-side code taking off Down Under – and then a 1907-08 tour to England and Wales.

When they arrived in England on 30 September 1907, the tourists spent several weeks adapting to league rules and watching several Northern Union games before taking on many of the competition's club sides, with mixed results. But that provided the perfect preparation for the international match against Wales at Aberdare on New Year's Day 1908. In what is recognised by the New Zealand Rugby League as their nation's first official Test match, the tourists were narrowly beaten 9-8 in front of a 20,000 crowd, with Turtill lining up at full-back. Co-incidentally, among the Wales tryscorers that day was Warrington forward George Thomas, who died on the Somme on 3 July 1916.

Turtill then lined up against England at Wigan on 11 January as the tourists again suffered another narrow defeat, this time going down 18-16. The first Test against the Northern Union took place at Headingley on 25 January, with the hosts taking the honours 14-6, although Turtill did have the distinction of scoring New Zealand's first ever try against what, in essence, was the Great Britain national side. He was also at full-back as the tourists won the second Test 18-6 at Chelsea's Stamford Bridge and third Test 8-5 at Cheltenham. Not surprisingly, Turtill and his fellow countrymen were wanted men by the Northern Union clubs.

Initially, Turtill continued to focus on his New Zealand rugby league touring commitments and was his country's captain in the 11-10 first Test triumph over Australia in Sydney on 9 May 1908. It was the first Test ever played between the nations. But once those commitments were complete, he returned to his country of birth with his pregnant, New Zealand-born wife Mabel Edith – who he had married in Christchurch in 1908 – to sign for St Helens ahead of the 1909-10 season. Records show they travelled to England from the port of Wellington aboard the *Corinthic*.

There had been talk of Turtill joining Salford, but instead he opted to link up with his good friend and fellow New Zealand tourist Arthur Kelly, who was already at Knowsley Road. Saints' capture of Turtill was announced on 17 July 1909, and was big news, with the *Athletic News* leading the plaudits. Under the headline 'The Coming of Turtill', they announced:

> The event of the week in Northern Union circles has been the 'settling down' of Hebert [*sic*] Sydney Turtill, the full-back who played in England during the tour of the New Zealand professional 'All Blacks'. Probably the announcement that Turtill has gone to St Helens, a by no means wealthy organisation, will cause surprise but there were other interests than football in the matter. Turtill's inclinations have been for St. Helens for some time, and when the club secured

him remunerative employment the rest was easy. Mrs. Turtill has accompanied her husband to England, but during the latter's northern expedition she has resided with relatives in Bedfordshire, where Turtill will be located until he takes up residence in St. Helens.

The *Athletic News* then went on to add that Turtill was one of many players who were part of 'The Colonial Invasion' at the time, stating:

Rumour has it that before next season is much advanced, Frawley and O'Malley, two prominent Australian professionals, will be seen at Warrington. This will bring the number of 'aliens' on the registers of Northern Union clubs to fifteen, and probably a good team could be selected from the following:- Bolewski (Leigh), Turtill and Kelly (St Helens), Devereux and Morton (Hull), George Smith, Anlezark and Deane (Oldham), Todd, Johnson and McCabe (Wigan), Trevarthen and Wrigley (Huddersfield), Lavery (at present unattached to any club), Frawley and O'Malley (Warrington). Perhaps some difficulty would be experienced in making a complete set of forwards, but the burly Wrigley might step up into that breach.

Turtill made his St Helens debut in a 30-7 League defeat at Hull KR on 2 September 1909, and went on to make a total of 140 appearances for the club, scoring three tries and kicking 200 goals for an overall points tally of 409. He also captained the side on numerous occasions. As well as playing for Saints, he owned and ran a pub, the Nelson Hotel, in the centre of town. Domestically he was well settled too with Hubert and Mabel having three sons, Alan Cecil, Roy Tyrell and Kenneth Sydney.

But events were changing on the rugby field. Turtill's last St Helens appearance was in a 22-8 home defeat to Warrington on 21 February 1914 – with the criticism he was receiving from the Saints faithful at the time proving the final straw, as the *Liverpool Echo* of 25 February explained underneath the headline 'St Helens Full Back Resigns.' It reported:

> At the meeting of the St. Helens Rugby Football Club Committee last night a letter was read from Mr. H.S. Turtill, the well-known New Zealander, stating that after the criticism levelled at him during the last few weeks, and especially this week-end, he had come to the conclusion that the best thing he could do in the interests of the club was to resign. During the years he had been with them he had always done his best to serve them faithfully, and he thanked the committee for the cordial manner in which they have treated him. The committee, after discussing the matter, passed the following resolution:- 'That having carefully considered the letter received from H.S. Turtill, the captain of the team, tendering his resignation as a present playing member of the club, the committee resolve that the same be accepted. At the same time we desire to record our sincere appreciation of Turtill's good services to the club in the past, and our keen regrets that circumstances have arisen such as mentioned in his letter to cause him to take the step he has done.'

The Greatest Sacrifice

Turtill enlisted in St Helens in the opening months of the war, moving up to the rank of Sergeant in the 422nd Field Company, Royal Engineers. In April 1918, Turtill and his company were located in the Givenchy and Festubert area of northern France. They were there when the Battles of the Lys commenced – the German Spring Offensive Operation Georgette phase. The opening phase, on 9 April, was the Battle of Estaires. Turtill was killed during the initial bombardment at the age of 38. There was also a brief mention of the incident in which Turtill lost his life in the unit war diary, which recorded:

> Enemy opened his offensive by an intense barrage. The officers billet was hit.[3]

The news of his death was reported across the country, typified by the *Liverpool Echo* of 1 May 1918, which stated:

> Sergeant H.S. Turtill ..... has been killed in action. He had been for over two years in the local Engineers, and had seen a great deal of fighting. He was widely respected in football circles, being a very clever player, and an excellent captain for the St Helens team.

This was followed by a far larger and more comprehensive piece in an article in the *St Helens Newspaper and Advertiser*, which included a letter sent to his widow from Company Quartermaster Sergeant Harry Mercer of the Royal Engineers, who was also secretary of the St Helens club. The letter read:

> Dear Mrs Turtill – I dread the task which I am now

performing, knowing as I do the news I am giving you must cause both yourself and the dear little kiddies Sid loved so well the greatest pain and suffering. Poor old Sid, he has had to pay a great price in sacrificing his life in the cause of humanity, fighting for freedom and his King and country. Small recompense though it is, I feel sure it will be some consolation to you to know that his death was painless. Sleeping calmly in his billet, after a most fatiguing day, he was struck in the temple by a piece of one of the hundreds of shells with which the enemy heralded his attempt to drive us back in the morning of the 9th inst., and died instantly. To yourself and his dear family his loss must be terrible to bear, as I know it will also be to the wide circle of friends he enjoyed both in England and New Zealand. Both myself and his colleagues tender to you our heartfelt and sincere sympathy. He was loved by all who knew him, and those who, like myself, have been privileged to be his comrades, both on the playing fields in England and the battlefields of France, will miss him more than mere words can express. I have recovered most of his personal belongings, and when things quieten down a little I will send them to you. In the meantime, please accept my deepest sympathy – Yours in sorrow. H. MERCER C.Q.M.S.

Hubert Turtill is laid to rest in Brown's Road Cemetery, Festubert. His family returned to New Zealand after the war, although there was more heartache to come in the Second World War, when Alan was killed in North Africa on 29 November 1941 at the age of 32, serving as a Captain with the 21st Battalion New Zealand Infantry, whilst Kenneth was taken a Prisoner of War. He was liberated in 1945.

Another Northern Union player to be killed in the same area as Turtill during the German Spring Offensive was Warrington's Stanley Young, who fell on 18 April at Vermelles – around five miles away from his St Helens rival.

The Cheltenham-born scrum-half looked set for an incredibly successful career at Wilderspool, having signed for the club in the autumn of 1913 as a 24-year-old from Abertillery Rugby Union Club and making his Northern Union debut in a 4-0 home win over Leeds on 29 November. That was to prove to be the first of 60 senior appearances for Warrington, as Young became a virtual ever-present for the team. In almost no time at all, he was shaping up to potentially be one of Warrington's finest signings – until the Great War claimed his life.

James Stanley Young was born in Cinderford, Gloucestershire, one of coal miner Thomas and Fanny Young's (née Bevan) 12 children. His birth was officially registered in early 1889. The family were living in Tamworth in 1891, and spent time at Kettlebrooke before returning to Cinderford, where their son was soon proving to be an outstanding athlete. That talent was allowed to blossom on the rugby field during his time at Double View School, paving the way for him to impress in the 15-a-side code for Cinderford, Cheltenham and Gloucester.

He then moved to top Welsh club Abertillery for the start of the 1913-14 season, where he was also given the opportunity to work in the coal mines. In fact, such was his immediate impact that after a couple of games he was being touted as a future Welsh Rugby Union international. But just as he was starting to take the Welsh scene by storm, Young was lured away by Warrington in what at the time was clearly a big-money deal, as the *Gloucestershire Echo* revealed on 14 November 1913 under the headline 'Thunderbolt for Abertillery'. The article said:

> A sensation was created in 'Rugger' circles in Abertillery on Thursday, when the information was circulated that the club's fine outside-half, Stanley Young, formerly of Cheltenham, had been induced to sever connection with amateur Rugby and sign professional forms for the Warrington N.U. club. Since joining Abertillery in about the second week of the present season, Young had shown great form, and it was largely due to him that the side had performed so well.... Indeed, he displayed such cleverness in the half-dozen games in which he played for the club, that he was even mentioned as a strong candidate for a Welsh international cap ..... His loss will now be severely felt. It is stated that Young received the most tempting terms. He got a lump sum of £200, and the other terms were £2 10s. for a victory, 35s. for a draw, and 30s for a loss, with suitable employment.

Young wore a Warrington shirt for the first time in a trial game against Broughton Rangers Combination on 13 November 1913 and was then almost immediately thrust into the Northern Union limelight against Leeds. That alone made it a memorable period for Young. But, on top of that, he also married Rosaline Elizabeth Wood around the same time.

On the other hand, the fact Young proved a Warrington star from day one meant the newly-weds had no time to enjoy a honeymoon, with the half-back featuring in 23 of the club's final 25 games of the season – although he had to wait until the last game of the season to open his tryscoring account in the 11-5 home win over Hull KR on 18 April 1914.

In the 1914-15 season, Young missed just two games all season whilst also working as a greengrocer in Stockton Heath, the district in which he lived with his wife and children. In his spare time, he coached the St Thomas' team to win the Junior League Championship. But all of this came to an end with the Great War. His 60th and final Warrington appearance – he crossed for just two tries during that time - came on 24 April 1915 and an 18-10 home win over Widnes, in the club's final official game before the competition re-commenced at the end of the war.

Although Young initially continued to work as a greengrocer, he eventually enlisted in Warrington as a Gunner with the Royal Field Artillery in 1916. Subsequently, he transferred as a Private to the 11th Battalion Manchester Regiment, attached to the 127th Light Trench Mortar Battery – and on 18 April 1918, he was killed by a mortar shell at the age of 29.

When Young died near the village of Vermelles, his name was not mentioned in the battalion's unit war diary entry for that day, but it was pretty conclusive as to who it was referring to when mentioning casualties. The entry says:

> April 18: Fairly Quiet Day. Enemy T[rench] M[ortar] activity. 1 O.R. killed, 2 O.R. wounded.[4]

His death was confirmed in the *Warrington Guardian* on 4 May.

> Another member of the Warrington Rugby team
> to pay the supreme sacrifice is Private Stanley
> Young, who was killed by the bursting of a shell

on April 18th. Private Young joined the Manchester Regiment last year and had only been at the front a short time. In a letter to Mr. T.P. Bradshaw, secretary of the Warrington Rugby Club, Sergeant Simpson states that his platoon, of which Young was a member, have lost a gallant soldier.

Stanley Young is buried at the Philosophe British Cemetery, Mazingarbe.

In contrast to Young, who was a relative newcomer to the Northern Union game after making his senior debut in late 1913, former England international John 'Jack' Flynn was at the other end of the spectrum. His professional career got under way in the 1904-05 season when he left his native Cumbria for Swinton, although both his and Young's playing careers were brought to an abrupt end on the battlefields of northern France. Half-back Flynn was to fall just over two weeks after Young, on 4 May, at the age of 34.

And his death was another to hit the Northern Union family hard, with the high-profile and highly-decorated Flynn one of the game's real characters, as reflected in the fact he earned the nickname 'Dandy' Flynn due to his appearance and antics.

Born in 1883, the son of Hugh and Athelia Thomas Flynn (née Hocking), by 1891 he and his siblings were living with their paternal grandparents. The Whitehaven-born ace was a natural star almost as soon as he took to the rugby field, playing at junior level with distinction as a utility back at local clubs Whitehaven Recreation and Parton. In fact, in a *Lancashire Evening Post* article on 27 February 1904, a glowing piece was penned about the then 20-year-old Flynn under the headline 'A Parton Celebrity'.

J. Flynn is one of the prominent members of the Parton Football Club. He scales about 11st. 3lb., and stands about 5ft. 6in., and commenced his football career in a Whitehaven junior team about five years ago. In the season 1901-02 he joined the Whitehaven Recreation, and from that time he has rapidly come to the front and is now one of the best three-quarters Parton possess. Whilst playing for the Recreation, the club had the honour of being the runners-up in both the Cumberland Senior League and the North-Western League, and in the same year the Recreation team unexpectedly knocked Idle out of the Northern Union Cup Competition, before they were defeated by Swinton, Flynn taking an active part in both these ties. Possessed of a good turn of speed, a powerful kick and plenty of dash, Flynn attracted the notice of others than Cumbrians, and last season he was approached by a prominent Lancashire Northern Union club, but he declined the offer. Had he accepted, it would have added another name to the long list of players which Cumberland has already supplied to the first-class Northern Union clubs, and there is not the least doubt that he would have given a good account of himself in any company. Flynn first played for Parton in the season 1902-03. He is a most useful and versatile footballer, having played for that club as a centre three-quarter, wing three-quarter, and full-back, playing in either of these positions with equal ability. The Parton club are this season making a

strong bid for honours, and there is no man in the
team who is a greater favourite than Flynn with
the supporters.

Although Flynn initially shunned professional Northern
Union advances, he was finally persuaded to make the move
south to join Swinton. His signature was secured on 11
October 1904 for a fee of 15 shillings, with Flynn almost
immediately promoted to the first team. In fact, his Northern
Union debut came whilst he was a trialist against Wigan at
Central Park a month earlier on 3 September.

By the time he made the move to Swinton's neighbours,
Broughton Rangers, in 1906, the young Flynn had rattled up
61 senior appearances. By that stage, Flynn had established
himself as a high quality half-back, the major attacking spark
for his side. The Cumbrian was regarded as the ideal size for
an elusive half and possessed all the tricks of the trade, as his
Broughton Rangers' pen picture from 1908 proved:

> Flynn can punt effectively from either foot, and
> is what should be described as a bustling outside
> half-back who, if supported effectively, will cause
> trouble to defenders.

In the five years he was at the club, he featured 111 times, and
earned his one England cap against New Zealand at an icy
cold Central Park at Wigan in front of a 12,000 crowd on 11
January 1908. Flynn played a leading role in a narrow 18-16
triumph that day against an 'All Golds' side who included a
certain Hubert Sydney Turtill. Flynn also helped Cumberland
win the County Championship on three occasions.

But even though he was such a key member of the
Broughton set-up, he re-signed for his first Northern Union

club, Swinton, in early 1911, with the *Athletic News* one of those making the announcement on 30 January in their round-up of the week.

> The other event of the week is the return of J. Flynn to Swinton, after a sojourn of four or five seasons with Broughton Rangers. The transfer fee in this case will not be large, but I believe Swinton have paid nearly half the amount they received from the Rangers when the Whitehaven player was originally transferred.

He made 19 appearances for Swinton during that second spell, before moving to Bradford Northern in September 1914. Unfortunately, they never got the chance to see him in action for them, with Flynn taking the decision to enlist in Carlisle with the locally-based Border Regiment, on 3 September 1914. Dark complexioned with brown hair and blue eyes, according to his surviving service records,[5] his occupation at the time was a miner, a change from the publican of the 1911 census.

After completing his training, where he rose to the rank of Sergeant but within a fortnight reverted back down to Private at his own request, he arrived in France in mid-July 1915. In his first 10 months, he was involved in a number of bloody exchanges with the enemy, but in June 1916 was hospitalised with a bout of influenza and bronchitis.

He then re-joined his unit and by June 1917 had been promoted to Lance Corporal for a second time. Two months later, he was wounded in action, but again returned to the front, where he was killed on 4 May 1918 as the Allies began to push the Germans out of the Somme region. The unit war diary describes the incident at Forceville which cost Flynn his life, referring to him by name. The entry states:

Shell of a H[*igh*] V[*elocity*] gun killed Corporal
Flynn of R[*egimental*] P[*olice*] and the Colonel's
servant just outside HQ mess.....[6]

John 'Jack' Flynn is buried at Forceville Communal Cemetery
and Extension in France, leaving a widow Martha, who he
had married in Whitehaven on 23 February 1903.

Then on 14 May, St Helens lost a second star player in
the year in Jimmy Flanagan. Like Saints teammate Turtill,
Flanagan was one of the Northern Union's most respected
backs, with the homegrown talent having scored 125 tries and
three goals in 231 appearances for the club. A total of 99 were
scored on the wing, 25 at centre and one at stand-off.

Born in St Helens to parents Dennis and Mary on 5
April 1886 and raised on Frederick Street, in the Windle area
of town, Flanagan played football during his junior days, but
he eventually made the switch effortlessly to the oval-ball
game, with his natural speed and balance proving highly-
effective weapons out wide.

The start to his Saints career did not bode well as he
made his debut in a heavy 38-0 home defeat to Oldham on 5
September 1908. But it was not long before the new winger was
proving his worth and crossing for tries on a regular basis, with
his wing-centre partnership with Halifax-born centre Jimmy
Greenwood proving one of the most lethal combinations in the
competition. In fact, on three occasions Flanagan scored four
tries in a game – against Barrow, Warrington and Hunslet –
while he also scored two further hat tricks for good measure.
The 1909-10 and 1910-11 seasons were particularly profitable
for the prolific three-quarter, who chalked up a highly-
impressive 60 tries in just 68 senior appearances.

Not surprisingly, his exploits earned him representative
recognition, with Flanagan being capped six times by

Lancashire between 1909 and 1914. Another highlight during his illustrious playing career came in February 1909 when he scored a try in St Helens' 9-0 victory over the touring Australians. It was after his exploits against the Australians that Flanagan began to earn 'star' status, with an *Athletic News* feature on 7 November 1910 telling the story.

> James Flanagan is one of Lancashire's most promising wing three-quarter backs ..... he commenced his football career when 16 years of age with a local Association club, and in turn played with Skelmersdale United, Hardshaw Juniors and St. Helens Town before the Rugby Club's officials recognised his abilities. This occurred during the Works Club Competition in 1908, when Flanagan was playing with a team boasting the title of 'All Blacks'. The club committee were on the lookout for promising talent, and Flanagan caught the eye. He was a registered member of the local Association team, but it was evident that there was the makings of a Rugby player in him. Flanagan then, as now, was of a very retiring disposition, and the St. Helens secretary tells how he and two members of the committee walked about near his home for several hours before the object of their visit could be induced to enter into a conversation. Then Flanagan was taken round to the secretary's office, and before midnight the necessary forms had been signed. At the practice games which followed, Flanagan showed grand form and was at once placed in the senior team. His first game was against Oldham – a formidable task for a

mere youth, and so well did he acquit himself that from that day he has been a regular member of the St. Helens team, and last year played in every match. He was a most prolific scorer. He placed 33 tries to his credit, and after his play in the county trial game he was selected for Lancashire against Yorkshire. He stands 5ft. 8½in., and weighs 10st. 10lb., and did not football claim his attention, Flanagan would achieve distinction on the running track.

But even though he was another leading Northern Union star, chemist's assistant Flanagan wasted very little time enlisting with the South Lancashire Regiment after the outbreak of war on 7 September 1914. Posted to the 11th Battalion (St Helens Pioneers), he was still able to play for Saints on a regular basis during his training. With training taking place locally, he actually featured 31 times during the 1914-15 season, including the heavy 37-3 Challenge Cup final defeat to Huddersfield's 'Team of All Talents' at Oldham on 1 May.

That was to be the Northern Union's final official competitive fixture during the war years, although the makeshift Northern Rugby Football Union Wartime Emergency League seasons did, of course, still take place between late 1915 and early 1919. And it would be fair say that St Helens' 1914-15 Challenge Cup campaign was a major tale in itself, with the backdrop of the start of the Great War dominating everyone's thoughts as Saints marched somewhat surprisingly towards their final showdown.

Despite an average season when they finished eighth, the Cup form of Flanagan's St Helens was in stark contrast. With the homegrown ace playing a key Cup role, the men from Knowsley Road overcame a challenging route to their

Huddersfield rendezvous, having to win away at junior club Featherstone in the opening round, followed by Swinton, Keighley and Rochdale (they beat the Hornets 9-2 in a semi-final replay at Wigan) to secure their final prize.

But, as John Huxley reflects in his book *The Rugby League Challenge Cup*, he believed a reporter in a prominent St Helens newspaper 'must have been cynical' as he wrote about Saints' successful cup run in the midst of the events taking place on the Western Front. The reporter wrote:

> I wonder what would have been the fate of any prophet who foretold this year's events. If such a prophet had begun by declaring that Germany would be fighting England in 1915, he might have been believed. If he had said Germany would have been fighting England, France, Russia and a few more – he might have stood a chance of saving his skin, provided he could run. But if he had said Saints would win every round of the Cup up to the final, away from home – he would probably have been extinguished on the spot as a dangerous lunatic at large.

As it was, St Helens were simply unable to match Huddersfield in that final, with their cause not helped by the threat of a player strike just minutes before kick-off. Because of a lack of club funds in the wake of the ever-growing wartime financial pressures, club chairman Tom Phillips announced to his players getting changed in the Oldham dressing rooms that there would be no extra cash bonus for winning the Cup. The rate would be the usual ten shillings (50 pence), even though it was traditional to offer more for important fixtures.

The players were stunned, and only the rallying words of Saints skipper Tom Barton, who pointed out that a Cup winner's medal alone was worth around £3, saved the day and gave the 8,000 crowd a game to watch. The Cup final was to be Flanagan's last major appearance before he lost his life in May 1918, just as it was for Huddersfield loose-forward Fred Longstaff, killed on the Somme just under two years earlier.

Flanagan impressed during his time in the Army, having being appointed Lance Sergeant on 30 January 1915. However, it was not until the end of the year – 6 November – that he and his battalion set sail from Southampton, reaching camp outside Le Havre the following day. Flanagan was then involved in the 1916 Somme Offensive, most significantly during the Battle of Albert, before the St Helens star suffered an accidental hand injury on 14 October 1916.[7] He was immediately admitted to 140 Field Ambulance and three days later shipped home for treatment aboard the HS 'Stad Antwerpen', with the news revealed in the *St Helens Reporter*.

Sergt. Jimmy Flanagan, of the South Lancs, the well-known St Helens three-quarter, has been wounded in France, and is now in the Northern General Hospital, Leicester. Writing to his wife this week, he says – 'Just a line to let you know I am doing well. You do not need to worry about me, as I am all right. I am in a very good hospital and the sisters are very kind. Let Mr Frank McCormick know where I am, for he comes here sometimes on business. Give the children my best love, and tell them I will soon be in St Helens to see them. It does your heart good to be in Old England again. I was very lucky coming away when I had got wounded, as the Germans were shelling all the

way, and it took me some time to get to the
dressing station. From there I went in a hospital in
France, and then got a boat for England.'

Although Flanagan appears to have played the injury down,
he did not embark for France again until 1 April 1918. After
a brief spell with the 2nd Battalion, he once more joined the
11th, allocated to their 'A' Company in mid-April. The unit
war diary entry reveals that when he received the wound that
was to prove fatal, the battalion were based at St-Jan-ter-
Biezen and taken by train daily to work on the Ouderdom
switch line near Reninghelst when he was struck in the left
breast by a piece of shrapnel from a shell on 8 May. He was
admitted to 99 Field Ambulance and then to 13 Casualty
Clearing Station, where he died of his wounds six days later.
On 20 May, his death was reported in the *Liverpool Echo*.

> Official news was received this morning by Mrs.
> Flanagan of Central-street, St. Helens, stating that
> her husband, Sergeant James Flanagan, the well-
> known three-quarter back of the St. Helens N.U.
> team, had died of wounds. He was one of the
> cleverest three-quarters St. Helens ever produced.
> He was 31 years of age, and had worked all his
> life at Gerard's Bridge Chemical Works.....

Flanagan is buried at Arneke British Cemetery in Northern
France. When he died he left a widow, Ellen (maiden name
Graham), who he married in 1909, and four children, James,
Patrick, Mary and Eileen. Amongst the personal effects
returned to Ellen were his disc, letters, a pocket book, badge,
cigarette case, three coins, a small bag, three religious medals
and a Rosary – the latter items indicating his Catholic faith.

Summer 1918 –
The Tide Begins to Turn

18

By the summer of 1918, the German Spring Offensive had lost its momentum. German casualties had been catastrophic, with estimates that the strength of their Army had fallen from five million in the March to four million by the autumn. On top of that, their lines had been stretched far too wide to be effective any more, and the fresh, enthusiastic and newly-trained Americans were starting to arrive in force to provide the Allies with a huge psychological boost. But even though it was the Germans who were now on the back foot, the Western Front was still a very dangerous place to be, with the British continuing to suffer a high casualty rate of their own.

In the final six months of the war, the Northern Union lost several more star men, including Wigan winger Lewis Bradley, who died of wounds on 20 June at the age of 29.

Bradley was yet another rugby league star who made the trip north after excelling in the rival 15-a-side code. Born in 1889 in Ruardean, Gloucestershire to parents John George and Ann[1]

Bradley – Lewis's mother's maiden name was actually Lewis – he was one of their eight children, although two died in childhood. Originally a coal miner, John George took over the family pub, the Roebuck Inn at Ruardean Woodside, in 1903.

From a very early age Bradley was impressing on the rugby field for local club Cinderford and, aged 18, joined top Welsh union club Pontypool, over the Gloucestershire/Wales border. In the 1910-11 season he was the Welsh side's top tryscorer, with an impressive 22 tries to his credit. The talented winger's exploits soon caught the attention of the Northern Union scouts, including those of Salford and Wigan, with Wigan finally winning the race to secure Bradley's signature in the winter of 1911, as revealed in the *Yorkshire Post and Leeds Intelligencer* of 2 December 1911. The headline read 'Important Capture by Wigan', with the report stating:

> Lewis Bradley, a well-known Rugby Union three-quarter back, reached Wigan last night in the company of two officials of the Wigan Football Club, for whom Bradley yesterday signed on. Although only 21 years of age, Bradley was regarded as the likely recipient of an international cap, and several Northern Union clubs had been most anxious to secure his services. He is 5ft. 7in. high, and weighs 11 stone. He is to make his initial appearance with the Wiganers at Central Park against Wakefield this afternoon. His capture is regarded as the most important for a considerable period.

By all accounts, his debut went exceptionally well, which was something the *Wigan Observer and District Advertiser* seized upon in their 5 December edition.

Lewis Bradley ..... who made a successful first appearance for the Wigan club on Saturday, is a native of Cinderford, and is consequently an Englishman ..... He is twenty-one years of age, and his business is that of a works stores clerk. After Saturday's successful start he returned to his home for a few days, but he will of course sojourn in Wigan during the football season. All the critics unite in saying that rarely has a three-quarter shown such promise on his first appearance with a Northern Union club. In all departments he was brilliant, and one would have thought he had been playing the Northern Union code for some time. If one can judge from first appearances, Wigan have obtained the services of an exceptionally capable player, and just at the right moment. The spectators in their appreciation of his play simply 'rose' at him. On his part, Bradley was highly gratified at their demonstration of approval, and was modestly inclined to under-rate his play. He wished he could have done better. Bradley is a left wing player, and on the right he is acting in an unaccustomed position. The opinion seems to have prevailed for some time in Wales that he would be induced to join some Northern Union club, but that if he remained in the Rugby Union he would be selected for the highest honours ..... It is interesting to know that Bradley is a teetotaller and non-smoker.

According to the *Gloucester Citizen* of 9 December 1911 'the price given to the ex-Cinderford player was £200 and £5 expenses.' That was clearly a large amount of money for the time, but from day one it was obvious it was a price worth paying as Bradley immediately became a massive crowd favourite, scoring tries at an incredible rate. In fact, in his 124 Wigan appearances he scored an amazing 136 tries – an average of 1.1 tries per game, which rates alongside Martin Offiah at 1.17.

Within a month of his arrival at Central Park, the flyer from the Forest of Dean was earning legendary status as he scorched over for five tries in a home win over Barrow on New Year's Day 1912. He then went even better in the 1913-14 season, equalling Jimmy Leytham's club record of six tries in a game in the 33-9 home destruction of Rochdale Hornets on 7 March 1914. That helped him to a season's haul of 39 tries, including three hat tricks.

Although war was declared just before the start of the following campaign, Bradley was still a virtual ever-present in the Wigan line-up, crossing for tries on a further 25 occasions. But he enlisted with the Royal Field Artillery (RFA), in Wigan in mid-1915, and during his military training at Leeds made several appearances in the Wartime Emergency League for the Headingley club, as well as for Wigan. He went overseas later in the war, possibly as late as March 1918, where he served as a Driver with the 410th Battery in the 96th Brigade. His responsibilities as a Driver with the RFA would have included moving the artillery pieces to wherever they were required, and the care and maintenance of the horses which were the transport mainstay for this task.

Bradley's luck ran out just as the war had swung the Allies' way. He was hit by an enemy shell on 18 June and transported back to a Casualty Clearing Station near Vignacourt, where he passed away on the morning of the 20 June.

The seriousness of his injuries were made clear in an article in the *Forest of Dean Mercury*, which published a letter from a Sister E.O. Schofield, the sister-in-charge at the hospital where Bradley died, to his parents at the Roebuck Inn. Addressing the letter to his mother, she wrote:

> Dear Mrs Bradley. Your son, Driver L. Bradley, 118613 R.F.A., was admitted here late on the 18th and died at 10.30a.m. to-day, the 20th. He had very severe multiple wounds of the back, head (which had fractured his skull), and both thighs. He was quite sensible until last night, and since then has been only semi-conscious. The poor boy had been badly infected with gas gangrene, and it rapidly spread and eventually caused his death. He left no messages, as yesterday he did not realise he was dying. He will be buried by our own Chaplain in the military cemetery near here, where so many of our fine men are lying. I hope it is a little comfort to you to know he was in a British hospital.....

Lewis's elder sister, Ellen, who was living in Gloucestershire, informed the Central Park club of his death. Her letter was printed in the *Wigan Observer and District Advertiser* on 27 June and included the following lines:

> His heart was in Wigan, and we should be grateful to you if you know of any of his friends if you will let them know ..... I have my youngest brother a prisoner of war in Germany; he wasn't sent out until 28th March and was missing between 9th and 18th April, and we have heard

> nothing since of him. It all helps to add to our
> burden. I don't know if you have a photograph
> of Lew; if not I will send you one. Poor Lew,
> perhaps it is better as it is than to be a cripple.

Lewis Bradley was the only one of the 21 Wigan players who enlisted to lose his life, and he is buried at Vignacourt British Cemetery on the Somme. Bradley's younger brother Sidney did survive the war.

Having mounted a successful counter-attack against what would prove to be the German's last offensive of the war at the Second Battle of the Marne during June and July, the Allies prepared to go in for the kill. With the German Army virtually on its knees and now with no hope of emerging victorious, the British, French, Belgian and American Armies mounted a series of offensives which were to force the Germans back towards their own borders and eventually force them to sue for peace.

The final push began with the Battle of Amiens on 8 August and signalled the start of the 'Hundred Days Offensive', which would end with the Armistice on 11 November 1918. The gains from 8 August onwards were huge, with German chief Ludendorff describing the Battle of Amiens as 'the black day of the German Army'. His troops took such a pounding that day against an unstoppable co-ordinated Allied attack that he was fully aware this was the beginning of the end.

But even though the Germans were now an Army in full retreat, they were determined to defend the Hindenburg Line whatever the cost, thus denying their opponent the opportunity to force them all the way back to Berlin. With many Germans seemingly prepared to fight to the death to defend their nation's honour – as well as their country from potential invasion – the Allies continued to lose men. Those included Leeds player Sidney Clifford Abbott on 18 September.

Born in Liverpool in late 1890, the son of George and Lucy Abbott, the family were soon in Leeds and this is where he was baptised on 4 January 1891 at All Souls' Church. Abbott excelled at his local Burley Vale club before making the move to Headingley on 23 January 1912. His registration to Leeds was confirmed in the Yorkshire Post and Leeds Intelligencer on 14 February that year.

Unfortunately for Abbott, although his signing had been well received, the winger had to bide his time in the reserves before finally making his Northern Union debut away at Coventry on 11 November 1912. It was, however, well worth the wait as Abbott announced his first-team arrival by scoring two tries in a 32-13 triumph, in which one of the home side's three tries was scored by Howard Davis, who went on to join Warrington and lost his life in the war in 1915.

Both of Abbott's tries came in the first half, as the *Leeds Mercury* reported in their match analysis the following day.

> Leeds, visiting Coventry yesterday, atoned somewhat for the defeat sustained against Batley on Saturday, by winning easily by 32 points to 13 ..... The Leeds three-quarters handled skilfully, and showed greater speed than the Coventry backs ..... Throughout the first half Leeds had the help of a rather strong wind and did most of the attacking. Abbott was the first to get over, but the place kick failed. Later Campbell crossed for an unimproved try. Operations continued in Leeds's favour, and Abbott was responsible for a further try that remained unimproved.

But despite that strong start to his Headingley career, Abbott was unable to retain his place in the side and found himself back in the second string, although he was kept on the senior books for Northern Union back-up. When war was declared, however, Abbott's time with his hometown club came to an abrupt end, with the Leeds three-quarter called upon as an Army Reservist.

As a 17-year-old, Abbott enlisted with the 3rd Battalion, York and Lancaster Regiment (Special Reserve) on 14 August 1908 for six years' service. His profession at the time was a labourer. The Special Reserve were part-time soldiers who attended annual training and could be called up in the event of general mobilisation. Although he was mobilised days after the declaration of war, he served at home in the early months and was appointed a Lance Corporal at his home headquarters at Hylton Camp, Sunderland on 18 January 1915. And later that year, on 13 August, he was discharged from the Army after serving his seven years, one year more than his original terms.[2] In his discharge papers it stated his character had been 'exemplary' throughout that time. The discharge papers described him as 5ft 6in, with hazel eyes and brown hair.[3]

However, with a war on, Abbott soon re-enlisted under the Derby Scheme on 11 December 1915. He was placed on the Class B Reserve, which meant he resumed civilian life as a bricklayer, and married munitions worker Lily Robinson at St Matthew's, Leeds in June 1916. A month after his marriage he was mobilised and posted back to the 3rd Battalion of the York and Lancasters. His recall earned him a £15 Bounty, an inducement introduced in 1916 to attract former soldiers.

He then embarked on a period of training in preparation for life on the Western Front, eventually going out to France at the end of March 1918 where he was initially with the 6th Battalion, before transferring to the regiment's 2nd Battalion, where he received his Sergeant's stripes in May 1918. On 18 September 1918 Abbott's battalion was part of a major early-morning attack, north west of St Quentin. Even in the assembly trenches just after midnight they were subject to a combination of high explosive and gas heavy shelling. The actual assault was described in the unit war diary.

> At 5.20a.m. under a splendid creeping barrage the battalion moved forward to the attack on enemy positions. The entire objectives allotted to the battalion, and named the GREEN LINE, being the line of DOUAI TRENCH, CHAMPAGNE TRENCH and FRESNOY TRENCH, ... were captured by the leading companies C & D. at 6.30a.m. At 10a.m. a determined enemy counter attack was delivered by the enemy from the direction of FRESNOY CEMETERY & WOOD. This counter attack succeeded in driving our left company back into CHAMPAGNE TRENCH. Mainly on account of casualties suffered during the advance, the left company was too weak to counter attack. From the junction of CHAMPAGNE TRENCH and BUGEAUD ALLEY, the GREEN LINE Southwards was held and consolidated. As a result of these operations about 50 prisoners were captured and many enemy dead left. The casualties suffered during the advance, by the battalion were:- OFFICERS: Killed 3, Wounded 2, Missing 1. OTHER RANKS: Killed 27, Wounded 140, Missing 43.[4]

One of those to lose his life during the attack was Sidney Clifford Abbott, who is commemorated at the Vis-en-Artois Memorial in France.

There was relatively little mention of his death in the Leeds papers, although there was a line in the *Yorkshire Evening Post* on 25 October 1918 under the list of war dead:

> Sergt. S.C. ABBOTT, York and Lancasters, of 3 Herbert Grove, Meanwood Road, Leeds, formerly employed by the Albion Brewery Co.

It was followed up with another *Yorkshire Evening Post* announcement on 16 December 1918, which read:

> ABBOTT – At 3, Herbert Grove, on the 11th December, to the wife of the late Sergt. S.C. Abbott (nee Lily Robinson), a daughter.

A daughter, Dorothy, he never got to see.

Bradford Northern's Fred Longthorpe was the next Northern Union loss. He was to die of his wounds on 20 September 1918.

Born in the Laisterdyke area of Bradford in 1889, he was the son of Joshua Priestley Longthorpe and his wife Emma (née England). His father appears to have been absent from the family home in census records, being based in Lockwood. Longthorpe grew up with his mother and older siblings in Laisterdyke. After completing his education at Belle Vue secondary school, he joined the family's greengrocer business. But in October 1907 he signed up with the Militia, in the Royal Army Medical Corps. Two months later he took a step further, enlisting for 12 years with the Royal Garrison Artillery (RGA) at Gosport. A strapping lad, even at this young age, he stood at 5ft 10½in and weighed in at 152lbs. He was also described as having grey eyes and light brown hair.[5]

He attended several military training courses, including map reading and telephony, and was specially commended on courses for gunnery, electricity and range finding. During his time with the RGA he served in Malta with the 99th Company and was promoted to the rank of Bombardier (Corporal) on 4 May 1912, although within a month he had decided to buy his way out of the Army and return to work at the family greengrocers. And on 17 September 1912, he was able to combine his 'day job' with a new career as a Bradford Northern rugby league player after signing from Westfield Albion.

The club had high hopes that their new homegrown three-quarter would prove a prize asset, with a promising 28 September 1912 debut in a 12-7 home defeat against Huddersfield backing that up, as the *Bradford Telegraph and Argus* proclaimed:

> He made a successful debut last week against Huddersfield. He is a player of great promise, a very steady and tricky man, and a fearless tackler, and is expected to prove a rare acquisition to the club.

Yet despite such a promising first appearance, he went on to make just nine further first-team starts, with six more coming during the 1912-13 campaign and three in the opening three months of the 1913-14 season. His last Northern Union match was a thumping 61-7 defeat to Huddersfield at Fartown on 19 November 1913. Although he did not play again following that embarrassing defeat to the men in claret and gold, Longthorpe remained on Bradford's books.

On 8 April 1913 at Low Moor Wesleyan Chapel, 23-year-old Longthorpe married Emily Lincoln, 12 years his senior. He subsequently moved to the Fartown area of Huddersfield. This was the address he gave on 30 December 1916 when he attested at Halifax as a Private with the 2/28th (County of London) Battalion (Artists Rifles). This was a route to becoming an officer, and he quickly applied for a Temporary Commission in the Regular Army. The paperwork claimed his father's occupation was a vocalist – not the fish and fruit shopkeeper shown elsewhere. His application was accepted and he joined Number 2 Machine Gun Corps Cadet Battalion at Pirbright at the beginning of March 1917. He obtained his commission to Temporary 2nd Lieutenant with the Machine Gun Corps (Heavy) with effect from 27 June 1917, the announcement being made in the 7 July 1917 edition of the *London Gazette*.[6]

By September 1917 he was out in France and the following February he found himself posted to Number 2 Gun Carrier Company, part of the Tank Corps. These gun carriers were tracked vehicles with lifting capabilities which were auxiliaries to tanks, following behind them in a supply role carrying troops, ammunition and artillery to support the infantry when they advanced beyond the range of regular guns behind the lines.

He was eventually injured on 19 September 1918 during a major six-day Somme offensive in heavy rain as the British broke through a 17-mile front to penetrate three miles into German territory, in preparation for the push towards the Hindenburg Line. The 29-year-old Longthorpe suffered a gunshot wound to the right thigh and was taken to No43 Casualty Clearing Station, but despite the medical staffs' efforts to save his life, he died the following day and is buried at Thilloy Road Cemetery, Beaulencourt, France. The inventory of personal effects sent to his widow make interesting reading and are reflective of his rank. They included a pair of gold links, one gold safety pin, one gold watch and chain (damaged), one metal watch (damaged), two plain gold rings, one silver sovereign case and two pipes. One can only wonder if the damaged items were a result of the events on the day he incurred his fatal wounds.

Then, just over a month later, on 21 October, James Patrick Breen of Widnes died of his wounds at the age of 27.

Paddy Breen was a Widnes lad through and through, having been born in the town in 1891 to parents James and Mary Breen. As a youngster he was educated at St Marie's School and learned his rugby trade at Ditton Recreation – Ditton was a residential area of Widnes – and then moved on to sign for Widnes as a centre on 20 January 1914. He was working as a labourer at the Pilkington Sullivan works in Widnes at the time.

His signature was secured just days after he had made a successful Widnes debut in a 9-0 reserve team triumph over Rochdale, which was recorded in the *Nantwich Guardian*. The report said:

> At Lowerhouse-lane on Saturday. The home team included Breen and W. O'Garra, their latest acquisition from Ditton Recs ..... In the second half W. O'Garra, Harding and Kelly scored tries for the home team, who won by nine points to nil.

Breen was unable to break into the first team that season and remained in the 'A' team for the rest of the 1913-14 campaign. But after impressing for the reserves, he was handed his Northern Union debut on the wing in a 7-0 home win over League champions Salford on 17 October 1914. He went on to make four more first-team appearances – three at centre and one at stand-off – before his promising Northern Union career was brought to an abrupt end by the hostilities.

During the war he continued to play for his hometown club in the Wartime Emergency League with appearances noted as late as April 1917. Unfortunately, that would be the final time he would be seen in Widnes colours. Breen enlisted in Widnes with the Royal Garrison Artillery and went out to France at Eastertime 1918, where he served with the 132nd Heavy Battery.

Breen was wounded as the big guns pushed the Germans further and further back. He was evacuated from the front, died at a Casualty Clearing Station and is buried at the Roisel Communal Cemetery Extension on the Somme. The news of his death was recorded in the *Widnes Weekly News and District Reporter* of 15 November under the headline 'Popular Widnes Footballer Dies from Wounds'.

Footballers and athletes in Widnes district will hear with sorrow of the death from wounds received in action in France of Gunner James Patrick (Paddy) Breen, the eldest son of Mr. and Mrs. J. Breen, of Victoria street, Widnes ..... At billiards he was known outside as well as inside the town as a member of St. Marie's C.Y.M.S. League team. In football he was prominent as a centre threequarter with the Widnes club for two seasons, following several seasons with the A team and with Ditton Recs. He was employed at Pilkington-Sullivan works before enlisting on the 18th October last, and he went to France on Good Friday last. A letter from the matron of the 41st Casualty Clearing Station stated that he was admitted on the 21st October, having been severely wounded in the abdomen, thigh and arm. His condition was very critical, and everything was done to save him, but he passed away quickly and peacefully at 11.30 at night. He was not able to speak, and did not leave any message; he was too ill to be conscious of any pain.....

Sadly, the Widnes player was the second member of the Breen family to lose his life, with younger brother John of the King's Own (Royal Lancaster) Regiment having been killed in action in Belgium on 8 May 1915 and commemorated on the Menin Gate at Ypres.

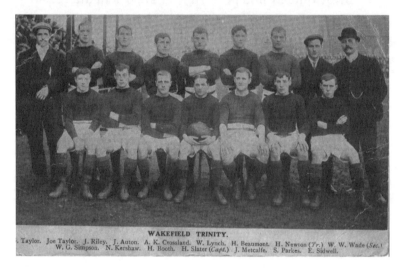

WAKEFIELD TRINITY.

. Taylor.   Joe Taylor.   J. Riley.   J. Auton.   A. K. Crossland.   W. Lynch.   H. Beaumont.   H. Newton (*Tr.*)   W. W. Wade (*Sec.*)
W. G. Simpson.   N. Kershaw.   H. Booth.   H. Slater (*Capt.*)   J. Metcalfe.   S. Parkes.   E. Sidwell.

Wakefield's Billy Simpson lines up with his pre-war teammates

courtesy of Wakefield Trinity Heritage

The Armistice but No End to the Deaths

19

It was not just on the Western Front where the Central Powers' resistance was crumbling rapidly in the second half of 1918. Like the Germans, the Austro-Hungarians, Bulgarians and Turks were struggling to keep their opponents at bay. In the Middle East, the British were enjoying major success against the ever-weakening Turkish Ottoman Empire, while the Austro-Hungarians and Bulgarians were finding it increasingly difficult to contain the resurgent Italians and Serbians.

It had, however, been a different story towards the end of 1917, particularly on the Italian Front where the tide was turning dramatically in the Central Powers' favour. To keep their ally in the war, the Germans joined forces with the stuttering Austrians to show their solidarity and mount a massive offensive against the Italians at the Battle of Caporetto in October and November of that year. It was a battle that virtually destroyed the Italian Army – and that was the last thing the British and French needed. Defeat for the Italians would enable the Germans and her allies to focus the vast majority of their attention on securing victory on the Western Front. As a result, both the British and French were forced to send troops to support the Italians and keep that front operational.

Among the British contingent was Bradford Northern's Harry Basil Wray. The 32-year-old Company Sergeant Major would be the last Northern Union player to die before the Armistice was signed, losing his life on 29 October 1918 – just six days before the conflict on the Italian Front came to an end. When he passed away, he had served a total of 14 years in the Army, having been a soldier both before, during and after his time in the Bradford Northern ranks.

Born in Malton to parents Mark and Mary Elizabeth Wray, his birth was registered in early 1887 and his baptism took place at Huttons Ambo parish church on 6 March 1887. He grew up in York and after leaving school enlisted in the West Yorkshire Regiment. By 1911 he was a Corporal in the 1st Battalion out in India.

When he returned home he played rugby union for Horton RFC before signing for Bradford on 3 March 1914. He was unable to break into the first team before the end of the 1913-14 season, but made his Northern Union debut in the second game of the following campaign, featuring in the second row in a 5-5 home draw with Huddersfield on 12 September. Unfortunately, however, it was already clear at that time that his appearances for Bradford would be limited due to his military commitments.

After war was declared he was back in the Army, spending his initial months training new recruits in York. That meant his time at Bradford was restricted, and he featured just six times in his debut 1914-15 season – although he would not have been proud to have been part of a Bradford side that lost five and drew one of the six matches in which he was involved.

His military duties meant he did not feature at all in the 1915-16 'friendly' matches – although he did marry Eliza D Worthington in 1915 and had a son, John, a year later. He then turned out for his club seven times in the 1916-17 Wartime Emergency League. However, the by now Sergeant Major Wray's most notable playing appearance in 1917 came in early May when he was part of a Yorkshire Northern Union team that beat the New Zealand Army, which included several All Blacks in its ranks, 19-8. It was a charity match played under Rugby Union rules with the proceeds going to war funds.

It was not long after this eye-catching success that Wray was preparing to be sent to the Italian Front, with the Bradford man and his fellow soldiers playing a huge military part in picking up the pieces after the Italian rout at Caporetto, and in doing so successfully preventing the Central Powers from making a decisive breakthrough.

Wray's service included time with the 10th Battalion of the Duke of Wellington's (West Riding Regiment).[1] But it was with the 11th Battalion West Yorkshire Regiment, in the final push to drive the enemy away from Italy, that cost the further promoted Company Sergeant Major Wray his life, during the Battle of Vittorio Veneto. The offensive got under way on 24 October 1918, with Wray's battalion stationed along the Piave River, which had been the scene of heavy fighting for several months. Led by the British, French and Italians, they were very quickly overwhelming their Austro-Hungarian foe in an onslaught that would hammer the final nail into the crumbling Habsburg Empire coffin. Victory was eventually achieved on 4 November.

The events of the 29 October, when Wray was killed, are recorded in E Wyrall's official regimental history *The West Yorkshire Regiment in the War*. It read:

The operations of 28th October were practically one success after another. At 12.30a.m. the attack was launched and, with the exception of an Austrian machine-gun nest which for a short while held up 'B' Company on the left, the assault proceeded and practically without opposition. By 2.30p.m., all objectives had been reached and patrols were pushed forward to discover the enemy. 'D' Company ..... captured and cleared Borgo Villa and later Soffratta, taking many prisoners. Finally (during the night 28th/29th), 'A' Company secured the southern bank of the Monticano, north of Soffratta, in order to enable the battalion to get across the river quickly on 29th. One hundred Austrians were taken in the latter affair, but C.S.M. Wray was killed.

Casualties in the 11th West Yorkshires between 27 and 29 October, when 1,000 prisoners and four guns were captured, were two officers and 58 other ranks wounded, and 11 other ranks killed. Wray was indeed unlucky. His actions in the campaign did not go unrecognised. The posthumous announcement of a Distinguished Conduct Medal for a previous incident was made in the *London Gazette*, ironically at around the time of his death. The citation read:

For conspicuous gallantry and devotion to duty when in charge of twenty men during a raid. By his dash and able leadership he set all ranks a fine example, was responsible for many prisoners being taken, and brought his party back without a casualty. He had previously done fine work.[2]

He was also awarded the Italian Silver Medal First Class.

Unfortunately, the announcement of his death was a mix-up, with the wrong Wray initially reported to have died, as described in the *Leeds Mercury* of 16 November:

> Information has reached Bradford to the effect that Sergt.-Major H.B. Wray D.C.M., a well-known Rugby Union football official, was killed in action on the Italian Front on October 29th.

But a week later, the *Yorkshire Evening Post* announced:

> The regretted death in action of C.S.M. Wray on the Italian Front has led in some papers to a confusion of names. It was Wray, the Bradford Northern forward, whose fall was announced, not S.H. Wray, the Bradford member of the Yorkshire Rugby Union Committee.

Harry Basil Wray is buried in Tezze British Cemetery, Italy.

Although Wray was the last Northern Union player to die while the war was still raging, he was not the last to die of wounds suffered during the conflict. In fact, two major names in the game lost their lives after the Armistice as a result of the injuries they suffered fighting for King and country. They were Hull's Fred Leonard Perrett and Wakefield's Billy Simpson.

Perrett was a player who excelled in both codes of rugby. The front-row forward shot to prominence in his native Wales where he won five caps for his country before switching codes in 1913, to have a brief spell with Leeds and then moving on to Hull. But he never had the chance to fulfil his league potential as his playing career was cut short by the war. He suffered serious injuries in the last few weeks of the conflict, finally losing his fight for life at a base hospital in northern France on 1 December 1918 at the age of 27.

Born on 9 May 1891 to George and Emma Perrett of Briton Ferry, South Wales, he began his rugby career with his hometown club, albeit at the relatively late age of 18, before he was signed up by Aberavon during the 1910-11 season, where he shone at both prop and hooker. He was employed as a steelworker at the time.

In the one-and-a-half seasons he was there, his stock rose all the time, gaining selection for a Rest of Wales XV in a charity clash at the end of the 1911-12 campaign. That was enough to convince the mighty Neath that this was the man they wanted, with Perrett joining them in September 1912. The 21-year-old went straight into Neath's first team and almost immediately earned his first Wales cap against the touring South Africans, before representing his country four times in the 1913 Five Nations Championship against England, France, Scotland and Ireland.

At that time, Perrett was one of Wales' brightest stars, helping his nation finish second in the Championships to England (they won three of their four games) and being one of only two men – Neath teammate Glyn Stephens was the other – to play in all four Welsh fixtures during that season's competition. His exploits as he broke into the Welsh national side had not gone unnoticed in the Northern Union heartlands, with Gwyn Prescott in his book *Call Them to Remembrance* (which honours the 13 Welsh Rugby Union internationals who lost their lives in World War One) revealing initial approaches from Bramley and Hunslet had been rejected. But when Perrett found himself out of work following the final international against Ireland in May, he was lured north by Leeds to guarantee his financial security.

The local press admitted the news of his defection had created shockwaves in the sport, as the *Cambria Daily Leader* of 20 May 1913 revealed:

> Something akin to a sensation was created at Neath and Brittonferry to-day when it became known that Fred Perrett, the Welsh international forward, had signed the professional ticket for Leeds. It is understood that Perrett will leave home on Friday next. Spoken to by a 'Leader' representative this afternoon, Perrett declined to say how much he was receiving. He, however, expressed the view that the amount was the biggest yet paid to a Welsh forward. A young forward of considerable skill, Perrett got his cap for Wales against the South Africans last season and kept his place right through the tournament. His secession will be a serious loss to Neath and to Wales, for whom he gave promise of several years of usefulness.

But on 30 May, the amount Perrett received was finally revealed, with the *Gloucestershire Echo* announcing:

> There had been some difference between him and the Northern Union club with regard to the amount to be paid him. That has been arranged, and Perrett has actually received £100 down.

At 5ft 11in and well over 15st, the burly forward looked ideally suited to the Northern Union game and, having focused so much of their scouting attention in Wales, Leeds were always in pole position to secure his signature, just like they had with the likes of Joseph Hopkins and Arthur Llewellyn, who also died during the Great War. Perrett wasted little time making his debut, starting at prop in the opening game of the 1913-14 campaign in a 23-2 home win over Broughton Rangers on 6 September. He followed that up with three starts at hooker, one in the second row and then two others at prop. Those seven appearances came in the first eight games of that season, and that was that for Perrett in the Leeds colours. It was announced in the *Yorkshire Evening Post* on 6 April 1914 that Perrett was on his way to Hull. Under the headline 'Leeds Forward Transferred', it said:

> Many supporters of the Leeds Northern Union club will regret to hear that Fred Perrett, the Welsh international forward who came to Headingley at the beginning of the season, has been transferred to Hull. For some reason or other, Perrett never impressed the Leeds Committee, but he is a rare scrummager, weighing over 15 stones and standing 5ft 11 inches in height, and last season he played in all the Welsh international matches. That was a distinction only shared by two other Welsh forwards. Only 22 years of age, and a teetotaller and non-smoker into the bargain, Hull have obtained in Perrett a forward who should yet 'make good' in Northern Union football. Before joining Leeds, he was a player of the Neath club.

The Welsh international initially had to bide his time with the

Black and Whites, not making his debut until the 13th game of the 1914-15 season and a 7-0 Yorkshire Cup triumph at home to Batley on 14 November. After that he became a Hull regular, going on to make a total of 28 appearances, with starts at prop, hooker, second row and loose-forward. Included in that was a two-try haul in a 20-10 Christmas Day defeat at Huddersfield. But on 20 July 1915 Perrett enlisted with the Welsh Guards in Llandudno, and his fledgling Northern Union career had come to an end.

This period also marked a change in his personal domestic circumstances. After enlisting, he married Hull-born Nora Gladys Dougherty on 24 November 1915, and the eventual family home was on St George Road, not far from the Hull ground. They were to have two sons, Frederick L Perrett, who was born in December 1915 and Bernard Perrett, who arrived in January 1918.

After completing his training with the 2nd (Reserve) Battalion at Caterham, Perrett arrived in France on 19 February 1916 and joined the 1st Battalion in the field at the beginning of March. However, on 3 April he was stricken with influenza requiring hospitalisation and a period of convalescence. It was not until mid-May 1916 that he was fit enough to rejoin his unit who appointed him to the rank of Lance Corporal in July.[3]

Throughout his time on the Western Front, Perrett had proved his capabilities as a soldier, and in late December 1916 he returned to England, recommended for a commission to become an officer. Within days of being accepted for training at Number 3 Officer Cadet Battalion at Bristol, the *South Wales Weekly Post* of 17 February 1917 announced the news.

Corporal Fred Perrett, the old Welsh international
and Northern Union Rugby forward, who joined
the Welsh Guards as a private, and has since seen

> service in France, has been recommended for a
> commission after the late Battle of the Somme,
> where he distinguished himself, and he has just
> joined a cadet corps at Bristol University for
> training.....

Over the next few months, he successfully completed the course, with the *Cambria Daily Leader* of 30 July 1917 confirming the *London Gazette*[4] in proudly announcing:

> Fred Perrett, Britonferry, the old Welsh
> international and Northern Union forward, who
> was with the Welsh Guards in France when he
> was recommended for a commission for special
> services, has just been gazetted second-lieutenant
> with the Royal Welsh Fusiliers.

The following year, 1918, proved to be a difficult one for Perrett. On 2 May he was admitted to hospital in Rouen with a gunshot wound to the right shoulder, fortunately described as slight. Shortly after returning to duty, he suffered another injury and was admitted to the Red Cross Hospital at Wimereux. The *Cambria Daily Leader* of 14 October reported:

> Lieut. Fred Perrett ..... who only returned to France
> about three weeks ago after recuperating from
> wounds in the shoulder, has again been wounded,
> this time in the neck caused by a German bomb.

He was discharged from hospital back to duty with his battalion, the 17th Royal Welsh Fusiliers, on 22 October 1918. He would be facing the final big push to force the Germans back to their own borders during the conclusion of the successful 'One Hundred Days' offensive. And it was just days before the Armistice was signed, on 4 November, that Perrett was to suffer the injuries that were to ultimately claim his life.

Charged with the task of taking German positions in the Forest de Mormal, the famous rugby forward led his men on the final part of the assault and was severely wounded in his left hand and right thigh by heavy machine-gun fire. He was immediately taken out of the front line and, after emergency treatment at an Advanced Dressing Station and Casualty Clearing Station, he eventually arrived at No8 British Red Cross Hospital at Boulogne on 8 November.

Such was the severity of his injuries that the authorities wasted little time sending a telegram to his wife Nora, granting her a pass to travel to visit her very sick husband. Another message to his wife on 29 November reported on her husband's condition at week ending 24 November. Although indicating he was still dangerously ill, it included a crumb of hope with the words *'condition better'*.[5] It proved a false hope. Despite the best efforts of the medical staff to save his life, Fred Perrett passed away on 1 December 1918 after suffering a secondary haemorrhage.

He is buried at Terlincthun British Cemetery at Wimille, on the outskirts of Boulogne, a cemetery chiefly used for hospital burials. His headstone inscription reads: 'One of the Best.'

In contrast, legendary Wakefield winger William Gordon Simpson (known as Billy), who did not die until 10 May 1919 due to a war-related illness at the age of 31, is buried under a Commonwealth War Graves Commission headstone in his home town of Gomersal.

Born on 16 January 1888 to parents James and Jane Simpson and baptised at Grove Chapel, Gomersal, on 25 June 1889, the cause of their son's death was nephritis, which is inflammation of the kidneys. He also had a heart condition. It is possible the fatal illness was a legacy of a life-threatening rugby injury he suffered in the opening game of the 1912-13 season when he ruptured a kidney in a home game against Bramley on 7 September.

The seriousness of the injury effectively signalled the beginning of the end of his playing career, although he did go on to play a handful of first-team games in the years that followed and still remained on the club's playing register at the time war was declared – despite announcing he was intending to retire in September 1913.

As it turned out, his final senior Wakefield appearance was in an 11-3 home win over Halifax on 13 September 1913, in which fellow fallen Trinity heroes William Beattie and Herbert Finnigan also featured. That was Simpson's 182nd first-team appearance for Wakefield in what was an excellent career which yielded 97 tries, including one in Trinity's 17-0 Challenge Cup final triumph over Hull FC at Headingley on 20 April 1909, in front of a crowd of 23,587.

He also crossed for the match-clinching score in his club's 8-2 Yorkshire Cup final triumph over Huddersfield, also at Headingley, on 3 December 1910, and featured in Wakefield's 20-13 victory over the touring Australians at Belle Vue on 19 December 1908. That appearance against the Kangaroos came two years after Simpson, a bootmaker in the boot repairing department of the Gomersal Co-operative Society, had signed for Wakefield as an 18-year-old from the Gomersal junior club. Standing around 5ft 4½in, he made his Northern Union debut on the wing in a 20-0 home defeat to Broughton Rangers on 24 November 1906.

He opened his Trinity tryscoring account in a 31-3 home win over York on 22 December and finished his debut campaign with a highly-encouraging seven tries from 17 appearances, including a hat trick in a 35-6 victory over Bramley at Belle Vue in March 1907. The tries continued to flow in the years that followed, with his most notable exploits coming in the 1910-11 season when he set a new club record for tries in a season with 32 – a mark that remained until Fred Smith crossed 37 times in 1959-60.

During this season Simpson married Mary Ann Sharp at the Registry Office in Bradford on 17 February 1912. Personally and professionally life was looking good. As the 1912-13 season got under way, Simpson had established himself as one of the most feared and respected wingers in the Northern Union competition, having notched 58 tries in his previous 78 games. But just when Simpson was setting his sights on achieving even more in the game, fate dealt him the cruellest of hands, with the details of the ill-fated injury that was to wreck his career recorded in detail on the Wakefield Trinity Heritage website.

> Billie[6] suffered a serious injury in the first game of the season at home to Bramley (7th September). In the last few minutes he was injured in a tackle and carried from the field with abdominal injuries. The committee ordered a cab to take him home, but he was later feeling seriously unwell and was admitted to Clayton Hospital with an initial diagnosis of broken ribs, but later found as a ruptured kidney. It was so serious that they thought he was going to die, and his family, as well as the Trinity committee, were by his bedside and the chaplain was called. The seriousness of his injuries eased over the next few days, but he remained in hospital for five weeks.
>
> Initial thoughts were that he would not play

again but he was sidelined for almost seven months, returning to the first team at Hunslet the following March. He would only play another five further games that season, followed by another two in 1913-14. He caused a stir when he demanded first-team money when returning in the reserves, but he never fully recovered from his injuries.

When war was declared, Simpson initially carried on working, having taken over as the licensee of the West End Hotel, Gomersal, in March 1915. However, he signed up under the Derby Scheme on 9 December 1915. He was mobilised in November 1916 and served with the Machine Gun Corps, being posted to France in April 1917.[7]

Private Simpson survived the war, getting his final posting home on 8 February 1919 as his battalion was being demobilised, but he was immediately admitted to the Northumberland War Hospital, Gosforth, Newcastle-on-Tyne, after falling ill. His condition deteriorated on a daily basis, with his medical records showing the hospital staff's desperate fight to try to save his life. The notes said:

> Patient had ..... Bright's Disease (chronic nephritis). He also had usual treatment for nephritis e.g. Hot drinks, Barley water, Lemon drinks and magnesium sulphate in morning. For his heart condition, he had Brandy and a Strychnine tonic. Owing to the serious condition of his heart it was impossible to employ drastic methods in treatment of nephritis.[8]

The efforts were in vain and William Gordon Simpson died

at 10.45am on 10 May. No family members were present. Arrangements were made to transport his body home by rail, arriving at Gomersal station in the early hours of 13 May.

His death, and details of his funeral, were announced in the *Cleckheaton and Spen Guardian* on 16 May 1919 and said:

> After having served in the Army abroad for two years, Mr. Wm. Gordon Simpson, of the West End Hotel, has passed away. He was well-known throughout the Heavy Woollen District as a footballer, and at the age of eighteen years he was engaged by the Wakefield Trinity Club to play wing three-quarter. For eight years he remained with them, being at the same time employed in the boot repairing department of the Gomersal Co-operative Society. In March 1915, he became licensee of the West End Hotel, and in December of the following year joined the Army. Shortly afterwards, he was transferred to France, and after two years' service went into hospital suffering from neuritis[9] [*sic*], to which he unfortunately succumbed early this week. The interment took place on Wednesday afternoon at the West-lane Wesleyan Chapel, the Rev. H.J. Haslam (circuit minister) officiating. There were wreaths from the Gomersal Working Men's Club and the Spen Valley Licensed Victuallers' Association (for he was a member of both these bodies), and one from the Wakefield Trinity Football Club. Deceased was 31 years of age and leaves a widow and two little children.[10]

Many other soldiers were to survive the war but were then

to die as a result of the Spanish Flu. It was given that name as it was in Spain where the virus was first reported in March 1918 (although it did not originate there, with the debate still raging to this day over where in the world the flu struck first) and quickly became a pandemic, going on to infect over a third of the world's population. By the time the pandemic had come to an end over a year later, it's believed more than 50 million had died, and included in that horrifying statistic was young St Helens forward George Sephton, who lost his life at the age of 19.

Born in St Helens on 24 July 1899, the former railway clerk became ill while serving as a telegraph operator with the Royal Naval Reserve. He passed away on 24 November 1918, with the cause of death on his service record stating it was *'influenza and bronchial pneumonia.'*[11]

Sephton never got the chance to test himself at Northern Union level. The fact the talented teenager made 28 'friendly' Wartime Emergency League fixtures for Saints between 1915 and 1917 – which is why he did not qualify for a St Helens Heritage Number – suggests he could have gone on to have a highly-successful career in the professional game. But, like so many other potential future rugby league stars, the Great War took that potential away. He is buried at St Helens Cemetery.

Missing the chance to fulfil his full potential was also the case for Hunslet's Percy Thompson, an almost forgotten Northern Union man in the conflict, whose death was recorded in the *Athletic News* on 10 March 1919. Percy Thompson's registration from the Maryport club Glasson Rangers was completed on 24 September 1914. He immediately proved his worth and started in the back row in the opening game of the 1914-15 season as his new club secured an impressive 17-3 home triumph over Bradford

Northern on 3 September. This was his only Northern Union appearance.

It is possible that he died on the morning of 31 December 1917, on board the *SS Osmanieh*. The troopship, carrying a mixture of soldiers, medical staff, including nurses, and crew was about to enter Alexandria harbour when she struck a German mine and quickly sank with the loss of 199 lives. One of those missing presumed drowned was a Sapper Percy Thompson, from Maryport. He grew up in the Netherton area of town, the son of Jonathan and Mary Ann Thompson. Married to Lily Henderson in 1916, the 25-year-old train driver was called up on 1 October 1917, a month before the birth of his daughter. He set off for Egypt on board the 'Osmanieh' on 17 December 1917, as part of the Royal Engineers 98th Light Railway Train Crew Company. He is commemorated on the Chatby Memorial, Egypt.

However, it has not yet been possible to definitively link this man with Hunslet's Percy Thompson.

St Helens Kiwi Hubert Turtill lost his life in the final year of the war

courtesy of Saints Heritage Society

The Aftermath – So Many Careers Destroyed

20

So many Northern Union players died during the Great War, lost to the game and their families way before their time. But it should not be forgotten that many others who survived the war were similarly never able to grace the field again due to the injuries they suffered fighting for their country. After all, while just over 700,000 British soldiers were killed, around two million returned home injured, many of them with life-changing consequences.

It is impossible to know how many professional rugby league careers were cut short due to wounds, but it is clear the number was large. Even a relatively minor injury could have a devastating effect on a player who clearly needed to be super-fit and 100% healthy to compete at the highest level. And the examples about to be given here underline some of the varying ways in which a career was cut short.

One man never to play again was Wigan forward Cuthbert Molloy. He broke into the first team and featured at prop in a 12-5 Northern Union defeat at Oldham on 21 November 1914 when he was just 19 years of age. He was clearly an immense talent, with the *Athletic News* having stated in its 25 August 1913 edition:

> In order to discover local players of merit, a practice game between teams of juniors was played on Saturday, and two forwards who gave a most promising display were signed on [*by Wigan*]. One of them, Cuthbert Molloy, who was attached to West End Stars, is very highly spoken of. He is only 18 years of age but weighs 12st 10lb.

But in 1915 Molloy went off to war and returned home a blind man. The Wigan-born talent enlisted on 28 January 1915 with the Royal Field Artillery and first arrived in France on 26 June later that year. It was while he was serving in France on 8 April 1916 that he suffered his life-changing injury when he was wounded in the head by a bursting German shell which, according to his service records, left him *'Totally Blind, Both Eyes'*.[1]

After receiving treatment, Molloy returned to England on 23 May 1916 and proceeded to Sir Arthur Pearson's Home for Blinded Soldiers at St Dunstan's, Regent's Park. St Dunstan's, as it came to be known, was set up in 1915 as a direct response to the numbers of men returning home blinded as a result of battlefield injuries. Its aim was to provide them with training, rehabilitation and lifelong support so they could live an independent and fulfilling life. The charity continues today as Blind Veterans UK.

Molloy was officially discharged from the Army on 4 July 1916. It must have been a tough time for the then 21-year-old, but he refused to let his blindness get the better of him.

In 1917 White Hall was acquired by Wigan Corporation to provide a workshop for the blind where they could be usefully employed and taught various handicrafts. These ranged from piano tuning and sock and stocking knitting, to boot heeling and soling and factory skip repairs. The workshop was officially opened in August 1917 and one of those giving a presentation to the assembled dignitaries was Cuthbert Molloy, who explained that although he had lost his sight there was no reason why his life should be darkened. He had been taught boot and shoe repairing and was receiving singing lessons. His best accomplishment, which he had been learning since March and the one he was demonstrating, was Braille shorthand and typing. He used the Braille shorthand machine to take down dictated letters then transcribed them using the typewriter. He was full of praise for St Dunstan's, who provided his tuition.[2]

Molloy also did not allow his blindness to affect his personal life, going on to marry and have children before his untimely death in 1940 at home in Rhyl at the age of just 45. This was announced in the *Liverpool Evening Express* of 1 November 1940 which stated:

> A well-known Wigan footballer before the last war, Mr. Cuthbert Molloy, has died at his home ..... at the age of 45. Mr. Molloy was blinded by a bursting shell when he was on active service at Arras in 1916. He was trained at St Dunstan's, where he was taught shorthand typing, mat-making and boot repairing. He went to live at Rhyl twelve months ago.

One of the most prominent players of the day to suffer a career-ending injury was winger Ben Johnson, who featured

76 times for Wakefield Trinity between 1912 and 1915. The highlight of his career was appearing on the wing for his club in the 1914 Challenge Cup final, when they were beaten 6-0 by Hull. But after fighting in the war, Johnson returned to West Yorkshire having lost a leg.

Other examples have been provided by the clubs themselves, including Halifax and Hull KR. Halifax RLFC historian Andrew Hardcastle reported that:

> Billy Williams lost an eye, Harry Haigh a limb and Fred Mallinson later had a leg amputated as a result of a war injury. James Brown was also injured and Harry Paterson suffered shellshock.

And Hull KR historian Roger Pugh added:

> Charlie Brain did return to action for one game for Rovers in 1919, but the physical demands on his body, and particularly his feet, after being taken prisoner at Mons early in the war proved too great for him to continue, while Robert Hicks and Leonard Trump were two others who returned home and couldn't continue their careers.

The *Athletic News* also gave several examples of players injured during the Great War and unable to continue, including two established members of the St Helens pack in Bill Tellyn (he played 36 times for Saints in the 1913-14 season but had to have a leg amputated) and Archie Waddell.

Tough New Zealand forward Waddell came over to play for Saints alongside his good friend Hubert Turtill for the start of the 1910-11 season. Turtill lost his life in the final year of the war, but Waddell's time at St Helens was cut short due to his experiences serving with the ANZACs at Gallipoli in 1915, as explained by Alex Service of the Saints Heritage Society after discovering a piece in the *St Helens Newspaper and Advertiser* of 25 February 1916. It said:

> Sergeant Waddell arrived in St Helens the other day having spent four-and-a-half months in hospital as a result of his experiences with the Colonial Forces at Gallipoli. He looked fairly well, however, but said he was not yet in form to play football, as he is suffering from the effects of concussion caused by the explosion of a high explosive shell, and also from the effects of dysentery. As the Newspaper representatives left, Sergeant Waddell said: 'As I said, I don't think I shall play football again, but I shall go to see the boys on Saturday when they play Barrow.'

The *Athletic News* also gave a brief mention to Bradford's F. H. Stead, saying:

> Early on in the war F.H. Stead returned home severely injured and discharged from the Army incapacitated for life.[3]

The same publication paid tribute to a player from Hull FC:

> Another brilliant player, Steve Darmody,[4] who came over to England with the New South Wales League team in 1911 and joined Hull, has been lost to the game, for as a result of wounds he has had to have a foot amputated. It was Darmody who introduced us [*to*] the 'loose forward' game.[5]

The Australian had volunteered for the Motor Transport Section in the British Army and, while serving in Belgium, he trapped a lower part of a leg in the fly-wheel of a motor vehicle he was repairing, severing off the foot completely. He was trapped for over two hours. Hull later staged a benefit game for their popular player between the East Riding and the West Riding at the Boulevard, which helped raise £220. Among those who volunteered their services that day were RFL Hall of Fame members Harold Wagstaff, Jonty Parkin, Billy Batten and Australia's Albert Rosenfeld.

These examples are the tip of the iceberg, with many other players on the books of NU clubs unable to resume after 1918. However, some who were injured during the conflict did manage to continue their professional careers – the most famous of which was Huddersfield's Douglas Clark.

The Cumbrian-born England forward was as hard as nails and as strong as an ox, and was a mainstay of the Fartown 'Team of All Talents' pack that secured a clean sweep of the trophies in the 1914-15 season. To say his life was colourful would be an understatement, and his exploits before, during and after the war are the stuff of legends, making him arguably one of the most famous rugby league players of all time. His heroics earned him a place in the Rugby League Hall of Fame, where he was inducted in 2005.

Even as a 14-year-old, it was clear Clark was a super-human being, able to carry a hundred-weight bag of coal under each arm, much to the astonishment of his seniors. It was no surprise, therefore, that he was soon making a name for himself as a feared junior rugby league forward, starring for the Brookland Rovers Under 18s at the age of 15. As a result, Huddersfield paid the princely sum of £30 to acquire his services a month before his 18th birthday in April 1909.

It was a decision the Fartown club would never regret. Before going off to the Western Front, Clark had collected a whole host of Northern Union winners' medals, and in the 1913 League Championship final had the distinction of scoring a hat trick of tries in a 29-2 defeat of Wigan at Wakefield. He also made five Great Britain appearances before 1914, with his most memorable match being the famous '*Rorke's Drift*' Test against Australia in Sydney on 4 July 1914, when Great Britain somehow managed to secure a 14-6 victory, despite being down to 10 men at one stage.

Playing in the second row, Clark broke a thumb in the first half and dislocated his collar bone at the start of the second. He briefly went off the field to be strapped up and then returned, only to find it impossible to continue. When he was forced to withdraw, hard-man Clark was in tears.

After the outbreak of war, Clark joined the Army Service Corps, alongside Huddersfield teammates Harold Wagstaff and Ben Gronow, with their regimental training tales reaching regal proportions, as revealed in John Huxley's *The Rugby League Challenge Cup*.

> While on convoy duty near Windsor, a halt was called and a gentleman approached their lorry. At the time, Clark and his colleagues were trying to open a tin of bully beef from the wrong end. The gentleman said: 'Don't you think sonny, you'd do better if you opened the other end?' Other questions followed, Clark ran out of patience and said to their questioner: 'Look here sir, we're busy.' The gentleman smiled and walked away. Clark's feelings can only be imagined when it was revealed that the gentleman had been none other than the reigning monarch, King George V!

But things got even more eventful for the man from Ellenborough when he arrived in Belgium in 1917 as part of the Army Service Corps Motor Transport Division, just ahead of the week-long Battle of Messines, which got under way on 7 June. Almost from the start, Acting Sergeant Clark came under heavy German artillery fire, with his experiences recorded in his remarkable personal war diary, as transcribed by the late Huddersfield RLFC club historian David Gronow. Several extracts were re-printed in *Standing on the Shoulders of Giants: A History of Rugby League in Huddersfield*.[6]

They included the two occasions he was injured whilst delivering vital supplies to the men in the frontline trenches. The first time was just outside Ypres on 24 July when he fell victim to a gas attack.

> Fritz sends over shrapnel. Gets in dump which spreads all over lorries and, of course, we get it. He kills one man and two lose their arms. I am very weepy. We help bandage poor fellow up. He sends over his beastly chlorine gas. We put them in a lorry. Driver missing. I take helmet off to call for driver, but have to put it on again. Driver turns up and takes wheel, nearly ditches us. I take off my helmet to drive, manage to get to hospital. Find two of wounded dead. I collapse and taken to gas hospital. Eyes, chest, throat very bad. Sick, sick.[7]

Clark was under treatment in the British base at Poperinge – around seven miles behind the British front line – for 10 days, before he returned to action and again spent every day subjected to heavy German shelling. Time and again, the

Fartown legend performed heroic acts under heavy artillery fire – until his luck finally ran out on 31 October 1917.

> We had not gone very far until we found the gas very bad ..... so we pulled up to warn drivers, Mr Preedy going back to following lorries. I took ours forwards to unload ..... the place was deserted, so first and second driver and myself started unloading. I pulled off my helmet 3 times, doing so I was almost overcome. At this point one of Fritz's green lights flared up, and then the place was turned into hell. I doubt if ever Fritz has sent over so many shells on such a small stretch as he did round us, even putting the shelling of the previous days in the shade. I received a nasty wound in the left arm and I thought it certain all would be killed. I ordered boys to go back and take cover near the other lorries. Here I found Mr Preedy and reported I was wounded. He wanted to take me to hospital, but I refused to leave the lorries. Shells were falling in front, behind and on all sides.....we decided to get lorries out of this..... [8]

After turning his lorry around, a shell burst close to Clark's vehicle, with shrapnel hitting him in the chest and abdomen. At the end of the war with a 95% Disability Certificate and fragments of shrapnel still left in his body, he was awarded the Military Medal for valour. But despite doctors questioning whether he should return to his physical pre-war pursuits – or if he may, in fact, be in a position to do so – he was back in the Huddersfield Northern Union fold, and in 1920 was again picked for Great Britain, winning a further six caps on the 1920 tour to Australia and New Zealand.

On top of that, he also resumed his distinguished pre-war wrestling career, emerging successful in the 1922 and 1924 Grasmere Cups and going on to become Champion of Great Britain. He later went on to be crowned All-in Wrestling Champion of the World, winning the championship belt outright after defeating two successive challengers and touring Australia in 1934 and 1936.

Douglas Clark died at his home in Huddersfield on 1 February 1951 at the relatively young age of 59, something his doctors had warned him could happen if he continued his rugby career after sustaining such serious war-time wounds.

Fortunately, his name lives on, with his incredible exploits recognised at the Imperial War Museum's northern base in Manchester, where there is a special panel commemorating his achievements. Included in the collection are his war medals, numerous wrestling trophies and several important rugby league items, including the Great Britain Test cap he was awarded for being part of the 1914 squad that toured Australia and New Zealand in the summer of that year. Interestingly, however, the cap has the year 1915 inscribed on it rather than 1914. That was because the start of the Great War had distracted Northern Union officials, who did not get around to sorting out the production of the caps until 1915 – and the manufacturers assumed 1915 was the year required for the Test memento!

Besides the game's biggest stars, many 'A' team players just starting out on the road to a potential professional career were also killed in action, as were many former Northern Union favourites who had lit up the sporting arena a number of years before the war clouds began to gather.

They include players such as Bramley's Harold Smith, who had been a Northern Union hero in years gone by. On referencing his death in early 1919, the *Athletic News* stated:

Smith, previous to joining the Army, was the
captain of the [Bramley] team, and he rendered
great service to his club.[9]

Then at the other end of the scale, the *Athletic News* featured
in the same publication the death of Broughton Rangers'
teenager Edward Gatley, who was on the verge of breaking
into the first team and was being admired from near and far.
The Northern Union correspondent said of Gatley:

He was one of the most promising players the
club ever registered. A local lad, he came to the
Rangers from intermediate football, and time
after time after watching him play, I expressed
the opinion he would be a brilliant stand-off half-
back. He was only in his teens, but he could take
a ball in almost any position, was quick into his
stride, knew the art of breaking through the
opposing centre three-quarter backs, possessed a
natural swerve, was dashing to a degree and, in
addition to being a dangerous attacker, was
sound in defence. Gatley was one of the best
discoveries Broughton ever made.[10]

Hull FC's Wilfred Allen was another who could have had a
bright Northern Union future as he looked to follow in the
footsteps of his older brother, Arthur '*Tim*' Allen, who had
been a regular in the first team for several seasons.

Back-row forward Wilfred had starred in his youth for
Hull Central and made his Junior Airlie Birds 'A' team debut
at home to Dewsbury in November 1912. But before he had
the chance to rise through the Black and White ranks,

stretcher bearer Private Wilfred Allen of the 13th Battalion
East Yorkshire Regiment was killed on the Somme on 13
November 1916. He was 24. Sadly, however, by the time
Wilfred had fallen, '*Tim*' had also passed away at home in
Hull, on 7 March 1915, at the age of 27 after developing a
sudden illness. Wilfred was at the funeral.

Who knows how far Gatley or Allen could have gone
in the game, or so many others who never had the chance to
fulfil their potential, for that matter?

Their chance of glory on the rugby field had gone. But
there is no denying, of course, that their First World War
sacrifice was just as great as those Northern Union stars who
died while they were still competing at the highest level
when war was declared, and no less than the former rugby
league 'greats' whose careers had ended by the autumn of
1914 and then gave up their lives on the battlefield.

As mentioned in this book's introduction, it is possible
some of the established Northern Union players of the day
who died in the Great War may have been missed – a far from
comprehensive list of historical records from that time mean
there is, unfortunately, a chance of this being the case – so
compiling an extra list of former first-team players or reserve
players really may be a 'mission impossible'.

But in closing, here at least are some of those fallen
rugby league heroes from the ex-first team or reserve team
category who made the ultimate sacrifice.

Their names should also never be forgotten, as outlined
in the *Athletic News* and by several professional clubs.

Batley: Herbert Childe, Joseph Wilson, Frank Brook Roebuck.

Bramley: D Hammond, Harold Smith.

Bradford Northern: F Craven.

Broughton Rangers: J Evans, I Frost, W Royle, Edward Gatley.

Dewsbury: Alfred Gildea.

Halifax: Arnold Nettleton.

Huddersfield: FC Haigh, Jack Hirst.

Hull FC: H Barker, WC Bemrose, WE Holmes, A Monod, WH Maskwell, W Mercer, CC Pearson, A Taylor, H Wallace, Wilfred Allen.

Hunslet: JR Birtles, H Cox.

Keighley: Richard Blades.

Leeds: HE Bannister, J Harkness, L Farrar, B Thorpe, N Parker, George Pickard, GR White.

Leigh: Benjamin Sumner, Frank Ganley, James Tobin, Billy Unsworth, Sam Whittaker, Harry Bilsbury, Ralph Makin, James Henry Threlfall.

Oldham: John Scott, Thomas Wainman, Herbert Mills, William Moore Bell Nanson, Adam Jardine.

Runcorn: Harry Farmer, Joseph Jolley.

Salford: E Brown, N Shaw, George Russell, Fred Hope, Tom Williams.

St Helens: James Ford, George Sephton

Swinton: Charles Battye, Joe Cartwright, Ezra Gee, Bill Lever, Albert Sanderson, Herbert Shedlock, Harold White.

Wakefield Trinity: B Ward, E Ward, Oakley, Ogley.

Warrington: James Andrews, James Berry, Joseph Oakes, Johnno Stuntz, John Cartwright.

Widnes: A Barrow, J Ditchfield, Lewis Griffiths, P Golding, WA Jackson, James Kinsella, N Lowe, J Rose, W Ratcliffe, David Tench.

Roll of Honour

Appendix 1

Re = Regiment; Ra = Rank*; SN = Service Number; D = Date of Death; B/C = Place of Burial or Commemoration; LC = Last Club.
*All ranks as recorded by the Commonwealth War Graves Commission. For the rank of Serjeant the main body of the book uses today's modern spelling, Sergeant

ABBOTT, SIDNEY CLIFFORD. Re – 2nd Bn. York and Lancaster Regiment; Ra – Serjeant; SN – 28615; D – 18 September 1918; B/C – Vis-en-Artois Memorial, France; LC – Leeds

ASHLEY, JOHN THOMAS. Re – 9th Bn. Cheshire Regiment; Ra – Private; SN – 13509; D – 25 September 1915; B/C – Lillers Communal Cemetery, France; LC – Runcorn

BAIRSTOW, HARRY. Re – 4th Bn. Seaforth Highlanders; Ra – Private; SN – 201713; D – 11 April 1917; B/C – Aubigny Communal Cemetery Extension, France; LC – Keighley

BEATTIE, WILLIAM LINDSAY. Re – 1st Bn. Border Regiment; Ra – Lieutenant ; D – 27 January 1917; B/C – Quarry Cemetery, Montauban, France; LC – Wakefield Trinity

BLAKEY, DAVID HARKNESS. Re – 11th Bn. Royal Inniskilling Fusiliers; Ra – Serjeant; SN – 18634; D – 1 July 1916; B/C – Connaught Cemetery, Thiepval, France; LC – Leeds

BRADLEY, LEWIS. Re – 410th Bty. 96th Bde. Royal Field
Artillery; Ra – Driver; SN – 118613; D – 20 June 1918;
B/C – Vignacourt British Cemetery, France; LC – Wigan

BREEN, JAMES PATRICK. Re – 132nd Heavy Bty. Royal Garrison
Artillery; Ra – Gunner; SN – 181029; D – 21 October 1918; B/C –
Roisel Communal Cemetery Extension, France; LC – Widnes

BROWN, ALEXANDER. Re – 10th Bn. King's Royal Rifle Corps;
Ra – Rifleman; SN – R/2566; D – 3 September 1916;
B/C – Thiepval Memorial, France; LC – Warrington

BURTON, CHARLES JOHN INGLIS. Re – 3rd Bn.
Worcestershire Regiment; Ra – Private; SN – 23263; D – 29 April
1916; B/C – Ecoivres Military Cemetery, Mont-St-Eloi, France;
LC – Rochdale Hornets

CHILD, JOSEPH. Se – 1st/9th Bn. Royal Scots; Ra – Private;
SN – 351764; D – 9 April 1917; B/C – Nine Elms Military
Cemetery, Thelus, France; LC – Batley

COCKCROFT, ARTHUR CLARENCE. Re – 11th Bn. attd. 10th
Bn. King's Own Yorkshire Light Infantry; Ra – Second Lieutenant;
D – 1 July 1916; B/C – Gordon Dump Cemetery, Ovillers-la-
Boiselle, France; LC – Wakefield Trinity

COOK, JAMES HENRY. Re – 1st Bn. King's Royal Rifle Corps;
Ra – Rifleman; SN – 5/4856; D – 3 July 1915; B/C – Cambrin
Military Cemetery, France; LC – Salford

CRABTREE, GEORGE WILFRED. Re – 3rd/5th Bn. Lancashire
Fusiliers; Ra – Private; SN – 202431; D – 20 April 1917;
B/C – Gorre British and Indian Cemetery, France; LC – Swinton

DALEY, JOHN. Re – 3rd Bn. Grenadier Guards; Ra – Private;
SN – 22807; D – 14 September 1916; B/C – Thiepval Memorial,
France; LC – Swinton

DAVIS, HOWARD. Re – 8th Bn. Rifle Brigade; Ra – Serjeant;
SN – S/978; D – 31 July 1915; B/C – Lijssenthoek Military
Cemetery, Belgium; LC – Warrington

DEBNEY, JAMES WILLIAM. Re – 6th Bn. York and Lancaster
Regiment; Ra – Private; SN – 11477; D – 29 September 1916;
B/C – A.I.F. Burial Ground, Flers, France; LC – Batley

DOOREY, ERNEST. Re – 1st Bn. King's Own (Royal Lancaster Regiment); Ra – Corporal; SN – 1753; D – 24 May 1915; B/C – Ypres (Menin Gate) Memorial, Belgium; LC – Leigh

EWART, JOHN LINTON. Re – 5th Bn. Cameron Highlanders; Ra – Private; SN – 16599; D – 21 March 1918; B/C – Pozieres Memorial, France; LC – Halifax

FINNIGAN, HERBERT. Re – 1st/4th Bn. King's Own Yorkshire Light Infantry; Ra – Serjeant; SN – 287; D – 19 December 1915; B/C – Hospital Farm Cemetery, Belgium; LC – Wakefield Trinity

FLANAGAN, JAMES. Re – 11th Bn. South Lancashire Regiment; Ra – Lance Serjeant; SN – 20984; D – 14 May 1918; B/C – Arneke British Cemetery, France; LC – St Helens

FLYNN, JOHN. Re – 7th Bn. Border Regiment; Ra – Lance Corporal; SN – 14849; D – 4 May 1918; B/C – Forceville Communal Cemetery and Extension, France; LC – Bradford Northern (Previously Swinton)

HARRISON, JOHN. Re – 11th Bn. East Yorkshire Regiment; Ra – Second Lieutenant; D – 3 May 1917; B/C – Arras Memorial, France; LC – Hull FC

HOPKINS, JOSEPH HENRY. Re – 2nd Bn. West Yorkshire Regiment (Prince of Wales's Own); Ra – Private; SN – 24487; D – 1 July 1916; B/C – Thiepval Memorial, France; LC – Leeds

JARDINE, WILLIAM BOYD. Re – 2nd/10th Bn. Manchester Regiment; Ra – Corporal; SN – 3015; D – 16 January 1917; B/C – Jedburgh (Castlewood) Cemetery, United Kingdom; LC – Oldham

JARMAN, SAMUEL WILLIAM. Re – 2nd Bn. Scots Guards; Ra – Private; SN – 6295; D – 15 August 1916; B/C – Thiepval Memorial, France; LC – Leeds

JOHNSON, WALTER. Re – 1st/8th Bn. West Yorkshire Regiment (Prince of Wales's Own); Ra – Rifleman; SN – 3885; D – 3 September 1916; B/C – Thiepval Memorial, France; LC – Batley

JONES, THOMAS OWEN. Re – 9th Bn. Welsh Regiment; Ra – Corporal; SN – 20970; D – 20 September 1917; B/C – Tyne Cot Memorial, Belgium; LC – Oldham

KAY(E), MARK. Re – 6th Bn. Cameron Highlanders; Ra – Private; SN – S/18817; D – 31 July 1917; B/C – Ypres (Menin Gate) Memorial, Belgium; LC – Hunslet

LECKENBY, LEONARD. Re – 8th Bn. Seaforth Highlanders; Ra – Serjeant; SN – S/10857; D – 23 April 1917; B/C – Guemappe British Cemetery, Wancourt, France; LC – Leeds

LLEWELLYN, ARTHUR. Re – 13th Bn. Rifle Brigade; Ra – Rifleman; SN – 6050; D – 1 June 1917; B/C – Arras Memorial, France; LC – Leeds

LLOYD, BENJAMIN. Re – 'D' Coy. 7th Bn. South Lancashire Regiment; Ra – Lance Corporal; SN – 16711; D – 20 July 1916; B/C – Thiepval Memorial, France; LC – Leigh

LONGSTAFF, FRED. Re – 1st/6th Bn. West Yorkshire Regiment (Prince of Wales's Own); Ra – Private; SN – 4940; D – 21 July 1916; B/C – Blighty Valley Cemetery, Authuille Wood, France; LC – Huddersfield

LONGTHORPE, FRED. Re – 2nd Gun Carrier Coy. Tank Corps; Ra – Second Lieutenant; D – 20 September 1918; B/C – Thilloy Road Cemetery, Beaulencourt, France; LC – Bradford Northern

MARSHALL, THEODORE. Re – 7th Bn. Cameron Highlanders; Ra – Private; SN – S/23836; D – 1 August 1917; B/C – Elland Cemetery, United Kingdom; LC – Huddersfield

MIDGLEY, GEORGE WILLIAM. Re – 1st Bn. The King's (Liverpool Regiment); Ra – Lance Corporal; SN – 11775; D – 26 October 1914; B/C – Ypres (Menin Gate) Memorial, Belgium; LC – Bramley

NEWALL, WILLIAM. Re – 9th Bn. Rifle Brigade; Ra – Rifleman; SN – Z/391; D – 15 September 1916; B/C – Thiepval Memorial, France; LC – Runcorn

OKELL, PETER. Re – 13th Bn. Cheshire Regiment; Ra – Private; SN – 243796; D – 10 June 1917; B/C – Ypres (Menin Gate) Memorial, Belgium; LC – Runcorn

O'NEILL, PATRICK. Re – 147th Heavy Bty. Royal Garrison Artillery; Ra – Gunner; SN – 292401; D – 27 September 1917; B/C – Belgian Battery Corner Cemetery, Belgium; LC – Dewsbury

PERRETT, FRED LEONARD. Re – 17th Bn. Royal Welsh
Fusiliers; Ra – Second Lieutenant; D – 1 December 1918; B/C –
Terlincthun British Cemetery, Wimille, France; LC – Hull FC

PICKLES, JOSEPH ROBERT. Re – 1st/5th Bn. West Yorkshire
Regiment (Prince of Wales's Own); Ra – Serjeant; SN – 1304;
D – 1 July 1916; B/C – Thiepval Memorial, France; LC – Leeds

PRESTON, DAVID. Re – 15th Bn. Lancashire Fusiliers;
Ra – Lance Corporal; SN – 25007; D – 1 July 1916; B/C – Thiepval
Memorial, France; LC – Salford

RANDERSON, ROBERT. Re – 6th Bn. Yorkshire Regiment;
Ra – Captain; D – 7 August 1915; B/C – Lala Baba Cemetery,
Gallipoli; LC – Batley

REES, HOWELL. Re – 10th Bn. Durham Light Infantry;
Ra – Private; SN – 23/335; D – 8 May 1917; B/C – Arras
Memorial, France; LC – Keighley

ROMAN, WALTER. Re – 1st Bn. Somerset Light Infantry; Ra –
Private; SN – 5592; D – 28 July 1916; B/C – Bridgwater (Wembdon
Road) Cemetery, United Kingdom; LC – Rochdale Hornets

RUCK, HAROLD JAMES. Re – 1st Bn. Grenadier Guards;
Ra – Lance Serjeant; SN – 12280; D – 26 September 1916;
B/C – Caterpillar Valley Cemetery, Longueval, France; LC –
Bradford Northern

SANDERS, JAMES. Re – 1st Bn West Yorkshire Regiment (Prince
of Wales's Own); Ra – Private; SN – 15/1765; D – 13 October 1916;
B/C – Thiepval Memorial, France; LC – Leeds

SHANNON, DANIEL. Re – 7th Bn. Cameron Highlanders;
Ra – Private; SN – S/15796; D – 25 September 1915; B/C – Loos
Memorial, France; LC – Oldham

SIMPSON, WILLIAM GORDON. Re – Machine Gun Corps
(Infantry); Ra – Private; SN – 85993; D – 10 May 1919;
B/C – Gomersal Methodist Chapelyard, United Kingdom;
LC – Wakefield Trinity

STEPHENSON, ERNEST. Re – 2nd Bn. Rifle Brigade;
Ra – Rifleman; SN – Z/769; D – 1 July 1916; B/C – Thiepval
Memorial, France; LC – Swinton

SWINTON, ERNEST. Re – Royal Field Artillery; Ra – Second Lieutenant; D – 28 May 1915; B/C – Farnworth (St Luke) Churchyard, United Kingdom; LC – Widnes

THOM, GEORGE. Re – Army Ordnance Corps; Ra – Armament Staff Serjeant; SN – TD/944; D – 30 December 1915; B/C – Salford (Weaste) Cemetery, United Kingdom; LC – Salford

THOMAS, PHILLIP. Re – Yorkshire Hussars Yeomanry: Ra – Private; SN – 2769; D – 25 May 1915; B/C – Ypres (Menin Gate) Memorial, Belgium; LC – Hull KR

THOMAS, WILLIAM GEORGE. Re – 8th Bn. South Lancashire Regiment; Ra – Private; SN – 15041; D – 3 July 1916; B/C – Thiepval Memorial, France; LC – Warrington

THOMPSON, PERCY. Details Not Confirmed; LC – Hunslet

TILLOTSON, THOMAS HENRY. Re – 2nd Bn. Coldstream Guards; Ra – Private; SN – 15361; D – 16 September 1916; B/C – Thiepval Memorial, France; LC – Hunslet

TINDALL, JOHN CLARENCE. Re – 1st/8th Bn. West Yorkshire Regiment (Prince of Wales's Own); Ra – Rifleman; SN – 1888; D – 9 May 1915; B/C – Ploegsteert Memorial, Belgium; LC – Batley

TOPPING, ROBERT. Re – 11th Bn. Royal Sussex Regiment; Ra – Private; SN – 3944; D – 30 June 1916; B/C – St. Vaast Post Military Cemetery, Richebourg-l'Avoue, France; LC – Leigh

TURTILL, HUBERT SYDNEY. Re – 422nd Field Coy. Royal Engineers; Ra – Serjeant; SN – 426516; D – 9 April 1918; B/C – Brown's Road Military Cemetery, Festubert, France; LC – St Helens

TWIGG, JOHN. Re – 2nd Bn. Leicestershire Regiment; Ra – Serjeant; SN – 7466; D – 13 March 1915; B/C – Le Touret Memorial, France; LC – Rochdale Hornets

VINTON, GEORGE. Re – 2nd Bn. Royal Munster Fusiliers; Ra – Private; SN – 7806; D – 27 August 1914; B/C – Etreux British Cemetery, France; LC – Broughton Rangers

WAGSTAFF, THOMAS. Re – 5th Bn. Cameron Highlanders; Ra – Private; SN – S/18732; D – 18 October 1916; B/C – Warlencourt British Cemetery, France; LC – Bramley

WARD, BELFRED. Re – 72nd Coy. Machine Gun Corps (Infantry); Ra – Private; SN – 11262; D – 30 April 1916; B/C – Bailleul Communal Cemetery Extension Nord, France; LC –Leeds

WEST, ARTHUR DOUGLAS. Re – 1st Bn. The King's (Liverpool Regiment); Ra – Serjeant; SN – 52763; D – 15 November 1916; B/C – Tilloy British Cemetery, Tilloy-les-Mofflaines, France; LC – Oldham

WEST, ERNEST THOMAS. Re – 10th Bn. King's Royal Rifle Corps; Ra – Rifleman; SN – R/2812; D – 29 September 1915; B/C – Royal Irish Rifles Graveyard, Laventie, France; LC – Rochdale Hornets

WHITFIELD, HAROLD. Re – 5th Bn. Cheshire Regiment; Ra – Private; SN – 2255; D – 22 April 1915; B/C – Spoilbank Cemetery, Belgium; LC – Runcorn

WILKINSON, JOHN. Re – X Coy. 8th Bn. Duke of Wellington's (West Riding Regiment); Ra – Private; SN – 11196; D – 12 August 1915; B/C – Helles Memorial, Gallipoli; LC – Bradford Northern

WISHART, GEORGE. Re – 56th Bty. 54th Bde. Royal Field Artillery; Ra – Gunner; SN – 56951; D – 7 October 1914; B/C – Nantes (La Bouteillerie) Cemetery, France; LC – Hunslet

WRAY, HARRY BASIL. Re – 1st Bn. attd. 11th Bn. West Yorkshire Regiment (Prince of Wales's Own); Ra – Company Serjeant Major; SN – 7764; D – 29 October 1918; B/C – Tezze British Cemetery, Italy; LC – Bradford Northern

YOUNG, STANLEY. Re – 11th Bn. Manchester Regiment attd. 127th Light Trench Mortar Bty.; Ra – Private; SN – 303170; D – 18 April 1918; B/C – Philosophe British Cemetery, Mazingarbe, France; LC – Warrington

Bibliography

Appendix 2

Books

- BECKETT, Ian F. W. *The Great War: 1914-1918*. Pearson Longman, 2007.
- DRUM, Neil, and Peter Thomas. *A District at War: Irlam and Cadisheads Part in the Great War 1914-1918*. Manchester: Thomas-Drum Publications, 2010
- CARTWRIGHT, Brian F. *A 'Ton' Full of Memories*. Batley: Author, 1986
- GARVIN, Ged, J. L. Garvin, and Christine Garvin. *We Hope to Get Word Tomorrow: The Garvin Family Letters, 1914-1916*. Barnsley: Frontline, 2009
- HEYWOOD, Brian, David Smith, Stuart Leslie Sheard, David Thorpe, David Gronow, Daniel Sheard, Rob Smithson, and Howard Taylor. *Standing on the Shoulders of Giants: A History of Rugby League in Huddersfield*. Upper Calder Valley Publications, 2015
- HUXLEY, John. *Rugby League Challenge Cup*. Enfield: Guinness, 1992
- MACLEOD, Norman, and James Walter SANDILANDS. *The History of the 7th Battalion Queens Own Cameron Highlanders*. By Colonel J.W. Sandilands ... and Lieut. Colonel Norman Macleod. Stirling: Eneas Mackay, 1922
- MASSUE DE RUVIGNY, Melville Amadeus Henry Douglas Heddle De La Caillemotte De. *The Roll of Honour: A Biographical Record of All Members of His Majestys Naval and Military Forces Who Have Fallen in the War*. Standard Art Book Co: London, 1917

- O'MEARA, W. A. J. *The Roll of Honour of the Institution of Electrical Engineers. (Contained Herein Are the Names of Members of the Institution of Electrical Engineers Who Gave Their Lives ...* 1914-1919. London, 1924
- PRESCOTT, Gwyn. *'Call Them to Remembrance': The Welsh Rugby Internationals Who Died in the Great War.* Cardiff: St. Davids Press, 2014
- SHEFFIELD, Gary. *The Great War 1914-1918: The Story of the Western Front.* London: SevenOaks, 2014.
- SLATER, Gary. *The Warrington Wolves Miscellany.* Stroud: History, 2012
- STRACHAN, Hew. *The Oxford Illustrated History of the First World War.* Oxford: Oxford University Press, 2016.
- WYRALL, Everard. *The History of the Kings Regiment (Liverpool) 1914-1919. By Everard Wyrall. With Maps and Illustrations.* 3 Vol. London: Edward Arnold & Co, 1928
- WYRALL, EVERARD. *The West Yorkshire Regiment in the War, 1914-1918, Vol. 1: 1914 -1916*
- *Historical Records of the Queens Own Cameron Highlanders Volume 4.* Edinburgh: William B. Blackwood, 1931
- *National Roll of the Great War*, various volumes: Naval & Military Press, 2006
- *RL Yearbook (Little Blue Books) 1912-1913*
- *RL Yearbook (Little Blue Books) 1913-1914*
- *RL Yearbook (Little Blue Books) 1914-1915*

Newspapers and Periodicals
- *Athletic News*
- *Bath Chronicle and Weekly Gazette*
- *Batley News*
- *Batley Reporter and Guardian*
- *Birmingham Mail*
- *Bradford Daily Telegraph*
- *Bradford Telegraph and Argus*
- *Cambria Daily Leader*
- *Coventry Herald*
- *Cricket and Football Field*
- *Dewsbury Reporter*
- *Dumfries and Galloway Standard*
- *Dundee Courier*
- *Exeter and Plymouth Gazette*
- *Forest of Dean Mercury*

Bibliography

- *Gloucester Citizen*
- *Gloucestershire Echo*
- *Halifax Courier*
- *Hawick News and Border Chronicle*
- *Huddersfield Daily Examiner*
- *Hull Daily Mail*
- *Jedburgh Gazette*
- *Keighley News*
- *Lancashire Evening Post*
- *Leeds Mercury*
- *Leigh Chronicle and Weekly District Advertiser*
- *Leigh Journal*
- *Liverpool Daily Post*
- *Liverpool Echo*
- *Liverpool Evening Express*
- *Manchester Courier and Lancashire General Advertiser*
- *Manchester Evening News*
- *Nantwich Guardian*
- *Newcastle Journal*
- *Pall Mall Gazette*
- *Rhondda Leader*
- *Rochdale Observer*
- *Runcorn Guardian*
- *St Helens Newspaper and Advertiser*
- *Salford Reporter*
- *Sheffield Daily Telegraph*
- *Shipley Times and Express*
- *South Wales Weekly Post*
- *Southern Reporter*
- *Swinton and Pendlebury Journal*
- *Warrington Guardian*
- *Widnes Weekly News and District Reporter*
- *Wigan Observer and District Advertiser*
- *Western Mail*
- *Western Times*
- *Yorkshire Evening Post*
- *Yorkshire Herald*
- *Yorkshire Post and Leeds Intelligencer*

The Greatest Sacrifice

Websites

- *Abertillery Online, Heroes of World War One* -
http://www.abertillery.net/oldabertillery/tales/wwwI.html
- *Auckland Museum, War Memorial, Online Cenotaph*
http://www.aucklandmuseum.com/war-memorial/online-cenotaph
- *Bradford Bulls Foundation, Birch Lane Heroes* https://bullsfoundation.org/
- *British Isles Family History Society of Greater Ottawa* https://bifhsgo.ca/
- *Commonwealth War Graves Commission* https://www.cwgc.org/
- *General Register Office* https://www.gro.gov.uk/gro/content/
- *Great War Forum* https://www.greatwarforum.org/
- *Huddersfield Rugby League Heritage, The Players Archive, Douglas Clark*
http://www.huddersfieldrlheritage.co.uk/Archive/Written/Players/D
ouglas_Clark.html
- *Huddersfield Rugby League Heritage, The Players Archive, Fred Longstaff*
http://www.huddersfieldrlheritage.co.uk/Archive/Written/Players/Fr
ed_Longstaff.html
- *International Committee of The Red Cross 1914-1918 Prisoners of the First
World War, ICRC Historical Archives* https://grandeguerre.icrc.org/
- *Leeds Rhinos Players Association, World War 1*
http://leedsrhinosplayersassociation.co.uk/worldwar1.html
- *Leigh Centurions* https://leighrl.co.uk/wp/
- *Ministry of Defence Blog - Decorated First World War soldier buried almost
100 years after he was killed, 8 October 2015*
https://modmedia.blog.gov.uk/2015/10/08/decorated-first-world-war-
soldier-buried-almost-100-years-after-he-was-killed/
- *NixonPicturesNZ, All Blacks At War*
http://www.nixonpictures.co.nz/All_Blacks_WWI_Hubert_Turtill.html
- *Papers Past, National Library of New Zealand Digitisation Programme*
https://paperspast.natlib.govt.nz/
- *Rugby League in World War One, Tony Collins* http://www.tony-
collins.org/rugbyreloaded/2014/8/5/rugby-league-in-world-war-one
- *St Helens Heritage Society* http://www.saints.org.uk/saints/index.php
- *St Helens Roll of Honour* http://www.sthelensrollsofhonour.co.uk/
- *Salford War Memorials* http://www.salfordwarmemorials.co.uk/
- *The Gallipoli Association Website, On This Day, 4 June 1915* -
http://www.gallipoli-association.org/on-this-day/june/04/
- *The London Gazette* https://www.thegazette.co.uk/
- *The Long, Long Trail – The British Army in the Great War 1914-1918*
http://www.longlongtrail.co.uk/

- *The Wishart Surname in the Great War* http://wishart1418.org/
- *Wakefield Trinity Heritage* http://www.trinityheritage.co.uk/

Unpublished Sources

Note all references prefixed with TNA indicates The National Archives are the document holders

- *Admiralty, Royal Naval Volunteer Reserve, Records of Service, First World War* – TNA ADM 337
- *Militia Attestation Papers* – TNA WO 96
- *Number 1 Canadian Casualty Clearing Station Unit War Diary* – Library and Archives Canada RG9-III-D-3. Volume/box number: 5032. File number: 838.Copied container number: T-10921.
- *Newspaper cuttings book and diary* – Robert Randerson
- *Officers' Services First World War, Lieutenant William Lindsay Beattie, The Border Regiment* – TNA WO 339/37683
- *Officers' Services First World War, 2nd Lieutenant Arthur Clarence Cockcroft, The King's Own (Yorkshire Light Infantry)* – TNA WO 339/4245
- *Officers' Services First World War, 2/Lieutenant Fred Longthorpe, Tank Corps* – TNA WO 339/89264
- *Officers' Services First World War, 2/Lieutenant Fred Leonard Perrett, Royal Welsh Fusiliers* – TNA WO 339/91349
- *Officers' Services First World War, Captain Robert Randerson, Alexandra, Princess of Wales's Own (Yorkshire Regiment)* – TNA WO 339/11831
- *Officers' Services First World War, 2nd Lieutenant Ernest Swinton, Royal Field Artillery* - TNA WO 339/635
- *Rugby Football League Archive, Registers of Players* – Heritage Quay, Ref RFL/HR/1/1
- *School Log Book* - St Mary of the Angels, Batley
- *Service Medal and Award Rolls, First World War* – TNA WO 329
- *Service Medal and Award Rolls Index, First World War* – TNA WO 372
- *The Leeds Rifles and their Antecedents 1858-1918* – Patricia Mary Morris
- *War Office: Soldiers' Documents from Pension Claims, First World War* – TNA WO 364
- *War Office: Soldiers' Documents, First World War 'Burnt Documents'* – TNA WO 363

And the following Unit War Diaries held by The National Archives (TNA)
- *1st Battalion Border Regiment, 29th Division, 87th Infantry Brigade, 1 April 1916-30 April 1919* – The National Archives (TNA) WO 95/2305/1

The Greatest Sacrifice

- *1st Battalion Grenadier Guards, Guards Division, 3rd Guards Brigade, 1 August 1915 – 28 February 1919 – TNA WO 95 1223/1*
- *1st Battalion King's (Liverpool Regiment), 2nd Division, 6th Infantry Brigade – TNA WO 95/1359*
- *1st Battalion King's Own Royal Lancaster Regiment, 4th Division, 12th Infantry Brigade, 1 August 1914 to 28 February 1919 – TNA WO 95/1506/1*
- *1st Battalion King's Royal Rifle Corps: 2nd Division, 6th Infantry Brigade – TNA WO 95/1358/3*
- *1st Battalion Somerset Light Infantry, 4th Division, 11th Infantry Brigade, 1 January 1915 – 31 December 1916 – TNA WO 95/1499/2-4*
- *1st Battalion West Yorkshire Regiment, 6th Division, 18th Infantry Brigade, 1 August 1914 – 31 May 1919 – TNA WO 95/1618/2*
- *1/4th Battalion King's Own Yorkshire Light Infantry, 49th Division, 148th Infantry Brigade – TNA WO 95/2806/1*
- *1/5th Battalion West Yorkshire Regiment, 49th Division, 146th Infantry Brigade 1 April 1915-28 February 1919 - TNA WO95/2794/1*
- *1/6th Battalion Prince of Wales's Own (West Yorkshire Regiment), 49th Division, 146th Infantry Brigade, 1 August 1914 – 28 February 1919 - TNA WO 95 2794/2*
- *1/8th Battalion, Prince of Wales's Own (West Yorkshire) Regiment, 49th Division, 146th Infantry Brigade - TNA WO 95 2795/2*
- *2nd Battalion Rifle Brigade, 8th Division – TNA WO 95/1731/2*
- *2nd Battalion Royal Munster Fusiliers, 1st Division, 3rd Infantry Brigade 1 August 1914-31 December 1915 – TNA WO 95/1279/1*
- *2nd Battalion Scots Guards, 3rd Guards Brigade, 1 August 1915 – 28 February 1919 – TNA WO 95 1223/4*
- *2nd Battalion West Yorkshire Regiment (Prince of Wales's Own), 8th Division, 23rd Infantry Brigade, 1 November 1914 - 31 July 1916 – TNA WO 95/1714/1*
- *2nd Battalion York and Lancaster Regiment, 6th Division, 16th Infantry Brigade, 1 July 1918 - 31 December 1918 – TNA WO 95/1610/8*
- *3rd Battalion Grenadier Guards, Guards Division, 2nd Guards Brigade, 1 July 1915 – 31 January 1919 – TNA WO 95 1219/1*
- *3rd Battalion Worcestershire Regiment, 25th Division, 7th Infantry Brigade 1 November 1915 to 31 October 1917 – TNA WO 95/2244/1*
- *3/5th Battalion Lancashire Fusiliers, 66th Division, 197th Infantry Brigade, 1 February 1917 – 28 February 1918 – TNA WO 95/3137/2*
- *5th Battalion Cameron Highlanders, 9th Division, 26th Infantry Brigade, 1 May 1915 – 28 February 1918 – TNA WO 95 65/1767/1*

- *5th Battalion Cheshire Regiment, 5th Division, 14th Infantry Brigade, 1 February 1915 – 31 December 1915* – TNA WO 95/1565/2
- *6th Battalion Border Regiment, 11th (Northern) Division, 33rd Infantry Brigade, June 1915- January 1916* – TNA WO 95/4299
- *6th Battalion Cameron Highlanders, 15th Division, 45th Infantry Brigade, 1 July 1915 to 31 August 1917* – TNA WO 95/1945/1-3
- *6th Battalion York and Lancaster Regiment, 11th Division, 32nd Infantry Brigade, 1 July 1916 to 30 April 1919* – TNA WO 95/1809/5
- *7th Border Regiment, 17th Division, 51st Infantry Brigade, 1 July 1915 to 31 March 1919* – TNA WO 95/2008/1
- *7th Battalion Prince of Wales's Volunteers (South Lancashire Regiment), 19th Division, 56th Infantry Brigade, 1 January – 31 December 1916* – TNA WO 95/2081/4
- *8th Battalion Seaforth Highlanders, 15th Division, 44th Infantry Brigade, Unit War Diary – 1 April 1917 – 30 June 1917:* WO 95/1940/2
- *8th Battalion Duke of Wellington's (West Riding Regiment), 11th Division, 32nd Infantry Brigade, June – December 1915* – TNA WO 95/4299
- *9th Battalion the Royal Scots, 51st Division, 154th Infantry Brigade, 1 January 1916 - 31 January 1918* – TNA WO 95/2887/5
- *9th Battalion Welsh Regiment, 19th Division, 58th Infantry Brigade, 1 July 1915 - 31 March 1919* – TNA WO 95/2092/2
- *10th Battalion King's Own Yorkshire Light Infantry, 21st Division, 64th Infantry Brigade* – TNA WO 95 2162/2
- *10th Battalion King's Royal Rifle Corps, 20th Division, 59th Infantry Brigade* – TNA WO 95/2115/1
- *11th Battalion East Yorkshire Regiment, 31st Division, 92nd Infantry Brigade, 1 March 1916 to 30 April 1919* – TNA WO 95/2357/2
- *11th Battalion Manchester Regiment, 11th Division, 34th Infantry Brigade, 1 July 1916 to 30 June 1919* – TNA WO 95/1821/1
- *11th Battalion Royal Inniskilling Fusiliers, 36th Division, 109th Infantry Brigade* – TNA WO 95/2510/5
- *13th Battalion Rifle Brigade, 37th Division, 111th Infantry Brigade, 1 August 1915 – 28 February 1919* – TNA WO 95/2534/1
- *15th Battalion Lancashire Fusiliers, 32nd Division, 96th Infantry Brigade* – TNA WO 95/2397/3
- *44th Brigade Royal Field Artillery (1914 Aug – Dec, 1915 Feb, Apr). Also includes diaries of 56th Battery Royal Field Artillery (1914 Aug – Dec)* – TNA WO 95/1327/2

353

The Greatest Sacrifice

- *72nd Machine Gun Company, 24th Division, 72nd Infantry Brigade – 1 March 1916-28 February 1918* – TNA WO 95/2215/2
- *422nd Field Company, Royal Engineers, 55th Division, 1 January 1916 to 30 April 1919* – TNA WO 95/2916/2
- *'A' Squadron, Yorkshire Hussars, 50th Division* – TNA WO95/2817/1

Other
- 1939 Register
- Army Registers of Soldiers' Effects, 1901-1929
- Censuses (England, Scotland, Wales) 1841-1911
- Census (Ireland) 1911
- General Register Office Indexes
- Parish Registers (various)
- School Admission Registers (various)
- Soldiers Died in the Great War Database

Also sources referred to in the book and its Endnotes

Acknowledgements

It is difficult to know where to start when it comes to offering our thanks to those who have helped us along the way. But what clearly needs emphasising immediately is what a privilege it has been to be able to call on the assistance of so many wonderful people. The way rugby league has come together to offer its whole-hearted support to this project has been unbelievable, nothing has been too much trouble. We just hope this book does justice to the way this book has been backed from day one.

Most of all, of course, we hope *The Greatest Sacrifice* does justice to the men who sacrificed their lives – and their rugby league playing careers – for all of us. We have used a variety of sources to paint a picture of their lives, beginning with their childhood, their successful rise to the top of the rugby league ladder and then their untimely deaths. One of the ways of doing this has been to re-produce the newspaper articles of the day. The extracts have been re-produced just as they would have appeared in their original form, hence some of the differences in grammar and general style of writing. Hopefully, the decision not to change any of the newspaper text will have helped bring a little more of the history to life.

There have been so many people who have helped, so apologies if we have been unable to mention all. So, where to begin with the thanks?

First of all, it has to start with publishers Phil Caplan and Tony Hannan, who saw the potential in this project and were prepared to give it – and us – their full backing, even before a word had been written. Then there are the numerous club officials and historians who have provided us with their own individual lists of players who fell and, where possible, provided photographs of them as well.

Mike Latham has been a real inspiration throughout this whole process, not only giving us information on the players from his beloved Leigh, but also providing painstaking support in making sure those players from Runcorn have not been forgotten. Swinton's Ian Jackson is another whose support has been unfaltering from the very start, as has that from the likes of Oldham's Michael Turner and Huddersfield's David Thorpe.

In fact, every club has been brilliant. There's Craig Lingard and John Mitchell from Batley, the whole team from the Bradford Bulls' Birch Lane Heroes project, Graham Morris, who led the way for Broughton Rangers and Salford, Andrew Hardcastle at Halifax, Hunslet's Peter Jarvis and Pat Benatmane, John Pitchford from Keighley, Hull FC's Bill Dalton, Hull KR's Roger Pugh, Rochdale Hornets' duo Neil Bruckshaw and Jim Stringer, Alex Service from the Saints Heritage Project, Lee Robinson of Wakefield Trinity Heritage, Warrington's Neil Dowson, Steve Fox at Widnes, Keith Sutch from Wigan, Yorks's Jon Flatman, and additionally David Makin, Bernard Shooman and Les Hoole.

Acknowledgements

Family members of players who have been honoured in this book have been unwavering in their support, several allowing access to their own personal collections. These include David Longstaff (Fred Longstaff), Marie Cousens (Fred Longthorpe), Paul Marshall (Theodore Marshall), Patricia Blackledge (Robert Randerson) and David Smith (Jack Tindall). Also thank you to Gill Ashcroft, who made a special trip to take a photograph of George Thom's grave at Weaste Cemetery, Andrew Howson, who photographed Theodore Marshall's grave at Elland Cemetery, and Charles Wheeler who photographed several headstones in France. Although in the final version it was not possible to include them all your help was much appreciated.

A special mention to The Green Howards Museum at Richmond, North Yorkshire who allowed us to use their photograph of Robert Randerson and to Ken Pearson for allowing us access to Randerson's pre-war playing diary.

Well-respected rugby league figures Tony Collins and Stuart Sheard are two others who have provided invaluable support and advice, while the British Library staff at Boston Spa have been great at making sure the many trips to study the newspapers from 100 years ago have gone like clockwork. That has also been the case for the visits to Batley, Huddersfield and Bradford libraries. Dave Smith and his team at the University of Huddersfield's Heritage Quay have also been amazing throughout.

Towards the end of the project, my former newspaper colleague Pete Barrow has been a very trusted proof reader, while, finally, a special mention goes to the Rugby Football League and Ralph Rimmer, in particular, who have also backed us from start to finish.

Chris Roberts,
August 2018

HUNSLET v. YORK: AN ATTENUATED MINSTER SIDE.

The management of the York Club, owing to [ma]jority of their players having joined the Colo[urs] [cou]ld only raise a side consisting of six men to f[ill] [thei]r return fixture with Hunslet at Parkside. [The Huns]let Committee made up the full complement [of play]ers by loaning some of their reserves, and [by] voluntary assistance from the onlookers, two [of whom] responded. The game was not as farcical as [one woul]d have expected in the circumstances. The f[irst half] was particularly well fought, and only eight poi[nts] [divid]ed the sides in this portion of the game. It w[as] [in th]e last 10 minutes when Hunslet piled up th[e score,] this being due to the brilliant combination [of Mitch]ell, Buck, and Hammill, all of whom were s[een at the]ir best. For the first time in two years Juk[es turned] out for Hunslet, and he played a promine[nt part in] [i]n the Hunslet first line. Mitchell, Hulligha[n] [(2) each], Jukes, Hammill (3), and Buck (2), were th[e scor]ers for Hunslet, and Bradford (1) and Buck [(1) were] [re]sponsible for the goals. Craven and Bloom[field ass]isted the Hunslet defence, and Naylor kicked [a couple] [of] goals. Result:—Hunslet 5 goals and 9 tri[es (33 poi]nts), York 2 goals and 2 tries (10 points[).]

[Hunslet]—Child, back; Andrews, Buck, Mitchell, an[d] [?], three-quarter backs; Buckley and Jones, ha[lf-backs; J]ukes, A. Walker, Hammill, Bradford, Copl[ey, ?] [?]ber, and Hulligham, forwards.

[York]—Phillips, back; Waite, Naylor, [Fisher, ?] [?], three-quarter backs; Kershaw and [? left-half]

Endnotes

Chapter 1

[1] *Rugby League in World War One* – Tony Collins http://www.tony-collins.org/rugbyreloaded/2014/8/5/rugby-league-in-world-war-one This figure contrasts with the 2,500 in the *Athletic News* of 10 March 1919

Chapter 2

[1] *Unit War Diary of the 2nd Battalion Royal Muster Fusiliers, 1st Division, 3rd Infantry Brigade 1 August 1914-31 December 1915* – TNA WO 95/1279/1 – Note all references prefixed with TNA indicate The National Archives is the holder of the document

[2] DRUM, Neil, and Peter Thomas. *A District at War: Irlam and Cadisheads Part in the Great War 1914-1918.* Manchester: Thomas-Drum Publications, 2010.

[3] *Unit War Diary of the 1st Battalion the King's (Liverpool Regiment), 2nd Division, 6th Infantry Brigade, 1 August 1914 to 31 December 1914* – TNA WO 95/1359/1

[4] Ibid

Chapter 3

[1] *Rochdale Observer* – 18 March 1914

[2] *Rochdale Observer* – 24 March 1915

[3] There is some discrepancy over Twigg's arrival in France. His Medal Index Card and Medal Award Rolls indicate 12 October 1914, but his service records state 9 November 1914 when he joined the 2nd Battalion Leicester Regiment, from the home-based training unit, the 3rd Battalion

[4] Promoted from Lance Sergeant on 9 November 1914

[5] Some reports incorrectly name him as John Clancey

[6] *Rochdale Observer* – 24 March 1915

[7] *Rochdale Observer* – 27 March 1915

[8] *London Gazette* – Publication 4 December 1914, Issue 28995, Page 10305

[9] *Officers' Services First World War, 2nd Lieutenant Ernest Swinton, Royal Field Artillery* – TNA WO 339/635

[10] Ibid

[11] Other sources in his service records clearly indicate his wounds were incurred on the 18th May. These include a letter from his Brigadier General to his father dated 30 May 1915.

[12] *Officers' Services First World War, 2nd Lieutenant Ernest Swinton, Royal Field Artillery* - TNA WO 339/635

[13] O'MEARA, W. A. J. *The Roll of Honour of the Institution of Electrical Engineers. (Contained Herein Are the Names of Members of the Institution of Electrical Engineers Who Gave Their Lives ... 1914-1919)*. London, 1924.

14 London Gazette – Publication 31 December 1915, Supplement 29422, Page 18

Chapter 4

[1] *Unit War Diary of the 5th Battalion Cheshire Regiment, 5th Division, 14th Infantry Brigade, 1 February 1915 – 31 December 1915* – TNA WO 95/1565/2

[2] There is some discrepancy as to his rank, with most official military records stating he was a Corporal rather than a Sergeant. This is how he is recorded by the Commonwealth War Graves Commission. However, the Soldiers Effects Register does agree with the newspaper report and indicates the rank of Sergeant.

[3] *Bradford Daily Telegraph* – 5 August 1904

[4] *Leeds Mercury* – 23 August 1904

[5] *Yorkshire Evening Post* – 15 January 1909

[6] *Yorkshire Post and Leeds Intelligencer* – 5 June 1915

[7] MASSUE DE RUVIGNY, Melville Amadeus Henry Douglas Heddle De La Caillemotte De. *The Roll of Honour: A Biographical Record of All Members*

of His Majestys Naval and Military Forces Who Have Fallen in the War.
Standard Art Book Co.: London, 1917.

[8] Ibid

[9] Ibid

[10] *Unit War Diary of the 1st Battalion King's Royal Rifle Corps: 2nd Division, 6th Infantry Brigade* – TNA WO 95/1358/3

[11] *Western Times* – 15 July 1915

[12] *Athletic News* – 30 September 1907

[13] This was second team player George Russell

Chapter 5

[1] *London Gazette* Publication Date 25 August 1914, Issue 28879, Page 6697

[2] *London Gazette* Publication Date 15 January 1915, Supplement 29043, Page 594

[3] *London Gazette* Publication Date 11 June 1915, Supplement 29192, Page 5736

[4] *Batley News* – 14 August 1915

[5] *Batley News* – 10 October 1914

[6] *Unit War Diary of the 6th Battalion Alexendra, Princess of Wales's Own (Yorkshire Regiment), 11th Division, 32nd Infantry Brigade, July-December 1915* – TNA WO 95/4299

[7] *Officers' Services First World War, Captain Robert Randerson, Alexandra, Princess of Wales's Own (Yorkshire Regiment)* – TNA WO 339/11831

[8] *Batley Reporter and Guardian* – 1 October 1915

[9] *Unit War Diary of the 8th Battalion Duke of Wellington's (West Riding Regiment), 11th Division, 32nd Infantry Brigade, June – December 1915* - TNA WO 95/4299

[10] *The Gallipoli Association Website, On This Day, 4 June 1915* – http://www.gallipoli-association.org/on-this-day/june/04/

[11] Ward's parents were dead and it was his brother, his next of kin, who lived at that address

Chapter 6

[1] *Historical Records of the Queens Own Cameron Highlanders Volume 4.* Edinburgh: William B. Blackwood, 1931

[2] *Unit War Diary of the 10th Battalion King's Royal Rifle Corps, 20th Division, 59th Infantry Brigade* – TNA WO 95/2115/1

[3] This was a well-used word of the period, with its meaning being

poignant, moving or piteous rather than the more common connotation of today.

[4] *Unit War Diary of the 1/4th Battalion King's Own Yorkshire Light Infantry, 49th Division, 148th Infantry Brigade* – TNA WO 95/2806/1

[5] *London Gazette* – Publication Date 13 June 1916, Supplement 29623, Page 5946

Chapter 7

[1] *Unit War Diary of the 3rd Battalion Worcestershire Regiment, 25th Division, 7th Infantry Brigade* 1 November 1915 to 31 October 1917 – TNA WO 95/2244/1

[2] *Unit War Diary of the 72nd Machine Gun Company, 24th Division, 72nd Infantry Brigade* – 1 March 1916-28 February 1918 – TNA WO 95/2215/2

Chapter 8

[1] *Yorkshire Evening Post* – 24 January 1914

[2] Fellow Abertillery signing Arthur Llewellyn who will sadly feature later.

[3] *Unit War Diary of the 2nd Battalion West Yorkshire Regiment (Prince of Wales's Own), 8th Division, 23rd Infantry Brigade, 1 November 1914 - 31 July 1916* – TNA WO 95/1714/1

[4] Ibid

[5] Ibid

[6] *London Gazette* – Publication 12 December 1916, Supplement 29864, Page 12220

[7] The identity tags used at the time were made of compressed fibres or paper which decomposed quickly, so the fact that he had a homemade metal tag was crucial to identification.

[8] *Unit War Diary of the 1/5th Battalion West Yorkshire Regiment, 49th Division, 146th Infantry Brigade, 1 April 1915-28 February 1919* – TNA WO95/2794/1

[9] See Eddie Toole in Chapter 2

Chapter 9

[1] *Yorkshire Evening Post* – 7 November 1914

[2] *London Gazette* – Publication 1 June 1915, Issue 29177, Page 5216

[3] *Officers' Services First World War, 2nd Lieutenant Arthur Clarence Cockcroft, The King's Own (Yorkshire Light Infantry)* – TNA WO 339/4245

[4] *Unit War Diary of the 10th Battalion King's Own Yorkshire Light Infantry, 21st Division, 64th Infantry Brigade, 1 September 1915 - 31 January 1918* – TNA WO 95 2162/2

[5] Ibid

[6] *Officers' Services First World War, 2nd Lieutenant Arthur Clarence Cockcroft, The King's Own (Yorkshire Light Infantry)* – TNA WO 339/4245

[7] It was actually 1 July 1916 that Cockcroft died

[8] This was the inscription used when someone is known to be buried in a particular cemetery, but the exact location of their grave is not known.

[9] George Thom, who of course lost his life in the war on 30 December 1915

[10] *Militia Attestation Papers, 20th Foot (Lancashire Fusiliers):* – TNA WO 96/415, POP – RIL

[11] *Unit War Diary of the 15th Battalion Lancashire Fusiliers, 32nd Division, 96th Infantry Brigade* – TNA WO 95/2397/3

[12] *Athletic News* – 17 March 1919

[13] *National Roll of the Great War, XIV Salford*, Naval & Military Press, 2006.

[14] His Medal Index Card and Medal Award Rolls do not show any entitlement to the 1914/15 Star, which he should have been awarded if the dates giving on the National Roll of the Great War were accurate.

[15] *Unit War Diary of the 2nd Battalion Rifle Brigade, 8th Division* – TNA WO 95/1731/2

[16] *Rochdale Observer* – 30 September 1914

[17] 'Gott strafe England' was a slogan used by the Germans during the First World War meaning 'May God punish England'.

[18] *Unit War Diary of the 1st Battalion, Somerset Light Infantry, 4th Division, 11th Infantry Brigade, 1 January 1915 – 31 December 1916* – TNA WO 95 1499/2-4

Chapter 10

[1] *War Office Soldiers' Documents, First World War 'Burnt Documents' for George William Thomas* – TNA WO 363

[2] Slater, Gary. *The Warrington Wolves Miscellany*. Stroud: History, 2012.

[3] *War Office Soldiers' Documents, First World War 'Burnt Documents' for George William Thomas* – TNA WO 363

[4] Her birth was registered in the Leigh Registration District in the September Quarter of 1910, and her death in the December Quarter.

[5] *Unit War Diary of the 7th Battalion Prince of Wales's Volunteers (South Lancashire Regiment), 19th Division, 56th Infantry Brigade, 1 January - 31 December 1916* – TNA WO 95/2081/4

[6] GARVIN, Ged, J. L. Garvin, and Christine Garvin. *We Hope to Get Word Tomorrow: The Garvin Family Letters, 1914-1916*. Barnsley: Frontline, 2009.

[7] *Leeds Mercury* – 20 December 1911

[8] *Unit War Diary of the 1/6th Battalion Prince of Wales's Own (West Yorkshire Regiment), 49th Division, 146th Infantry Brigade, 1 August 1914 – 28 February 1919* – TNA WO 95 2794/2

[9] Ibid

[10] Lloyd George was at the time the Chancellor of the Exchequer, who would subsequently become Secretary of State for War and then Prime Minister in December 1916

[11] *Huddersfield Rugby League Heritage, The Players Archive, Fred Longstaff* http://www.huddersfieldrlheritage.co.uk/Archive/Written/Players/Fred_Longstaff.html

Chapter 11

[1] Named after the famous 1879 Zulu War Battle of Rorke's Drift when a small garrison of British soldiers repelled a huge Zulu force

[2] *Unit War Diary of the 2nd Battalion Scots Guards, 3rd Guards Brigade, 1 August 1915 – 28 February 1919* – TNA WO 95 1223/4

[3] *Unit War Diary of the 1/8th Battalion, Prince of Wales's Own (West Yorkshire) Regiment, 49th Division, 146th Infantry Brigade* – TNA WO 95 2795/2

[4] *Unit War Diary of the 10th Battalion, King's Royal Rifle Corps, 20th Division, 59th Infantry Brigade, 1 July 1915 – 28 February 1918* – TNA WO 95 2115/1

[5] An engineering company whose products included boilers, chimneys, condensers, water or gas coolers and heaters

[6] *Unit War Diary of the 3rd Battalion Grenadier Guards, Guards Division, 2nd Guards Brigade, 1 July 1915 – 31 January 1919* – TNA WO 95 1219/1

[7] Ibid

Chapter 12

[1] Known as the Heidenkopf by the Germans

[2] *Unit War Diary of the 1st Battalion King's Liverpool Regiment, 2nd Division, 6th Infantry Brigade* – TNA WO95/1359

[3] *National Roll of the Great War, VIII Leeds,* Naval & Military Press, 2006

[4] *Gloucester Citizen* – 16 May 1902

[5] *Unit War Diary of the 1st Battalion Grenadier Guards, Guards Division, 3rd Guards Brigade, 1 August 1915 – 28 February 1919* – TNA WO 95 1223/1

[6] He is double counted in the census, also featuring in the entry compiled by his father at home in Darfield

[7] *War Office Soldiers' Documents, First World War 'Burnt Documents' for James William Debney* – TNA WO 363

[8] Wyrall, Everard. *West Yorkshire Regiment in the War, 1914-1918, Vol. 1: 1914 -1916.*

[9] *Unit War Diary of the 1st Battalion West Yorkshire Regiment, 6th Division, 18th Infantry Brigade, 1 August 1914 – 31 May 1919* – TNA WO 95/1618/2

[10] *War Office Soldiers' Documents, First World War 'Burnt Documents' for Thomas Wagstaff* – TNA WO 363

Chapter 13

[1] *War Office Soldiers' Documents, First World War 'Burnt Documents' for William Jardine* – TNA WO 363

[2] *Death Certificate for William Jardine, January 1917, District of Jedburgh* – Statutory Registers Deaths 792/3

[3] The appointment was on 30 January 1915

[4] *London Gazette* – Publication 22 August 1916, Supplement 29722, Page 8382 and Publication 16 January 1917, Issue 29904, Page 606

[5] *Unit War Diary for the 6th Battalion Border Regiment, 11th (Northern) Division, 33rd Infantry Brigade, June 1915- January 1916, Unit War Diary* – TNA WO 95/4299

[6] *Officers' Services First World War, Lieutenant William Lindsay Beattie, The Border Regiment* – TNA WO 339/37683

[7] *Unit War Diary for the 6th Battalion Border Regiment, 11th (Northern) Division, 33rd Infantry Brigade, June 1915- January 1916, Unit War Diary* – TNA WO 95/4299

[8] *Unit War Diary for the 1st Battalion Border Regiment, 29th Division, 87th Infantry Brigade, 1 April 1916-30 April 1919* – TNA WO 95/2305/1

Chapter 14

[1] *Unit War Diary for the 9th Battalion the Royal Scots, 51st Division, 154th Infantry Brigade, 1 January 1916 - 31 January 1918* – TNA WO 95/2887/5

[2] *Unit War Diary for the 3/5th Battalion Lancashire Fusiliers, 66th Division, 197th Infantry Brigade, 1 February 1917 – 28 February 1918* – TNA WO 95/3137/2

[3] Ibid

[4] *Leeds Rhinos Players Association, World War 1, Leonard Leckenby* – http://leedsrhinosplayersassociation.co.uk/Leonard-Leckenby.pdf

Chapter 15

[1] *Unit War Diary of the 11th Battalion East Yorkshire Regiment, 31st Division, 92nd Infantry Brigade, 1 March 1916 to 30 April 1919* – TNA WO 95/2357/2

[2] *London Gazette* – Publication 17 April 1917, Supplement 29720, Page 8372

[3] *London Gazette* – Publication 12 June 1917, Supplement 30130, Page 5866

[4] *London Gazette* – Publication 8 June 1917, Supplement 30122, Page 5705

[5] Turkish-held Mesopotamia, which was the old name for Iraq, was vital to the British to supply the oil for their modern naval fleet. If the troops of the Ottoman Empire could capture the Allies' oilfields in the south it would prove disastrous to the Allies

[6] *London Gazette* – Publication 8 June 1917, Supplement 30122, Page 5704

[7] *War Office Soldiers' Documents, First World War 'Burnt Documents' for Howell Rees* – TNA WO 363

[8] *Leeds Rhinos Players Association, World War 1, Arthur Llewellyn* – http://leedsrhinosplayersassociation.co.uk/Arthur-Llewellyn.pdf

[9] *Abertillery Online, Heroes of World War One* – http://www.abertillery.net/oldabertillery/tales/wwwI.html

[10] It is more likely that he was by now already in the 4th Battalion of the Rifle Brigade

[11] *Leeds Rhinos Players Association, World War 1, Arthur Llewellyn* – http://leedsrhinosplayersassociation.co.uk/Arthur-Llewellyn.pdf

[12] *Unit War Diary of the 13th Battalion Rifle Brigade, 37th Division, 111th Infantry Brigade, 1 August 1915 – 28 February 1919* – TNA WO 95/2534/1

[13] Ibid

[14] Ibid

Chapter 16

[1] Sometimes referred to as O'Kell in military records

[2] Kaye in military records

[3] *Unit War Diary of the 6th Battalion Cameron Highlanders, 15th Division, 45th Infantry Brigade, 1 July 1915 to 31 August 1917* – TNA WO 95/1945/1-3

[4] *War Office Soldiers' Documents, First World War 'Burnt Documents' for Thomas Owen Jones* – TNA WO 363

[5] *Unit War Diary of the 9th Battalion Welsh Regiment, 19th Division, 58th Infantry Brigade, 1 July 1915 - 31 March 1919* – TNA WO 95/2092/2

[6] *Leigh Centurions Remembrance Sunday Blog, 10 November 2017* – https://leighrl.co.uk/wp/blog/2017/11/10/remembrance-day-sunday/

Chapter 17

[1] *War Office Soldiers' Documents, First World War 'Burnt Documents' for John Linton Ewart* – TNA WO 363

[2] *Unit War Diary of the 5th Battalion Cameron Highlanders, 9th Division, 26th Infantry Brigade, 1 May 1915-28 February 1919* – TNA WO 95/1767/1
[3] *Unit War Diary of the 422nd Field Company, Royal Engineers, 55th Division, 1 January 1916 to 30 April 1919* – TNA WO 95/2916/2
[4] *Unit War Diary of the 11th Battalion Manchester Regiment, 11th Division, 34th Infantry Brigade, 1 July 1916 to 30 June 1919* – TNA WO 95/1821/1
[5] *War Office Soldiers' Documents, First World War 'Burnt Documents' for John Flynn* – TNA WO 363
[6] *Unit War Diary of the 7th Battalion Border Regiment, 17th Division, 51st Infantry Brigade, 1 July 1915 to 31 March 1919* – TNA WO 95/2008/1
[7] *War Office Soldiers' Documents, First World War 'Burnt Documents' for James Flanagan* – TNA WO 363

Chapter 18
[1] In some records Anne
[2] He had been granted leave from annual training in 1913.
[3] *War Office Soldiers' Documents, First World War 'Burnt Documents' for Sidney Clifford Abbott* – TNA WO 363 AND *War Office Soldiers' Documents from Pension Claims, First World War* – TNA WO 364
[4] *Unit War Diary of the 2nd Battalion York and Lancaster Regiment, 6th Division, 16th Infantry Brigade, 1 July 1918 - 31 December 1918* – TNA WO 95/1610/8
[5] *Officers' Services First World War, 2/Lieutenant Fred Longthorpe, Tank Corps* – TNA WO 339/89264
[6] *London Gazette* – Publication Date 7 July 1917, Supplement 30171, Page 6801
[7] *Officers' Services First World War, 2/Lieutenant Fred Longthorpe, Tank Corps* – TNA WO 339/89264

Chapter 19
[1] This is indicated on his Medal Index Card and his Service Medal and Award Rolls
[2] *London Gazette* – Publication 29 October 1918, Supplement 30983, Page 12845
[3] *Officers' Services First World War, 2/Lieutenant Fred Leonard Perrett, Royal Welsh Fusiliers* – TNA WO 339/91349
[4] *London Gazette* – Publication 27 July 1917, Supplement 30210, Page 7782
[5] *Officers' Services First World War, 2/Lieutenant Fred Leonard Perrett, Royal Welsh Fusiliers* – TNA WO 339/91349

[6] The website spelling of his name.

[7] *War Office Soldiers' Documents, First World War 'Burnt Documents' for William Gordon Simpson* – TNA WO 363

[8] Ibid

[9] The paper was wrong with its cause of death. It should read nephritis.

[10] Hannah Jane born in 1913 and Sydney Gordon in 1915

[11] *Admiralty, Royal Naval Volunteer Reserve, Records of Service, First World War, Sephton George, Z/3633, Mersey* – TNA ADM 337/58/33

Chapter 20

[1] *War Office Soldiers' Documents, First World War 'Burnt Documents' for Cuthbert Molloy* – TNA WO 363

[2] *Wigan Observer and District Advertiser*, 18 August 1917

[3] *Athletic News*, 10 March 1919

[4] He was a regular in the Black and Whites' back row

[5] *Athletic News*, 10 March 1919

[6] Heywood, Brian, David Smith, Stuart Leslie Sheard, David Thorpe, David Gronow, Daniel Sheard, Rob Smithson, and Howard Taylor. *Standing on the Shoulders of Giants: A History of Rugby League in Huddersfield*. Upper Calder Valley Publications, 2015

[7] Ibid

[8] Ibid

[9] *Athletic News*, 10 March 1919

[10] *Athletic News*, 17 March 1919

The Authors

Jane Roberts is a professional genealogist whose love of rugby league stems from childhood Sunday afternoons watching Batley with her dad. She has a passion for history, particularly First World War and is a frequent visitor to the battlefields. After graduating from Liverpool University with a modern history degree she worked as a civil servant. She began researching her own family history over a decade ago and this developed into a wish to find out about the lives of ordinary people who do not normally feature in history books. It led her to researching the men on her local church War Memorial in Batley, and formally studying family history to obtain a qualification. She left the civil service to become a professional genealogist in 2017. She writes regularly about family history and wider northern history in her blog at https://pasttopresentgenealogy.wordpress.com

Chris Roberts, her husband, has been a rugby league journalist for over 30 years, having covered the sport at all levels, from local amateur fixtures to World Cup finals. During his time working on local and regional newspapers, he has followed the fortunes of Huddersfield Giants, Batley Bulldogs, Dewsbury Rams and Hunslet Hawks. Before embarking on a career in journalism, Chris studied for a BA (Honours) degree in sport and recreation at Staffordshire University. Besides having a passion for rugby league, Chris shares Jane's fascination with history and, in 2017, completed a First World War In Perspective online course through the Oxford University Department for Continuing Education to further increase his knowledge and understanding of the conflict.

Investigate our other titles and
stay up to date with all our latest releases at
www.scratchingshedpublishing.co.uk